D0838008

PROMISES KEPT

PROMISES KEPT

ONE MAN'S JOURNEY AGAINST INCREDIBLE ODDS

Pg 180- Reader's Pg 196 - Pg 204 Begin speech
Digest Michel's
article Speech

ERNEST W. MICHEL

Foreword by Leon Uris

BARRICADE BOOKS

Fort Lee, New Jersey

Published by Barricade Books Inc.
185 Bridge Plaza North
Suite 308-A
Fort Lee, NJ 07024

www.barricadebooks.com

Copyright © 2008 by Ernest W. Michel
All rights reserved.

No part of this book may be reproduced, stored in a retrieval system, or transmitted in
any form, by any means, including mechanical, electronic, photocopying, recording, or
otherwise, without the prior written permission of the publisher, except by a reviewer
who wishes to quote brief passages in connection with a review written for inclusion in
a magazine, newspaper, or broadcast.

Library of Congress Cataloging-in-Publication Data
A copy of this title's Library of Congress Cataloging-in-Publication Data is available on
request from the Library of Congress.

ISBN 13: 978-1-56980-338-7
ISBN 1-56980-338-2

10 9 8 7 6 5 4 3 2 1

Manufactured in the United States of America

This book is dedicated to the blessed memory of my parents, Otto and Frieda Michel, who were killed in Auschwitz in August 1942.

My life's greatest regret is that they died without knowing that their two children, my sister Lotte and I, would survive the Holocaust. Between us we have seven children, nineteen grandchildren (sixteen of them in Israel), and, as of 2007, seventeen great-grandchildren—a total of seventy-two descendants.

This book is also dedicated to my children, Lauren Shachar, Joel Michel, and Karen Daniels, and to my six grandchildren, Noga, Rachel, Yair, Nesya, Gil, and Jonah. I hope and pray that they and their descendants shall always remember our miraculous survival as proof of the strength and continuity of our people.

Last, but not least, part of this dedication belongs to my wife, Amy, who has given me a new life.

CONTENTS

INTRODUCTION

My previous book, *Promises to Keep*, was published in 1993 by Barricade Books. The manuscript had been turned down by every publisher I sent it to.

Through a good friend, I met Lyle Stuart, publisher of Barricade Books, and his wife, Carole. There is only one way to describe Lyle: unconventional. He was a character, and a liberal, with a big "L." He died in 2006.

Lyle often published books that nobody else would touch. Among them was *The Turner Diaries* by Andrew MacDonald. It was an obviously racist and anti-Semitic diatribe. Lyle insisted upon writing an introduction to the book, explaining that while he abhorred the author's point of view, as a believer in the First Amendment he felt the reader should know that these views existed.

When he read my manuscript, he told me that although he lost money on every single book on the subject, he had a deep concern about those who denied that six million Jews were murdered during the Holocaust, and he felt an obligation to continue publishing stories of survivors. *Promises to Keep* is now in its fourth printing.

A professor at Arizona State University whom I came to know during a winter stay in Arizona felt strongly that students should know more about this dark period and how it was possible for such an unspeakable tragedy to have taken place in the twentieth century, and that such genocide is continuing today in Darfur.

With the support of Carole Stuart, I decided to bring the original book up-to-date, eliminating some chapters and adding several new ones. The result is the publication of this book, *Promises Kept*.

Over the years, I have spoken on the subject of the Holocaust and my miraculous survival after five and a half years in forced labor and death camps at countless high schools, colleges, and universities all over the country. Part of my presentation, which is reflected in this book, includes not only the Holocaust but the lessons of the Nuremberg War Crimes Trial, which I covered as a special correspondent for the German news agency DANA. The book also deals with the phenomenon of genocide and the incredible story of the man who almost single-handedly and against great opposition led the way for the United Nations to make the crime of genocide part of international law and to make those found guilty of this crime subject to severe penalties.

I have received hundreds of letters from students with their reactions to my first book. Many have brought tears to my eyes.

It won't be long before there is not a survivor left. Most of us are now in our eighties and nineties. Time is running out. After we are gone, only books, films, and documentaries will be left to tell the story. I am among those survivors who feel strongly that as long as we are able, it is our obligation to tell our stories in the hope that they will contribute to a better understanding and provide a lesson for future generations so that what happened during those dark years will never happen again, to anybody, anywhere.

I want to thank Carole Stuart and her able staff for their work and support. I want to thank Professor Barbara Veltri for her foresight and guidance, my friend Gerda Klein, a fellow survivor who continues to inspire audiences all over the world, and my friend Sam Harris.

Finally, my deep gratitude to Judy Sherak, my assistant and friend, without whose advice and devotion this book would not have been realized.

FOREWORD

The word *survivor* has gained an extended meaning in the Jewish and much of the world's lexicon. It implies a European Jew who outlived the Nazi Holocaust and most likely one who endured a concentration or extermination camp, as well. These men and women are to be looked upon with wonderment.

My dear friend, Ernie Michel, is such a man.

For every survivor there is a tale that sears the soul. A half century after the event, it is still impossible to fully comprehend.

Each person who escaped Hitler's death machinery brought a slightly different version of his or her personal story of survival. Yet all the stories had a convergence of common factors.

To have lived through this, the darkest pit of man's depravity, he or she had to be touched by an unseen golden hand. Call it fate, luck, divine intervention, or a miracle. Every survivor will relate to you his or her particular miracle or miracles. Ernie Michel is no exception. He was chosen to live by a force beyond his own power.

Not everyone so blessed got through. In addition to that moment of fate or luck, he or she had to have supreme willpower and the presence of mind to impose it.

It is a glory to the Jewish people that those who survived came through with their human dignity intact, and many went on to live prominent and useful lives.

I first met Ernie Michel in the late 1950s, when the revelation of the Holocaust first staggered the imagination (as indeed it still does). At the time I was living in the San Fernando Valley and researching and writing my novel *Exodus*. Ernie Michel worked for the United Jewish Appeal in Los Angeles. We became fast friends almost immediately, and although we have spent most of our friendship living in different places, we always stayed in communication.

I left for Hollywood and Ernie eventually went to Paris to help establish a prototype of the UJA in France. Later he returned to New York and spent over two decades as head of that organization for the city. His tenure was truly distinguished and marked by enormous love and affection from the community he served.

I caught up with Ernie about five years ago when I moved to New York and we reestablished our relationship. Ernie was now retired and donating his time to help build a Holocaust Museum in New York City. Nonetheless, the UJA would not entirely let him go. He retained his office and used his skills and devotion to do whatever might be asked of him. One of Ernie's vows when he was in the camp was to bear witness. In keeping that promise he agreed to lead a UJA mission to Warsaw and Auschwitz. I wondered, how did the man have the courage to return to that, the most hideous piece of ground on the planet? As you will read, few human beings among us have ever suffered more profoundly. Only if you know of Ernie Michel's courage and of his devotion to his people can you conceive of an answer.

In my own years of research, I had visited several extermination camps: Maidanek, Dachau, Mauthausen. I had interviewed dozens of survivors.

I had also stood the longest libel trial in British history. In the pages of *Exodus* was a passage referring to a Dr. Dering, who had performed experimental surgery on Jewish men and women in Auschwitz in a grotesque scheme to sterilize the Jewish race and use them as neutered slave laborers. Only the strongest of the stock would be spared for the purpose of breeding new slaves. I knew that Dr. Dering had been indicted but never tried as a war criminal. What I did not know was that he was not German, but Polish and a prisoner himself—one who willingly performed castrations and ovariectomies on Jews.

Lo and behold, Dr. Dering had escaped extradition to Poland, fled to a British colony, and years later was knighted on the Queen's birthday, after which he returned to London and eventually brought suit against me.

I could not prove the numbers of my charges and I admitted openly that I had libeled him. I decided to defend the case on the premise that he was not entitled to damages because his character was worth nothing. After a short deliberation, the jury agreed with me. Dr. Dering was awarded a half-penny—the value of his character, in contemptuous damages.

The trial became the basis of my novel *Q.B. VII.* In the charged moments of the trial, none was more electrifying than when my barrister arose to argue before the jury. Lord Gerald Gardiner was a consummate Englishman, a brilliant legal mind who later went on to become the Lord Chancellor. He was a Quaker, absolved of combat duty in the war, but he was in command of a medical unit which was part of the liberation of Bergen-Belsen. He never forgot what he witnessed. He faced the jury and said, "When the history of mankind is writ, there will be no darker chapter than what an advanced, civilized, Western, Christian nation did to the Jews in the middle of the twentieth century."

When Ernie Michel asked me to join an upcoming UJA mission to Warsaw and Auschwitz, I agreed. In addition to the meaning of the mission itself, I felt a need to resolve my own experience with Dr. Dering and the London trial.

Auschwitz is now one of the major tourist attractions in Europe with lines of tour buses from all over the continent. I wondered: Do they come out of curiosity?

Block X, where Dr. Dering performed brutal surgery on Jewish men and women, was shuttered, but one did not have to listen hard to hear the ghosts, the echoes of their screams. Between Block X and the next barrack, the SS torture chambers, was an execution yard.

I had satisfied my curiosity to come to Auschwitz.

I had been to many concentration camps, but I had never been in the company of someone who had been a prisoner there. Ernie Michel then took us to nearby Birkenau, where inside one of the few remaining wooden barracks, he told us what day-to-day life had been like. Herein lies his remarkable story.

Back in Warsaw the mission was to go to the monument to the Warsaw Ghetto Uprising, a few blocks from Mila 18, the headquarters of the Jewish fighters. I was to give a short presentation, which I wrote out on stationery from the Warsaw Holiday Inn. By the time it was my turn to speak, it had grown dark and I could not see my notes. A number of those present lit torches and formed a semicircle behind me. The light and shadows of their flames cast an eerie background against the monument.

I had read a passage from my novel *Mila 18*, in which a young Jewish boy is spirited out of the ghetto and into hiding because it was deemed that he had the best chance to survive because of his strength. His uncle, Andrew Androfski, a leader of the Jewish Fighters, commands him to survive...to survive and to live for a hundred thousand children who will not survive...who will be murdered in Treblinka. The boy vows he will survive.

Just as I was reading that, I felt something hot fall on my hand and then little red blobs fell on my notes. At first it appeared to be blood. As it congealed I realized it was wax that had dropped from someone's torch. I looked over my shoulder. It was falling from Ernie Michel's torch.

I was flushed with a tremendous moment of revelation. The boy I was reading about from *Mila 18* could have been, may have been, Ernie Michel being ordered to survive.

We Jews have survived through conquest. Not the conquest of armies but the conquest of ideas given to mankind as mankind groped for the moral definition of humanity. We have survived because we are family and each generation of Jews has done what was necessary in their lifetime for that survival. We have survived because of men and women like Ernie Michel. This is the story of his survival and of his triumphant return to human dignity.

Leon Uris

PROLOGUE

BONN, GERMANY: NOVEMBER 1988

t was a clear, blue, sunny November morning. Our group of twelve men and women, Americans all, stood talking in subdued tones in the lobby of the Steigenberger Hotel in Bonn. We were waiting for the minibus that would take us to Villa Hammerschmitt to meet with the president of the German Federal Republic, Richard von Weizsaecker. It was one of the controversial aspects of our *Kristallnacht* Memorial Trip.

We would be received by the president and we would shake his hand. It was a "photo opportunity" that would go over the newswires to newspapers throughout the world. The caption would read, "Delegation of New York Jews, including a Holocaust survivor, greeted by West German president." News stories would explain the purpose of our visit—the fiftieth anniversary of *Kristallnacht*—one of the darkest nights in all Jewish history, the night of November 9–10, 1938, the prelude to the Holocaust.

We wanted the story to be told in Germany. We wanted to make certain that *Kristallnacht*, named for the shattered glass of the Jewish synagogues and shops destroyed that night, would not be consigned to history and forgotten. We came to see the president of West Germany to commemorate that event in Germany, to keep it within the memory and conscience of Germany and the entire world, and for the Jews, as well. It was a story we felt we had to tell.

I knew, ever since the plans were made, that this would be a tough trip for me. As a Holocaust survivor and then as executive vice-president of New York's UJA-Federation, the largest philanthropic organization in the Unites States, I had met with Presidents Eisenhower, Johnson, and Carter and every Israeli president and prime minister since the founding of the State of Israel in 1948. But this was different. Very different. I was going to confront my personal past.

The minibus slowed to a stop outside the hotel entrance and we edged to the door. My feet dragged reluctantly. We were all quiet, our faces somber. I was sure I was pale and drawn. Why was my anticipation dampened? Why didn't I feel vindicated? Why was I so uncomfortable?

We were going to meet the president of Germany on the fiftieth anniversary of the day that his countrymen began the systematic killing of Jews, a killing that resulted in the greatest mass murder in history. That systematic killing was designed to wipe me, my parents, friends, and relatives, all the Jewish people, off the face of the earth. I was about to meet the president of a people who built a macabre museum during the Nazi era, a museum of relics and religious items "of an extinct race." I was going to meet the president of the nation that robbed me of my education, violated my youth, and murdered my parents. He was the president of a country whose land seemed soaked beneath my feet, because it was soaked with the blood of those I loved.

"What am I doing here?" I wondered. Was I being presumptuous? What right did I have to be here? Was I doing the right thing? It was half a century, to the day, since the Gestapo agent punched my mother in the face. It was fifty years, to the day, since my father's arrest. My home, my innocence, and simple happiness died that day, 50 years ago. Fifty years ago today I wondered where my father was; I saw my mother's bruised face. I watched my grandmother collapse and my community die. Fifty years ago I felt my life was over.

We had just lunched with the Israeli ambassador to West Germany, a native of Austria. As he told us how significant and vital our presence in Germany was on that day, I thought about thin potato soup and sawdust bread, about cattle cars and lice. About Jews dying. And I thought of my friend Walter. I was thinking about escape and close calls, about lies and fate and about friends, those who died and those who didn't. I was thinking about my life and its worth.

So here I sat, in an efficient minivan, with a group of my American peers, on our way to see the president of Germany. I was thoroughly disoriented. Did I have the right to come back to the country that destroyed nearly six million of my fellow Jews and their 1,400 synagogues?

Instead of the neat, postwar streets of Bonn, I was seeing in my mind's eye that bitterly cold night so long ago. I saw the flaming synagogue. I heard the sirens. I ran back to the cardboard factory, to our shattered apartment, to my worn-out Papi, the friends who died in my arms, and the brutal medical experiments. I returned to the trucks and the ovens and the trains. I looked out the minivan window and saw Auschwitz.

I saw my father's sad face, drained of all hope, on the morning I was deported.

I saw my sister Lotte, age ten, put on a brave face on the night my father put her on a train to France—and none of us knew if she would get there.

I saw my dear friend Walter's ashen face as he died, totally emaciated, in my arms at Auschwitz.

I felt the weight of thousands of corpses I carried in my arms and loaded into trucks during my 22 months in the death camps.

I remembered running through the woods, shoulders hunched, as Honzo, Felix, and I made a desperate dash for life.

At the entrance to the presidential compound, the German police, prim in their immaculate green uniforms, stopped us, checked our names, and waved us in. The minibus halted in front of the president's villa, a sturdy, impressive building.

"What am I doing here?" I asked myself. I stepped off the van and waited for the others. My sense of disorientation grew stronger; I felt trapped. Why did I allow myself to enter yet another compound under German authority?

The president's young, well-dressed personal assistant, Berthold von Pfeffen Arnbach, greeted us. "Welcome to the president's home."

I made the introductions. I entered the villa and the door closed behind us. I was prepared, but I also dreaded this moment. I was about to come face to face with the president of Germany, a direct successor of Adolf Hitler. I was shivering, just as I had shivered in my night-clothes, fifty years ago to the day, when I woke suddenly, looked out the window, and saw the wild flames.

1

KRISTALLNACHT– GERMANY

I knew it was the synagogue that was lighting up the darkness on that cold November morning in 1938. I knew it immediately. It was the logical target for what the Nazis called their counterattack. It was their revenge for the death, three days before, of a minor German consular official. He was shot at point blank range in the German embassy in Paris by a young Jew, Herschel Grynszpan.

Last night, the radio blared out the ominous words:

"The international Jewish conspiracy will find out once and for all what will happen when they attack an innocent German official. The full wrath of the German people will be felt soon."

Now, hours later, our synagogue in Mannheim was aflame. That couldn't be...it was too far away. Mutti and Papi must be awake also. They would know what...

I turned and started toward the door before I realized I wasn't in my own bedroom in Mannheim. I was in my rented room in Bruchsal, some 20 miles away, where I lived and worked as an apprentice in a cardboard factory.

Fully awake now, I fought off a fifteen-year-old's sharp pang of panic at being far from home at a moment of great danger, unprotected and unable to protect those I loved most dearly. I hurried back to the window. Sadly, the light came from the right direction—it had to be the Bruchsal synagogue blazing out there. I dressed quickly and ran out into the street.

I raced toward the flames, now shooting high up into the sky. Others were running alongside me, but I failed to recognize any of them. I got the impression of wide eyes all around me, filled with excitement or concern. Why were they running? To help? To gloat?

Suddenly it was right in front of me. The entire building was engulfed. The brownshirts of the SA had taken out the prayer books, the prayer shawls, the Torah scrolls, everything they could get their hands on, and dumped them in a pile on the street, now, laughing boisterously, they were trampling on them, enjoying themselves. I could see little specks of spittle coming out of the corners of their mouths.

"Burn the Jews!" they kept chanting. "Burn the Jews! Burn the Jews!"

Within a few minutes, fire engines arrived to protect the neighboring buildings. They made no effort to save the synagogue. Small children ran shouting happily through the crowd, fascinated by the fire, turning the disaster into a carnival. Men and women stood watching, talking in little groups. Some of the faces were deeply flushed, looking almost joyful. Despite the heat from the fire, the scene sent chills through me, and I turned away.

Nobody made a move to help. Or to protest.

There was a low rumbling. The walls of the synagogue had begun to crack apart. Parents snatched up their children and we all stepped back as far as we could before the entire structure came tumbling down. A large cloud of smoke and dust, with flaring flames at the center, shot up toward the sky. Slowly the flames died down and the cloud of smoke became a sprinkling of dust over smoldering ashes.

With the fire dying, the early morning cold penetrated my hastily thrown-on clothing. The onlookers withdrew, their faces now drained of excitement or shock. It was quiet. Even the children were completely silent.

I don't remember how long I stood there. There was nothing left of the synagogue. Where the entrance gate had been was a gaping hole. Strangely, only a stone altar showing the Star of David remained. Everything else was smoking rubble. Pinpoints of flame spurted up, only to die down again. Dawn's gray light cast a chilling pallor over the scene.

The SA men were standing in a little knot, talking. I thought they looked over at me and the handful of others still clustered near the scene, so I walked away.

The sun was coming up. I went to my room to change, then decided to go to the cardboard factory.

Mr. Kaufman, the owner, was ashen-faced and unshaven. Standing close beside him were his son, Franz, and his daughter-in-law, Lisa. The building heat had not yet come on, and they were wearing their coats. They looked as if they were huddled together for warmth, but they were really huddled against something terrible that had been unleashed in the night. We were panic stricken, wondering what would happen next. We didn't have long to wait.

The radio commentator was calling it an act of justice and revenge. It was carried out in Germany and Austria, and there was already a name for it: *Kristallnacht*. Crystal Night. The night of the shattered glass.

The synagogue was not the only Jewish building to "feel the full wrath of the German people." The few stores in Bruchsal whose owners were Jewish had been demolished, looted, and torched. People had been beaten, jailed, and worse.

As we shivered in that cold office, I decided to get to Mannheim as fast as I could. I made a conscious effort not to think about what I would find when I got there.

Suddenly the door burst open and three men, obviously Gestapo, stamped in. They wore long, black leather trench coats with swastika buttons on the lapel. One was tall, the other two were stocky, and all were unshaven. One stepped toward Mr. Kaufman, his gun drawn, his jaw set, and his eyes gleaming.

"Jew Kaufman, this place is taken over by order of the Gestapo. You are under arrest!" he barked. He sounded exhilarated.

"Can I call…?"

"Shut up!" and turning to Franz Kaufman, he spat. "You are under arrest too!"

The other Gestapo men moved swiftly. One grabbed Mr. Kaufman's arm, the other pulled Franz. Roughly, they shoved them into a corner. The man with the gun slipped it back in its holster and turned to me. I stood next to Lisa Kaufman, shaking with fear.

"You! How old are you?" he shouted.

"Fifteen."

Without a word he turned away.

Franz tried to say something to Lisa, but the guards stepped between them and thrust Franz and his father through the open door. We heard their footsteps, two men firmly treading, two men stumbling and scurrying, echoing down the stairwell until they were out of earshot.

The remaining Gestapo man turned to Lisa.

"You! Jew pig! Hand over the keys!"

Lisa started to say something, thought better of it, and reached silently into a desk drawer and brought out the keys. He snatched them away and pounded strongly on the desk with the keys clenched in his fist. "Now get out! This place does not belong to you anymore! Out! You're lucky I don't kill you!"

We grabbed our coats and left. We had no choice. Lisa bit her lip, trying not to cry in front of me. I didn't know what to say. "You'd better get home to your family," she said softly. "I'll go to our apartment." I tried to comfort her with a hug, then bid her farewell. I ran all the way to the railroad station, arriving just in time to catch the train.

I dug my shoulder into a far corner seat, turning away from the welter of voices thickening the air like smoke.

Whispering voices. Loud voices. Gloating voices. Laughing voices. Full of talk about *Kristallnacht*.

"They finally got what was coming to them!"

What would I find in Mannheim? I couldn't erase five years of Hitler hatred and imagine it would be without change. I couldn't pretend it was a nightmare and I would wake up knowing that things would be all right.

It was too real. To be a Jew under the Nazis after 1933 was dangerous. Deadly, even. And it didn't matter that my father's family had lived in Germany for more than 300 years. It didn't matter that my father had served his country bravely in the First World War and was always proud to be a German, as he was to be a Jew. It didn't matter that my grandfather, now dead, had been a dashing, mustachioed cavalry officer in the 1870 Franco-Prussian War and a communal and Jewish leader in his native town of Norden. It didn't matter that two of my closest friends in Mannheim were Kurt Hess and Heinz Manz, both non-Jews. We were inseparable—we were in the same class, belonged to the same sports club, played soccer on the same team.

None of that mattered once Hitler came to power in 1933. I first felt the change on the playground. My once inseparable buddies joined the Hitler Youth Movement and turned their backs on me, and so did all the other non-Jewish children. When sides were selected for a game, I was the invisible man.

It hit home and hit hard. My father's cigar business was aryanized, taken over by non-Jews. What they paid him didn't last long. Our food became plainer, less plentiful. Little treats for my younger sister Lotte and me became rare and finally disappeared. Mutti and Papi seldom smiled. Our grandmother—we called her Oma—was a beautiful white-haired lady in her eighties, who was frightened and unable to understand what was happening around her.

On the radio, tirades against Jews by Hitler, Goebbels, Streicher—wave after endless wave of them—became more and more strident. Signs were posted at entrances to parks and playgrounds that said, "Dogs and Jews Not Allowed." Jews were barred from local cinemas and theaters. One day I was told I could no longer play on the school soccer team. The team must be *Judenrein*, free of Jews. It was the biggest blow of my young life. I was thirteen years old.

To feed the family, my mother sold some of her jewelry and my father parted with prize stamps from his large and valuable collection. The talk in the house, and anywhere Jews met in Mannheim, turned to ways of getting out of Germany. A visa became the most precious commodity in the world. I shared my grandmother's room because mine was taken over by a young couple from another town who were forced to give up all their belongings and were waiting for their visas.

The last thing I saw each night before I went to bed was a framed photo of my grandfather sitting proudly on his cavalry horse. I wondered what he, a proud German, would think about what was happening. I was glad that he didn't live to see it.

In 1937 a new edict was issued: Jewish children could no longer attend a public school. I was in the seventh grade, and the attempt to organize a special school for Jewish children didn't last very long. With children from all grades thrown together, classrooms were chaotic and learning became impossible.

When the Jewish school dissolved, life seemed to come to a complete halt. It was unbearable for me to sit at home with nothing to do. When I did go out, I was, at best, ignored by our non-Jewish neighbors. More often they jeered at me. Beurkel, a man who lived in our building, was always strutting around in his SA uniform, snooping around with sharp, sinister eyes. I was always afraid I would run into him.

The only pleasant moments I remember from those days were the times I spent with my close friend Maxi, and the times Walter came to see us. Maxi lived just down the street. Born with one foot slightly shorter than the other, he walked with a decided limp. In the days before Hitler, he would come to watch us play soccer and other games in the playground. Now he was never seen limping through the streets to the playground or anywhere else. Those streets, with swaggering bands of Hitler Youth in their uniforms and swastika armbands, were no place for Maxi, Jewboy and cripple. He was a perfect target for attack, so he stayed home all the time, and when I visited him, it was to exchange one cage for another.

We read books and magazines, talked about the good old days (imagine, at fourteen!), and played the only game young German Jews were allowed to play—fantasizing what it would be like to live in a free country—England, America, or Australia.

Another close friend was Walter, a boy of incredible strength. Orphaned at infancy, with no home of his own, he was always welcome at ours when he came to visit, which was often.

"Walter, do your trick," Lotte and I would plead with him.

He didn't need much encouragement. He'd take a sizable table, rest it on his chin, and balance it for several seconds. We stood there in total awe of his strength and dexterity. He was a sports fanatic who excelled in everything. When anything needed to be fixed—a bike, a radio—it was always, "Call Walter," and Walter would come and fix it.

After we were ejected from school, he took a job as a mechanic for a non-Jewish shop, but when the Jews were no longer permitted to work and the orphanage where he lived closed, Walter left town. When he came to say goodbye, I felt as though I was losing a brother. I didn't know if I would ever see him again.

Some of our friends were getting out of Mannheim, alone or with their families. As 1938 began, we heard news that my friend Robert Suess and his family were about to get their visas. Robert was a boy more seriously handicapped than Maxi. Paralyzed from birth, he used a small motorized vehicle to propel himself through the streets. Now, of course, it was safer for him to stay home. Unable to walk at all, Robert was the most severely imprisoned of us all. But I was jealous. If he could get out, why couldn't I?

My parents tried everything they knew to get Lotte and me out of the country. To obtain an affidavit, we needed someone in another country to guarantee our stay, but the only relatives we knew abroad had themselves managed to emigrate in the preceding year or two and they weren't in a position to help us.

With more and more of my friends gone, the chances of my being able to leave Germany became increasingly slimmer and I was becoming desperate. I kept after my father to try to find something for me to do, anything, although we all knew how difficult that was. His persistence brought results when he succeeded in locating one of the few businesses in our part of Germany still in Jewish hands. The Kaufman Kartonagenfabrik, a cardboard-box plant in Bruchsal, was not far from Mannheim.

I started work on January 2, 1938, and found room and board with a very nice elderly widow. It wasn't easy being away from home for the first time and in strange surroundings, but at least I now had something to do. The factory wasn't big, but Mr. Kaufman ran it well, with help from his son, Franz, and Lisa, Franz's wife. The workmen all respected him. I wasn't earning much, but it was enough to pay for my room and board with a little to spare.

Every other week I went home to Mannheim. More and more Jewish families were leaving for America, Indonesia, Shanghai, or South America. There was a chance that Lotte and I could get out separately. A children's refugee program in France just might open up for her.

One day I came home to hear the shocking news of Robert Suess's suicide. He had sat in his room, in his motorized chair, put his father's service revolver to his head, and fired. Robert left a note. He was sure that his condition was the reason his family was being denied their long-awaited visa. He was putting himself out of the way. Robert was just fourteen.

In October 1938 a new regulation came into effect. All Polish-born Jews living in Germany would be deported to Poland. Overnight. No exceptions. Among them was a family named Grynszpan. Their only son, Herschel, eighteen years old, was living in Paris at that time. It was his act of rage and retaliation at the German consulate in Paris that gave the Nazis an instant martyr—and the excuse they wanted to launch *Kristallnacht*.

These were my thoughts on the short ride home from Bruchsal. I was afraid of what I would find. As soon as the train slowed down enough, I swung off and ran toward home. On the way, I saw some of the few remaining Jewish shops in ruins, shattered glass all around, crates and boxes opened and rifled clean. Brownshirts were everywhere. Most of them were flushed and grinning.

I dreaded to see our apartment. The sidewalk in front of our building was littered with broken furniture and a layer of broken glass from smashed windows. The door to our apartment had been battered down. I looked around but I didn't see anyone.

"Mutti! Where are you?" My heart was pounding furiously.

I heard sobbing from the bedroom.

My mother was lying on the bed, her face swollen, holding my grandmother, who was sobbing uncontrollably.

"Mutti, are you all right? What happened?"

She got up and put her arms around me. She was bloody, her dress was torn, she was shaking.

"Ernst, Ernst." She looked up at me with the saddest, most stunned look I had ever seen in her eyes. "They came in this morning...broke in...Buerkel smashed open the door."

"Where is Papi?"

"They took him. I don't know where to." She wasn't shaking any more, but now her voice began to tremble. "Before that, they forced him to open the safe where he keeps his stamps. They took out the whole collection, threw it out in the street and burned it. Papi couldn't stop them, two big SA men were holding him. I tried and one of the men hit me in the face. That's when they took Papi away. Oma became hysterical and I had to hold her. Buerkel, the SA man who lived in our building, brought some more of them in, with clubs and guns. They went through the apartment, destroyed it piece by piece."

Her voice had fallen to a whisper. Now fatigue overwhelmed her and she sank down on the bed. Oma was moaning.

"Mutti—where's Lotte?"

"I sent her to one of her friends. I thought she would be safer there. Not so many Jewish families in that building." She looked at my anxious face and managed a feeble smile. "Don't worry. She called. She got there safely. She's all right."

I stumbled through what had been our apartment. Broken dishes, pictures, silverware were scattered all over the floor. Chairs were broken. Mirrors were smashed. Nothing had been left untouched. The apartment was a shambles.

"Mutti—the synagogue?"

She shook her head. "That was the first to go. I heard on the radio that most synagogues in Germany were destroyed last night. It's a pogrom, just like the ones in Russia and Poland. And we thought it couldn't happen here."

Mutti was calming down. Oma, exhausted, had fallen into fitful sleep. Mutti put her finger to her lips and got up, and we tiptoed out of the bedroom. When I saw her looking around at the devastation and then bend down to pick up the pieces, I knew she would be all right.

I went to see my friend Maxi and found him and his mother pale and shaken, but their apartment was intact. We didn't know then, and will never know, why some Jewish homes were selected for destruction while others went untouched. Maxi's father, like mine, had been arrested. His mother was on the telephone with another woman whose husband had been taken. There was no way of knowing where they were, or what was in store for them. The report was that all Jewish men over sixteen were being rounded up.

The walk to the synagogue took me through side streets where every Jewish store had been demolished. Primitive signs were painted on doors and over windows: *JUDE VERRECKE* (JEW DIE). The Nazi assault on Jewish businesses had been less random than the attack on Jewish homes. Not a single Jewish store was left intact.

Police and the SA had cordoned off the street around the synagogue. Hundreds of people were still milling around. There was nothing left of the synagogue except the bare four walls. Exactly like at the synagogue in Bruchsal, everything had collapsed into a charred pile of smoldering rubble. The benches, the books, the Torah scrolls, the Holy Ark. All reduced to ashes. All gone. I stood there, transfixed.

I was in tears when I got back to the apartment. Mutti was still trying to clean up. Her mouth was set firmly. Her face was still swollen.

I don't know how we got through the night.

Two days later there was a knock at the door. It was Papi, but I hardly recognized him. He had aged years. There was an empty look in his eyes, as if the life had gone from them. Mutti rushed into his arms. His suit was dirty, he was unshaven, gaunt.

"What happened to you? Where were you?"

"Let me have a bath and something to eat. Then I need some sleep. I haven't slept since it happened."

Mutti took him to the bathroom, helped him undress, tossed his suit into a heap in the corner of the room, and let him get some sleep. After he ate, we walked around the apartment on tiptoes as he slept.

The next day Papi told us he had been taken to Gestapo headquarters, where there were hundreds of Jewish men of all ages. They were lined up in the courtyard and left standing for hours. Some of the younger men were taken away, nobody knew where to.

Nobody was allowed to call home. There was no food. Permission was required to go to the bathroom. At night they were transported by truck to a large hall, where they slept on the floor.

The next day there was another lineup. The prisoners were interrogated. Name. Address. What bank accounts do you have? What property do you own? What insurance? The selections continued, seemingly at random. Nobody knew why some were picked and some were not.

The prisoners received some coffee and a piece of bread, nothing else. By the second morning, less than one third of the original group remained. A Gestapo man came into the room and told them to go home and wait for instructions. Papi had no idea why he was not sent away. There was no explanation.

Slowly, we picked up the pieces of our lives and put the apartment back in order.

A few days later I returned to Bruchsal to get my belongings.

I visited Lisa at her apartment and hardly recognized her. She looked years older, drawn, with dark shadows under her eyes. She paced back and forth in the empty apartment. She was alone, with no word from her husband or her father-in-law. Along with most Jewish men from Bruchsal, they had been sent to a concentration camp called Dachau. We talked for a while and I tried to comfort her, but there was nothing I could do. I went back to Mannheim.

I had no job, nothing to do but stay home and watch my parents suffer and my grandmother deteriorate, and sense the hopelessness growing in Lotte. Weeks went by with no word of how we could get her out of Germany. There was nowhere to go.

The results of that tragic night, undoubtedly one of the most horrendous in all of Jewish history:

More than 1,400 synagogues in Germany and Austria were totally destroyed.

Thirty thousand Jewish men were arrested and sent to concentration camps.

Hundreds committed suicide.

Unknown numbers died in the camps. The bodies were shipped home with explicit orders not to open the coffins.

Fifty Jews were killed in the streets.

Seven thousand five hundred Jewish businesses were destroyed.

Thousands of Jewish homes were vandalized.

German Jewry was fined one billion marks.

All Jewish businesses were closed, and property was transferred to non-Jews.

Jews were forbidden to be employed.

Kristallnacht, November 9–10, 1938, was the foreshadowing of the Holocaust.

At the age of fifteen, my life was in suspended animation.

I had only one faint hope for a way out. It lodged with a kind stranger from America, a non-Jew I had met for one brief moment in the summer of 1937.

2

THE LINDSAY FAMILY OF WILMINGTON, DELAWARE

PART I: MY PEN PAL, BOB LINDSAY

I t was summer 1937. I was riding my bicycle to my weekly afternoon Hebrew lesson at the synagogue. On my way, I stared in astonishment at a foreign automobile. It was larger than any European car I had ever seen. The men standing next to it were foreigners who were consulting a large open road map, pointing, and looking in several directions, shaking their heads.

I got off my bicycle and moved closer. They were speaking English. Not really confident that my school English would be good enough, I took a deep breath and walked over.

"Can I help you?" I asked.

The men smiled with relief at hearing English. One of them, a tall, distinguished-looking man of about 60, said: "We want to go to Heidelberg. We're lost. Do you know the way?"

"That's easy," I said. "Turn the car around and drive until you see a sign to the Autobahn. That will take you directly to Heidelberg."

The man thanked me and asked where I learned to speak English.

"I study in school and my father taught me a little," I replied.

He asked my name and how old I was. When I told him I was fourteen, his face lit up. After they climbed back into the car, he turned to me and said, "I have a son your age. How would you like to write to him? His name is Bob. We live in Wilmington, in a state called Delaware, in the United States, and I know he would like to get a letter from you. Would you like that?"

I nodded eagerly. A pen pal in the United States—wouldn't that be great! The man took a scrap of paper from his briefcase and wrote the name Robert Lindsay and his address in Wilmington.

"Go ahead, young fellow, and write to Bob. Thanks again for your help."

It took me some weeks to get up enough courage to sit down and write the first letter. When I mailed it, I knew it was filled with mistakes. I could speak some English, but writing was something else. My grammar and spelling left much to be desired. Years later, when I finally met Bob in the United States, he showed me the letters (he kept every one of them), and we had a few good laughs. We particularly enjoyed this paragraph from my first letter:

> A girl friend of me is also in U.S.A. in Franklin, Michigan. Do you know that? Do you like any sport? I play very likely football, I swim, play table-tennis, drive bicycle and so on. I have looked at the map where is lying Wilmington. Mannheim is lying on the Ryne. It is built 1600 and has 300,000 inhabitants. It is in South Germany near Frenche. We have no high-screaper, and our largest house has 13 stories. I very like to read, at most criminal-romanses. Our oculist has forbided me to read so much.

Throughout our correspondence between 1937 and 1939, I wrote at night in my rented room in Bruchsal with a German-English dictionary at my fingertips. I worked hard to improve my English, and Bob assured me that I was making fewer and fewer mistakes. Now I was glad, because I had decided to write one particular letter. It would have to be perfect. It would have to be the letter, I dreamed, that would get me out of Germany.

Soon after my fifteenth birthday, July 1, 1938, I sat at my father's typewriter, in the bedroom I shared with my grandmother whenever I came home, and pecked out my "Freedom Letter." I typed it over and over again, until the English was perfect. There were four letters, all the same, and I still remember the text, word for word.

To the President of the United States, Washington, DC
Dear President Roosevelt:

To the King of England
Buckingham Palace
London, England
Your Majesty:

To the Prime Minister of Canada
Montreal, Canada
Your Excellency:

To the Prime Minister of South Africa
Johannesburg, South Africa
Your Excellency:

I am a young Jewish boy. I am 15 years old and I live in
Mannheim, Germany.
I am desperate, trying to emigrate. I can no longer go to school.
My parents have difficulties feeding the family. I am healthy. I
will do any work.
We have no relatives outside of Germany to guarantee us. Sir,
please help me to leave here before things get worse.
I hope you will help me. Thank you.

I was so naïve.

There were no replies. Perhaps my letters were intercepted by the Gestapo and never reached their destinations. If they did, maybe they were ignored. I don't know. I only knew that all attempts to get out got me nowhere.

In desperation, after coming home from his arrest on *Kristallnacht*, my father wrote to the one person in America who could possibly help, Mr. Lindsay of Wilmington, Delaware. He wrote from the heart, one father to another. He wrote as a Jew who urgently sought to save his son from certain danger in Germany. Although they never met, although he knew nothing about Mr. Lindsay, in his best English he appealed to a Christian an ocean away. It wasn't a long letter. It was clear and direct and did not waste words. It began:

> I am the father of the young boy you met on the street in Mannheim last year. As you know, we are Jewish. You also are aware of what is happening to Jews in Germany.

My father, who led a life of total pride and quiet dignity, went on to do something he had never done before. He asked a favor of a stranger: Could Mr. Lindsay put us in touch with a Jewish family in Wilmington who might be willing to provide an affidavit enabling his son to get permission to come to the United States?

The next morning I mailed the letter at the local post office. I remember standing there, pasting on the necessary postage stamps. With the envelope went my hopes and prayers.

Weeks went by. A month. No answer. It was too much to hope for a response. And yet, every day I anxiously waited for the mailman. Finally, after two months, one Saturday morning a letter arrived. It was addressed to my father and came from Mr. Herbert V. Lindsay, Wilmington, Delaware, USA.

Papi was careful not to tear the stamp even as he ripped open the envelope. Lotte, Mutti, Oma, and I gathered around, and Papi read it out loud. Although I could not understand every word, I got the gist.

Mr. Lindsay wrote:

> I received your letter and read it with great feeling. Indeed, I remember your son, and I can tell you how much Bob enjoys reading the letters from his pen pal Ernst. You should know that the letters are read by everyone in our family. We think we know all of you.

Then he went on—it was good news: Mr. Lindsay had arranged, through his attorney and the appropriate office of something called the U.S. Department of State, for an affidavit on my behalf. I was going to get out! I was going to America!

Papers were being sent to the U.S. Consulate in Stuttgart, Germany, and we would be informed when and where to appear to fill out the necessary forms.

The letter concluded:

It is our hope that Ernst will be able to come to the U.S. quickly. He will stay in our house and go to school with Bob. With his knowledge of English it should not take him long to adjust to life in the United States.

Looking beyond his expected arrival, we would also hope to assist you, your wife and Ernst's sister to join him eventually. I have been in touch with people in the Wilmington Jewish community who want to be of assistance. Our family prays for your well-being, and we hope that with God's help you can begin a new life in our country.

After the letter was read aloud, we were speechless. My father had tears in his eyes. My mother read the letter a second time and started sobbing. My grandmother kissed me and stood there looking at me and nodding her head.

I was dumbfounded. A total stranger, who knew me only from correspondence with his son, was providing a lifeline for me and my family. Living with Bob! Going to school! In America!

We had a family celebration that evening, the first in many years. Papi and Mutti exchanged smiles. I couldn't remember the last time I had seen such happiness on their faces.

We were euphoric for several days. Then, as always, there came the waiting that went on too long, the letdown, the disappointment. There was no word from Stuttgart.

Every German Jew was given an additional middle name by Nazi edict. Males were called Israel; females, Sara. My name was now Ernst Wolfgang Israel Michel. My sister was Lotte Bertha Sara Michel.

Special ration cards for Jews were distributed. We were denied butter; we were permitted a little milk and meat once a week. Potatoes and bread were severely rationed. The laws banning Jews from employment and from any contact with non-Jews would be strictly enforced.

To keep the family going my father resorted to the one item of value he had left—the remnants of his stamp collection. Although Buerkel had stolen and destroyed most of the collection during *Kristallnacht*, some of the stamps had been out on consignment. As he got them back, Papi was able to sell a few at a time, bringing in barely enough to feed the family. I earned a few marks working at the Jewish cemetery. I had no idea how long we could last. Neither did my father.

He, however, was determined to last long enough to get me to Wilmington. He called the U.S. Consulate in Stuttgart, again and again. Each time, he got the same answer. No. No affidavit had been received. They were swamped with applications and it takes time to process the papers. When the papers were received, we would be informed by mail and told when to appear.

How long would that take? The man at the consulate couldn't say. It all depended. On what? The papers had to be properly filled out, the guarantees adequate. There was the quota to take into consideration. Quota? What was that? The number of German citizens permitted to emigrate to the United States annually under U.S. law was limited.

I tried not to lose all hope. In March 1939 I wrote to Bob:

> *I hope I can come in the shortest time to the U.S.A. But I don't know how long I have to wait till my number at the Consulate in Stuttgart is called. And who knows what will happen in this time? I have written to a cousin of mine, which is living in England, and she tries to find a situation for myself, that I can come to England, till I can come to the united states. But there is the great question, who will pay my living there in England? And I think, on this question, this fine scheme wrecks. But I wait for a chance, and I do hope it will come.*

In the spring of 1939 there was talk of war. "Soon it will break out," everybody said, "very soon." Once it did, we knew there would be no hope of getting out at all.

The strain began to tell on my father. One night he said something very strange. He told me to take lessons in calligraphy.

"Lessons in what?!" I was astonished.

My father was serious. Calligraphy was the ancient art of producing handwritten lettering for clarity and beauty. There was a Jewish art teacher who was giving calligraphy lessons to get by. He wasn't charging much and so we could afford it.

"But why calligraphy, Papi?"

"You never know when it might come in handy," he replied. "Besides, it will give you something to do."

At first I went to the weekly lessons just to please Papi. Then I got to like it, and I became good at it. Besides, it got me out of the apartment once a week. I could walk somewhere with something to do. It was my little escape, although I had to look around carefully whenever I left the apartment.

One day there was a phone call. Good news. A French-Jewish relief organization was ready to accept my younger sister, Lotte. I wasn't eligible. At fifteen, I was too old for a children's transport. Too old!

Papi and Mutti were torn between their desire to see at least one of us leave Germany and their concern about letting Lotte, at ten, travel alone to a foreign country. But there was no choice. The handwriting was on the wall. We had to get her out while there was still a chance. No matter how difficult or dangerous it might be, the alternative was worse.

Lotte would take a night train. The only information my parents were given was that she would be met at the train station in the first French town across the border. They were given no names or addresses—nothing.

At dinner that evening—the last we would ever have together as a family—everyone was silent except Lotte herself. She was flushed, excited, and restless.

My mother washed Lotte's hair, all the while giving her last-minute instructions on what to do and what not to do. "Be a good Jewish girl, and remember to brush your teeth regularly."

"Yes, Mutti." Lotte sounded very confident and more than a little impatient with adult advice. "I am not a baby. I will be all right."

That night I took a photo of my parents and Lotte. I don't know how, but somehow a print was preserved by a member of our family and came back to me after the war. Unmistakably, there is a look in my parents' eyes which speaks of the agony they felt that night.

"Lotte," my father kept saying over and over again, "you must let us know where you are as soon as you arrive."

"Yes, Papi, I know." Lotte sounded almost grown-up. Papi took her hand. "It is important that we know where you are at all times," he cautioned her. "I still hope all of us can get to the United States. That's why we must always know where you are." He was trying very hard to sound confident. Maybe he even believed what he was saying.

Later that evening we all went to the railroad station. Lotte carried a knapsack. I carried her suitcase, carefully packed so she could handle it herself. When she kissed Mutti goodbye, she clung to her for a long moment. She hugged me and I could feel the tremendous effort she was making not to cry.

The warning whistle blew and Lotte put on her bravest, most grown-up face, stepping quickly into the train. I handed Papi her suitcase and he followed her. I saw them through the window as they looked for a place to sit down. When the train started to gather speed, Lotte came to the window, tears running down her cheeks. She waved slowly with one hand and wiped her tears with the other. Mutti stood on the platform, motionless, staring at the train as it disappeared around the bend. Wordlessly, she hugged me and we made our way back to our apartment.

Papi did not come back until the next evening. He accompanied Lotte to the last station before the French border and returned to Mannheim later the same night. He stayed at the station for 24 hours, pacing back and forth, looking for Lotte on every train coming back from the border, hoping that he would not see her, praying that she had made it safely across the border.

"It was the most difficult thing I ever had to to," Papi confided. "First Lotte did not want to let me go. 'I want to stay with you!' she kept crying. 'Don't leave me alone!' But we knew there was no choice. I just hope that we made the right decision."

Exhausted from his all-night, all-day vigil, Papi still could not rest. He sat down and wrote once again to Mr. Lindsay, thanking him once more for his magnificent gesture and describing the delay. Could Mr. Lindsay do anything to speed up the process?

More waiting followed. March. April. May. My father phoned Stuttgart every week.

Finally, at the end of May we received a reply. Yes, the affidavit was received. Yes, everything seemed to be in order. Yes, we could come to the Consulate to fill out the papers.

Early in June 1939, Papi and I took the train to Stuttgart. We sat in a separate compartment. People stared at us, but nobody said a word. When we arrived, we walked to the Consulate because Papi was afraid to take a streetcar. At the Consulate there were long lines of people waiting. They all had the same expression of fear and concern on their faces.

The line moved slowly. It took several hours before we were ushered into the office of a representative of the United States Consul. He seemed harried and impatient.

"Yes," he said, "your affidavit seems to be in order...but I must tell you there is a long waiting list."

Now he looked at my father. "As you probably know, many German Jews want to leave for the United States, and all rules and regulations have to be observed."

He said something about making sure we were not Communists. I tried not to laugh. The few Communists in Mannheim were arrested immediately after Hitler came to power. Besides, how could a Jewish 16-year-old boy in Germany be a Communist?

We filled out all the papers, and then came the words I will never forget as long as I live. They were spoken softly, impersonally, but sounded like a death sentence.

"You will receive a number today," the Consul said. "If everything goes as expected, your number should be called some time in 1942."

Nineteen forty-two! In three years!

"Three years!" I jumped from the chair, tears streaming down my face. "But Mr. Lindsay wrote us."

My father pulled me down on the chair. He too was choking. "Is there anything that can be done to speed it up?"

My father showed the American the letter from Mr. Lindsay saying I would be able to stay in his home and go to school. All the assurances were there.

"Why three years? How can we last for another three years? Don't you know what is happening to the Jews in Germany?"

Usually quiet and composed, my father had risen from his chair, his voice almost shrill. The consul just sat there, unmoved. His reply was quiet and chilling. "You have to wait, just like everybody else. That's the way it is!"

My father got up from his chair and tried to grab the consul's arm. His action was meaningless. He stopped, realizing its futility. The interview was over.

Slowly we walked down the steps. My father held my hand. He was devastated. We took the train home, hardly exchanging a word.

Three months later, on September 1, 1939, Germany invaded Poland. Two days later England and France, honoring their commitment to Poland, declared war on Germany. The Second World War had begun.

Despite the affidavit, despite Mr. Lindsay's offer, my hope for a new life of freedom in America was over. I wouldn't be going to school with Bob in Wilmington.

It wasn't until many years later, when I studied the historical events leading to the Holocaust, that I became aware of the name Breckenridge Long, assistant secretary of state in the Roosevelt administration. He was responsible for the issuance of visas under the quota system authorized by Congress. Long, an anti-communist and reputed anti-Semite, issued strict orders to limit immigration of German Jews to the United States. The result was that despite the desperate attempts by Jews to get out of Germany, the quota for visas was never filled. Between 1933 and 1938 over 129,000 slots were available. Only 27,000 were ever issued. Thousands of Jews with valid U.S. affidavits, including me, were thus prevented from reaching the shores of America. Most were eventually deported to the extermination camps and killed.

3

ARREST BY THE GESTAPO, SEPTEMBER 1939

F or the first two days of the war we were glued to the radio, tracking the onslaught of the German troops through Poland. I wondered what they did to the Jews in their path.

On September 3 came an unceremonious banging on the door. I knew it was the Gestapo before I opened the door.

"Ernst Israel Michel?" the man barked. He was short and heavyset and wore ill-fitting civilian clothing. There was a large swastika button on his lapel. His lisp blurred my name.

"Yes."

He shoved a piece of paper at me.

"Be at the train station at six in the morning! One suitcase, working clothes, 50 marks. That's all!"

"Where...?"

"Quiet, Jewboy," he hissed. "Don't ask questions."

Then he was gone.

I stood trembling. I couldn't focus on the piece of paper in my hand. Papi came to the door, gently took my arm, and led me back to Mutti in the living room. Her face was chalk white. Thank God Oma was napping and hadn't experienced the Gestapo visit. She was so depressed, she slept almost all the time.

By order of the Mannheim Gestapo I was to follow all instructions in the letter. Any resistance or failure to obey any order would be severely punished.

I wrote one last letter to Bob Lindsay, to let him know what was happening. I entertained thoughts of escape, perhaps getting to the French border. I knew it was futile. My papers were stamped with the requisite "J" for Jew. There were checkpoints everywhere. Capture meant prison or worse.

My mother and I carefully chose what I would pack. All the things that told me I was me—my books, photos, clippings, soccer ball, board games, pages of calligraphy—stayed behind. I was saying goodbye to my childhood. My mother made my favorite meal. I knew it would be my last full meal for a long time. The menu was my favorite: thick, rich mashed potatoes with lots of gravy, dumplings, pudding, and a cake with whipped cream. I loved whipped cream and I often wonder what she bartered for that farewell treat.

We didn't talk much. What could we say? The air was permeated with exhausted silence. Mostly, we looked at each other. Mutti was close to tears. I tried to put on a good face, to be a man. None of us slept that night.

It was still dark when I rose from my bed. My suitcase was packed. Mutti had baked cookies and made sandwiches. As a last loving gesture, she added the bar of chocolate she had been saving for a special occasion. I held my Oma and murmured goodbye.

She reminded me to be a good boy. Her last words were, "Remember your Hebrew."

It was too early for the streetcar. Mutti and Papi slowly walked me to the station, savoring each step. Papi and I took turns carrying my suitcase. Our hearts were heavy and so was my bag. At the station, there were 30 of us in the same age group. I recognized some faces but we kept apart, in family clusters, saying little. Guards hurried us along to the station house. They checked off our names and ordered us through the door. They pushed our parents aside. I don't think full reality sank in until that moment of separation.

My father wore his gray, crumpled suit with a vest and his best tie. "Take care of yourself. Let us know where you are as soon as you can. Maybe we can still get you out." His hands shook. He looked at me, embraced me once, and turned away to hide his tears.

My mother could not say anything. Neither could I. Finally, she blurted out: "Be a good Jewish boy, Ernst. Don't..." She couldn't finish. Everyone on the platform was going through the same torture. As I was pushed through the door, I turned my head and watched my parents disappear around a corner. I tried not to deal with my fear that I would never see them again. What would happen to them? They were alone, and so was I.

After our parents left, the Nazis kept us waiting. In late afternoon we were escorted, under heavy guard, to the train. We gave up exchanging guesses about where we were headed. After a night on the train, we arrived at Fuerstenwalde; a Nazi nobleman's estate, not far from Berlin. There, in exchange for harvesting his potatoes, we were served edible food and had lenient guards. When we finished the harvest, we cut trees in a forest, and after that we were sent to another estate to do spring planting. We were permitted to stay in touch with our parents by post and telephone.

My parents were barely surviving. They hadn't heard from Lotte after France declared war on Germany, and they were deeply worried.

In October 1940, a letter to my parents came back to me stamped, "MOVED. NO FORWARDING ADDRESS."

That night I frantically called Mannheim 40968 (after all these years I still remember our phone number). An operator answered, "The number you are calling has been disconnected." Click.

The next morning I learned that 30,000 Jews, including my parents, had been deported from southern Germany. They were given two hours' notice and allowed 50 marks, one suitcase per person, and food for a few days. All other possessions were left behind and confiscated by the Gestapo.

I never heard from my parents again. After the end of the war I learned that they had been sent on a harrowing trip to Gurs, a concentration camp in the south of France, near the Pyrenées.

Oma, 85 years old, lived for a few months, then died of hunger and deprivation. Her grave still exists, not far from the camp. At least she was spared the fate of Mutti, Papi, and thousands of others.

In August 1942 Mutti and Papi were sent, via Drancy, to Auschwitz. In the meticulously kept Nazi files recently made public, I found the exact dates of the final deportation and their transport numbers. My father, Otto Israel Michel, born in Bad Kreuznach, Germany, age 64, arrived in Auschwitz on August 26, 1943. My mother, Frieda Sara Michel, *née* Wolf, born in Norden, Germany, age 55, arrived two days later.

I have never been able to find out why they didn't arrive on the same day. No one from these transports was found listed as an inmate of Auschwitz, so I assume that immediately upon arrival, they were sent to the gas chambers. The official Red Cross records read, *"Fuer Tod erklaert."* Determined to be dead.

Seven months later, ignorant of my parents' fate and drained from dragging through half a dozen labor camps, I arrived at that place called Auschwitz.

4

ARRIVAL IN AUSCHWITZ, MARCH 1943

Rtata...Rtata...Rtata...The train slowly crawled through the night as one station after the other disappeared in the dark. We knew we were traveling east.

"Gleiwitz." A voice came from the slit on top of the cattle car.

The train stopped, as it had many times during the three days and nights since we left Paderborn. We were never permitted to get off the train.

"Perhaps we'll get something to drink. I can't take this thirst much longer," someone remarked at the far end of the car.

The train started to move again. Three nights in a cattle car. I had worked in Paderborn for over a year since the fall of 1941. Was it my sixth or seventh labor camp since the deportation from Mannheim in September 1939? I lost count. It made no difference. One camp was like the other. Work. Never enough to eat. Sleep. With 10 to 15 men in one room, there was no privacy. No change of clothing. Day after day, week after week, it was the identical routine. We didn't work on Sundays only because the German guards wanted their day off.

Work in Paderborn was particularly difficult and distasteful. We were street cleaners, garbage collectors, and canal sweepers. I spent my days standing in human excrement, cleaning the sewage pipes with brushes. No matter how often I washed myself, I could not rid myself of the smell and I could never get used to it.

We were a *Kommando* of about 100 men and women, all Jews. We lived in four small wooden barracks, just outside the city. We wore our yellow stars at all times, and in the evening we were confined to the camp.

The only news we received was from the German radio, which proclaimed one victory after the other. We knew Jews were being deported to the east, and there were rumors of mass killings in a place called Auschwitz. We tried not to believe it and continued our routine. We existed. Who knew for how long?

In late February we were told that the camp was closing and that we were to be deported. We were allowed to bring food for three days and one suitcase of clothing. Then, at midnight and under guard, we were marched through familiar and deserted streets to the train station. I suppose the authorities didn't want us to be seen by the local populace.

At the station the local police put 50 of us into two cattle cars, men and women together. The cars were totally barren—except for a small pail for waste. There was no straw. Nothing. The doors were locked. It was dark. After a long wait our two cars were hooked onto other cars. Suddenly, the train started, and slowly, with its frightened human cargo, it began its journey.

After two days, whatever food we had brought with us had been eaten. Only a few of us brought something to drink. We shared precious water and rationed it to a few drops for everyone in the cattle car. Soon there was none left.

More than 72 hours had passed since we left Paderborn. A few of the older men were getting weak. The stench of urine and excrement in the car was getting unbearable. Privacy did not exist. We stood, we sat. There wasn't enough room to lie down. My bones ached. Sleep was impossible.

Those of us who had the strength took turns climbing on top of each other in order to read the names of the towns and cities we were passing through.

One of the women was in bad shape and needed medical attention. We made room for her, covered her, but there was nothing we could do. She soon slipped into a coma.

We were dirty, tired, cold. The wind whistled through the cracks. I found a place next to Ruth, a girl I met in Paderborn shortly after my arrival. She was the first girl I was ever attracted to. She was my age, my height, very bright, and very pretty. She came from Frankfurt, only a short distance from Mannheim. I liked her immediately and we spent a lot of time together in Paderborn. Now we sought each other out in the dank cattle car.

"They can't keep us like this much longer," she whispered to me. "Another day, and nobody will have any strength left. We'll die."

What could I say? She was right. I could hardly stand up. I was thirsty, hungry. I needed to sleep. "Let me just get out of here," was the nonstop refrain that pounded through my head in time with the wheels. I realized I was stuck. There was no way out.

Day 4.

Rtata…Rtata…Rtata…

One word gets whispered. "Auschwitz!" Nobody remembers who said it first.

None of us knew very much about it. It was supposed to be the largest camp for Jews in Poland. That's all we knew.

"Beuthen!" someone called out. We were in eastern Germany.

By now it was clear that we were traveling into Poland. Slowly, I made my way through the car, trying not to step on any bodies. I found my friend Gerd, who watched through the small slit as lights and silhouettes of chimneys and factories appeared and then quickly faded into the night. Gerd was one of my friends from the Hachsharah group, which had been assembled in an agriculture camp in 1940. The two of us had spent 1940–1941 together, preparing for *aliyah*, immigration to Palestine.

"What do you make of this?' I asked him.

"Ernst. I have a strange feeling. This doesn't smell good. If the Germans are serious about taking us to another labor camp, why did they lock us up? Why no food or water for four days?"

I could only nod.

"Do you remember the time we were stuck in the canal and the stream of shit almost drowned us?" he asked.

How well I remembered! It was probably one of the most horrifying moments in my entire life. We were some 25 feet below street level, in the bowels of the Paderborn canal system when suddenly, without warning, we were hit by a stream of hot water, mud, and excrement.

The canal was five feet in diameter. We were thrown by the force of the onslaught and almost drowned in it before we could fight back. We hung on to one another for dear life and slowly fought our way into one of the main canals. We were terrified of drowning in the excrement of the Paderborn canals. Totally exhausted and covered from top to bottom with stinking filth, we eventually made it to safety.

I tried to be cheerful. "Gerd, we got out of that mess. We'll get out of this one too. After all, the war must end some time."

Rtata…Rtata…Rtata…

Two of the women died. One of the men was in a coma. Others weren't going to make it either. They didn't know how lucky they were.

One of the boys wrote a postcard to his mother.

> *Dear Mom:*
> *Don't worry about me. We are on our way to another labor*
> *camp. We'll see each other again soon.*
> *Be strong.*
> *Your loving son.*

He threw it through one of the cracks as the train passed through a village, hoping that someone with a kind heart would find it and mail it.

At the next stop they threw open the door to our cattle car. Three SS men in black uniforms with the death head insignia on their collars stuck their heads in.

"We have three dead bodies in here. Is it possible…?"

They didn't even listen. "Who threw a postcard out of the train?"

No answer. The commander yelled, "I'll count to three. If nobody comes forward, we'll shoot!"

We froze.

"One!"

Nobody moved.

"Two!"

The three SS men raised their revolvers.

"Don't!"

The boy who wrote the card raised his hand. One of the SS men took aim. One shot. Right through the head. The boy stumbled, then crashed to the floor, on top of some of those lying nearby. He was dead before the door closed.

"Don't worry, Mom. We will see each other soon!" We covered him and put him in the corner. We now had four dead.

Rtata…Rtata…Rtata…

Five nights.

We had finished the last scraps of bread the day before. More painful than hunger was thirst. There wasn't a drop of water to be had. It was difficult to swallow.

"When we arrive, let's stick together." Ludwig, one of the senior leaders in Paderborn, gave us instructions. He was tall, gangly, and very serious. He was always concerned about us and tried to ease our pain by keeping our hope alive.

We understood. We knew each other and could help one another. I was sure that there would be a need for that.

"Bismarkhuette!" Gerd announced from his viewing post.

I couldn't keep my eyes open and tried to find some place to lie down and get some sleep.

"Sosnowitz!" a voice woke me up.

"Isn't that Polish?"

After a while—I had no idea how long—I sensed that something was wrong. I heard voices yelling and the train had come to a halt. I heard dogs barking. Angry dogs. Dogs that meant trouble.

"The first thing I'll do is go to a hotel, take a long shower, real hot, then…"

The door was thrown open. There were SS men, dogs, and men in striped clothing.

"Out! Everyone out! Move! Move! Leave your baggage behind. Out!" I heard the word that would follow us every day. "Move!"

Everything was happening so quickly, I could hardly take it in. I saw barbed wire and rows of lights. "K.Z.! Concentration Camp! What did I tell you?" No one doubted it any longer.

"How about our luggage? What will we do without our luggage?"

We hesitated briefly. What would happen to the dead bodies in the car? The dogs were barking, baring their teeth.

"Out, I said. Out! Don't you hear well?"

The beatings began as we jumped from the train. Keeping a small bag under my arm, I jumped down, grabbed a fistful of snow, and shoved it into my mouth. It was the first liquid I had tasted in over 36 hours. I wanted another fistful, but before I could reach for it, I received a blow on my back.

"Stick together!" Ludwig tried to keep some sense of control, but his voice was drowned out by the screams and the barking dogs.

As far as I could see, there were cattle cars with hundreds, possibly thousands, of men, women, and children looking around in total confusion and fear. I forgot my hunger and thirst as Gerd and I tried to stay together in the unfolding chaos.

Men in striped clothing were collecting the baggage from the cars. Others were throwing the dead bodies onto carts. As far as I could see, there were endless rows of cattle cars being emptied. The old, the infirm, men, women, children, babies, created a seething mass of humanity. It was mayhem. The SS beat those who did not move fast enough. There were bodies on the ground. We saw other prisoners, obviously camp inmates, herding people along.

The noise was like nothing I had ever experienced.

"Mom! Where are you?"

"Don't leave me, please."

"Hold on."

"Karl, Karl, here!"

It was a scene from Dante's *Inferno*. More and more people joined the procession, which slowly moved forward. I could not see where it was going. Men and women were searching for each other, crying and yelling. Then the SS loosed the dogs on the crowd. Some were bitten. More SS men beat us with their sticks.

"Let's go! Move! You can look for each other in hell!"

I lost Gerd in the commotion. Some others I knew were nearby. I stumbled over the body of an older man. Before I could help him up, the crowd pushed me forward. The only one I held on to was Ruth. She was as confused and as scared as I was. The hunger and fatigue were gone. This was strictly a matter of survival.

Adrenaline kept us moving.

More and more bodies littered the ground. What would happen to them? They were parents, children...The yelling and screaming died down. A sense of foreboding, of the inevitability of what this would lead to permeated the crowd. We were numb.

I passed a woman leaning against one of the now-empty cattle cars. Her empty eyes stared ahead; "Please, let me go home. Please, let me go home." She repeated it incessantly. Then she disappeared in the swarm of humanity pushing forward.

Then I heard someone shouting: "Women...Men..."

I tried to raise my head but couldn't. Too many people were shoving around me. "What does this mean? Men...Women..."

Ruth looked at me. There was naked fear in her eyes. What could I answer? I did not know. Nobody did. Except those SS men in their long leather coats with whips in their hands.

We continued to move slowly forward and now we heard the order clearly.

"Women to the left. Men to the right! Women to the left! Men to the right!"

I swallowed hard. What did this mean?

If I thought the situation was helpless before, the next minutes were the worst I had ever experienced. We reached the point of separation, all of us shuddering with fear. Children were torn from their parents' arms. One little girl did not want to leave her father. The SS men grabbed her and threw her to the ground, where she crumpled in a heap. Her father ran to her. Before he could reach her, a shot rang out and down he went, a few feet from his motionless daughter.

I had no time to absorb the scene when Ruth reached out to me one last time. We couldn't speak. I tried to grab her once more but then she was gone. There were now two columns, both moving slowly forward. Men on one side, women on the other.

Left and right. SS men held their snarling dogs on leashes. "Go! Go! Move!" Some spoke with Bavarian accents, and they were all young, well dressed, and looked well fed.

Husbands held their wives. Brothers held sisters. Children clung to parents. I clenched my teeth to keep the tears in. Izzy now shuffled next to me. The most charismatic, dependable leader in Paderborn, he had been dynamic, optimistic, and always helpful. He was also strong as an ox. He had married Lilo in Paderborn a few weeks before we were deported. She was already on the other side. Tears were running down his face. I reached over to touch him. He only nodded.

No one spoke. The incessant screams and barking wore us down. It was bitter cold. I felt chilled. "Let's go. Stand straight. You can sleep later."

The SS men pointed to Ludwig. He was one of the oldest in our group.

"What is your job?"

"Teacher."

"You will answer, 'Yes, sir,' stand at attention, and take off your hat when you are addressed by an SS officer, understood?"

"Yes, sir." Ludwig did as ordered.

"Here, so you remember!" The SS man hit him in the face with the gun. Ludwig tried to keep from falling, blood pouring down his face. He managed to remain standing.

"Form single rows. Stand straight. Move!" We fell in line.

Gerd was next to me. He pointed to the left. "Look! Our girls!"

I saw them. They were already on trucks, pushed together, with hardly any breathing room. Then the trucks moved and disappeared in the dark. Our girls. Ruth. Lilo. Would we ever see them again?

At that moment I decided to take in every detail, every move of what was happening so that when this hell was all over, if I survived, I would be able to remember it, maybe write about it. What I felt, what I saw. Everything. Whatever else it was, it was also history. Human history. Jewish history.

"Move!" The beatings continued.

What an idiot I am, I told myself. I think about writing of this when it's all over, but I don't know if I'll be alive in half an hour.

As we slowly moved forward, I heard first faintly, then louder, numbers being called out.

"Eighteen."

"Thirty-four."

"Nineteen."

We came face to face with a handsome, exquisitely dressed officer in a long gray coat, wearing leather gloves. His hat was cocked a bit to the left, and he was of medium height.

Now it was my turn. "How old?" He looked briefly at me.

"Twenty." In a split second his thumb pointed up. "Right." I followed the column to the right, not knowing that in that split second I was given a chance to live.

Gerd was behind me. "Twenty-one." Thumb up. "Right."

"Thirty four." Thumb down. "Left." What did this mean? Right? Left? Thumb up? Thumb down?

The line was now divided in two. I was in the column to the right. So was Gerd. Others were moving to the left. Ludwig was sent to the left. Most of our group was sent to the right. Most of us were in our twenties, Ludwig was older.

We had to do something. Things happened fast. After we passed the SS officer, one of our friends dropped his hat to the left, called out "Ludwig," and pointed to the cap. Ludwig got it, moved a step to the right to pick up the cap, and immediately joined our column. The SS officer didn't see it. At least we were still together. I looked around and recognized most of our Paderborn group. A few were missing, but we expected that they would catch up with us later.

Suddenly I become aware of an unusual smell. It was sweet and yet unpleasant. I couldn't figure it out, and pushed it out of my mind. On the left I saw a row of trucks. They were being loaded with older people and children. One man didn't have the strength to climb on the truck. I saw him turn to one of the SS men and I could hear his plea. "...war injury...shot in the leg...I can't."

"You can't!" the SS man mocked him. "I'll show you!"

He repeatedly hit the man with his gun. When he fell down, the SS officer kicked him in the groin and then picked him up and, head first, threw him on the truck in the midst of all the other people. The truck took off. Another came forward.

There were bodies everywhere. Men, women, children. Some were dead. Some were moaning.

This wasn't a work camp. This was worse. It was something no one in his right mind could imagine. What would become of us?

I was freezing, so I rubbed my hands and stamped my feet to keep warm. "Stay still!" an officer screamed, touching his machine gun. Those nearest to him were clubbed.

I wondered what had happened to my luggage and my warm sweater. The only clothes we had were on our backs. The empty trucks came, were loaded, and carried away their human cargo. There was some commotion in front of us. We began to move again. I was totally numb from the cold, the hunger, and the fear. None of us had enough strength to talk.

"Come on, move! What do you think this is? A sanitarium?" Then he laughed, "You're lucky you're still alive!"

It was our turn to climb into a truck. SS men surrounded us, beating those of us who didn't move fast enough. One man just stood there. "I won't go. I don't care. Do what you want." One quick bullet in the head killed him instantly.

We were jammed in so tightly that I could hardly breathe. Gerd was nearby.

I tried to figure out how long we had been here since the train arrived. It was less than two hours. I looked around at the sea of humanity. Prisoners in striped uniforms were cleaning up the place. Some were picking up bodies, others were hauling suitcases.

The train with the now empty cars was leaving, making room for the next arrival. Our trucks lurched forward. This was our welcome to Auschwitz-Birkenau.

5

FIRST DAY IN AUSCHWITZ

Only my eyes moved freely. The rest of me was hemmed in against the others. They packed the truck so tightly, we couldn't even squirm. We rode through a little village, its outlines blurred in the pitch dark. Skeletons of half-constructed, low buildings and darker shadows of heavy machinery were scattered along the route.

In a few minutes we saw lights, double rows of barbed wire, and guard posts manned by soldiers with guns drawn. We drove through a wide gate and jolted to a halt. The gate slammed shut behind us. No doubt about it. We were in one of the feared concentration camps.

"Out. Move!" Did they really expect us to react? We were disoriented, hungry, and weak. Did they think we would go up against their guns with our bare hands? Did they really believe their own lies about us? I jumped off the truck, almost fell, and tried to get some circulation back into my limbs.

"Forward. March!"

We were in an open plaza, lit with kleig lights and enclosed by rows of wooden barracks. We were surrounded by SS and prisoners in striped blue and white uniforms. It seemed like days since our arrival, but it was only a few hours. We halted in front of one of the barracks. Most of the Paderborners were there and I had no idea where the others were. All of us were in our twenties or thirties.

Where were the thousands of other men, women, and children who entered the camp with us? As if to answer my question, one of the prisoners in the striped uniforms came over. "Welcome to Auschwitz-Buna! You are the lucky ones!"

"Why lucky?" one of our bolder comrades asked.

"Because the others already went up the chimney!" He said it in German: *"Die Anderen sind schon rauf in Kamin!"* I didn't understand. What did he mean by "up the chimney"?

I looked at Gerd. He was as perplexed as I was. Before we could find out more, the SS guards pushed us into the barracks. Home. Plain wooden bunks lined the walls, three levels high with very little room between them. No mattresses. Just straw. Thin dirty blankets lay on top of the straw.

"Everyone undress. Everything. All clothing to be brought to the front!"

We looked at each other. This could not be real. Undress? Everything? Were we supposed to run around naked? In March? In frigid weather?

"I said undress and I mean undress!" the SS man shouted. "Do I have to show you?"

There was nothing to do but follow orders. Coat. Pants. Jacket. Sweater. Shirt. Underwear.

"Keep your shoes, belt, and glasses. Everything else goes."

Some of the uniformed prisoners collected our things and carted them away. Izzy asked one of them about the girls and the others who came with us. The answer defied belief, and word spread quickly.

"Dead. All of them. Gassed!"

Gassed? I remembered that peculiar, sweet smell as we got off the train. They were all dead? Those hundreds and thousands sent to the left at the selection were all dead? Not even the Nazis would do that, would they? I shuddered and remembered "You're the lucky ones! The others went up the chimney!"

Ruth, Lilo. The others. The enormity and monstrousness of our situation was overwhelming. Dazed as we were, we felt the horror. The Nazis were going to kill us all. It would take a little longer but the end result would be the same—being snuffed out, just like that!

War was understandable. Deportation was understandable. Hard labor was understandable. But murder? Gassing? They were doing it, and my fellow Paderborners and I were living in the middle of a killing factory.

"Barbers up front!"

The command interrupted my thoughts. Barbers? What for? In less than an hour all our body hair was gone. We stared at each other, naked, bald, stripped of everything, holding our shoes and belts. It was a classic comedy situation. What was I supposed to do with my hands?

Two prisoners sprayed us from head to toe with an acid liquid. It burned my skin. We were sent, still naked, out into the cold to an icy shower. We rinsed off the burning liquid and were chased by whip-snapping guards through the snow and back to our barracks. It would have been better, perhaps, if we weren't so lucky. We would have been spared such pain and torture.

We ran through the snow, naked and barefoot. Some men fell and barely moved. They froze stiff in minutes.

After what seemed like an eternity, we were allowed to enter our barracks. Another prisoner threw us bundles of clothing. "Get dressed."

We put the stuff on—thin, striped pants, striped jackets, torn underpants, shirts, and thin coats—all the same blue-gray stripe, with matching caps. My pants were too short, the jacket too big, the cap hardly covered my head. All of it gave off a heavy, sick smell. We had no choice. I dressed.

It had been six nights since we left Paderborn. We had had no food or sleep for three days. The only water I had was what I managed to scoop up in a handful of snow. We stood in front of the bunks in the barracks, our teeth chattering in the frosty air. There was just enough room to walk between bunks. There was nothing else, not even a toilet.

We were so utterly exhausted that some of us collapsed onto lower bunks. I tried to guess how many of us there were. There were four rows of bunks and three levels. Three in a bed. There were almost 1,000 of us in the room. Suddenly there was a commotion at the door.

"Who said you can lie down? Who gave permission?"

The voice came from a small, well-dressed prisoner who walked down the aisle while we got to our feet. I noticed that he spoke with a heavy Berlin accent. His head was shaven, just like ours. In his hand he held a rubber truncheon. The barracks fell silent.

"Are you out of your mind? Do you think this is a sanitarium? You are in a K.Z. In Auschwitz. This is Auschwitz-Monowitz. Or Buna. And you are lucky to be here."

He walked through the barracks. "Behave yourself and you may have a chance to live. Maybe. You understand?" We nodded. "Here are the ground rules. You listen. You don't ask questions. Keep your eyes open and your mouth shut. Anyone who can't do that is dead. Understood?"

"Mister…"

"I am not a mister. I am the Blockaelteste [the barracks commander], responsible for this barrack [Block no.10], and I want no trouble. What do you want?"

"My jacket is too small. Where can I change it for a larger one?"

The Blockaelteste laughed. "In Auschwitz everything fits. If it does not, I'll make it fit. One more piece of advice. Your bunks are to be made every morning. Tip top. Blankets lined up carefully. One exactly like the other. Anyone whose bunk is found messy gets twenty-five."

"Twenty-five what?" someone asked.

"Twenty-five lashes. Listen carefully. You are to line up alphabetically. A through Z."

We lined up again and German bureaucracy took over. Name, name of parents, birth date, last residence, profession—everything had to be written down. The procedure took hours. We stood at attention the entire time.

Years later I was able to obtain my Auschwitz registration papers through the archives of what is now the Auschwitz Museum. Many of the records have been preserved.

Slowly, ever so slowly, the sun rose on our first morning in Auschwitz. A new day. When all procedures were completed we lined up for ersatz coffee and a piece of sawdust bread. It was bitter, but who cared. It was the first hot liquid we had had in almost a week, the first food we had eaten in days. We drank from a tin bowl which we were to keep with us at all times.

There was nothing as tiring or demoralizing as roll call. We had to get used to it. Roll call twice daily. It was always the same.

"Move. Line up. Stand still. Close ranks. Attention! *Achtung!*"

We stood for hours through the count. It was bitter cold and my cap was too small. We had no gloves, and we weren't permitted to put our hands in our pockets. We tried, of course. Hell must be a 24-hour roll call.

Some men were weak, on the verge of keeling over. Many were feverish. It made no difference, roll call was mandatory. It was a ritual, and our lives depended on whether or not we lasted through it. After dismissal, we dragged the sick ones back to the barracks.

The Blockaelteste explained: "You are to sleep two or three in a bed. It will be warmer that way." Gerd and I shared an empty bunk and tried to sleep, but before we could close our eyes, another command was issued.

"Out! Roll call! Line up the way you did before—alphabetically." I didn't think I could go on. It was too much. It was amazing what we could endure. We dragged ourselves out. The SS surrounded us again, their guns at the ready. It was evident we terrified them, or they wouldn't have needed all that firepower to control us.

"Roll up your left sleeve."

A number of prisoners were sitting at a row of tables laden with tattooing equipment. We were being tattooed! One by one, digits were quickly and permanently injected into my left forearm. I clamped my teeth so that I wouldn't scream with pain.

1...0...4...9...9...5.

Once upon a time, Ernst Michel was a human being, a kid in school who loved to play soccer and looked forward to growing up. Now I was Auschwitz prisoner number 104995. That was me. My arm swelled as I looked at the ugly blue numbers which would forever be part of me.

We held our aching arms and filed slowly back to the barracks. As we entered, two prisoners carried a body out the door. He still had his belt around his neck. Suicide. I remembered seeing him on the truck. I told myself he was better off and wondered what would happen to me. The SS man nearest the door laughed. "This one didn't last long."

When we got back, Ludwig gathered all the Paderborners together in a corner of the barrack. His face was still black and blue from the blow he received on arrival. He was one of the oldest in our group—quiet, serious, and full of inner strength. He was one of the few who was married, and he had two small children with him in Paderborn. They were gone, just like Ruth and Lilo and the others who came with us. I couldn't imagine how he felt, and yet he tried to give us hope.

"Listen," he looked around to be sure that most of us could hear him in the tight space between the bunks. "We must try to help each other as much as possible. I know how you feel. Believe me, I feel the same way. But there is no point in letting go. Evidently we were sent here to work. Otherwise, the SS would not bother with all these details. The first few days are the worst. None of us expected this." He pointed to the surroundings.

"Men manage to live even here. You see them all around. It is important that we try to remain decent, just as we were in Paderborn, each helping the other. That is the only chance we have. Now let's get some rest."

The Blockaelteste, a non-Jewish Communist who I later learned had been in the camps for ten years, made one more announcement. "I'll be brief. I tolerate only discipline. Those who steal a piece of bread will deal with me. Make your beds carefully. No shortcuts. The SS demands it. You will obey orders. Tomorrow is your first working day in Buna."

I didn't care anymore. Nothing mattered. As one of the youngest, I was assigned a top bunk. When Ludwig finished speaking to us, I climbed up, lay down, found someone next to me, was pushed by another, and finally fell asleep. Shots were fired outside, but before I could figure out what was happening, I fell into an exhausted stupor. It was my first 24 hours in Auschwitz-Buna.

When daylight broke, we had to line up again. We were issued small yellow and red Jewish stars with our numbers stenciled on them. My arm was now swollen to twice its normal size.

We learned the significance of the different colored triangles that made up our stars. Jews: yellow. Red: political prisoners. Black: antisocials. Lilac: religious prisoners, priests. Pink: homosexuals. Green: professional criminals and murderers. There were variations even in these categories. Sometimes the color was on the top, sometimes it was on the bottom. It was an ingenious way to recognize immediately why someone was in Auschwitz. Most of us wore yellow.

We also learned there were privileged ranks in Auschwitz. The greens had the cushiest jobs. Many of these criminals had been imprisoned for years and there seemed to be a clear rule that the green triangle gave you certain privileges, including immunity from the gas chambers.

We learned that Auschwitz was actually three separate camps, Auschwitz I, Auschwitz-Birkenau, and Auschwitz-Monowitz or Buna. Auschwitz I was the main camp, where the administration was located. The camp commandant was Rudolf Hoess of the SS. We were told he had a villa just outside the camp where he lived with his wife and five young children. Imagine bringing up kids here!

Auschwitz-Birkenau was where we arrived. It was by far the biggest of the three compounds. It had four gas chambers and five crematoria where the mass killings took place. Auschwitz-Monowitz was considered the best of the three (if you could call it that) and it was where the Buna factories were. Buna is artificial rubber. Since Germany had no access to natural rubber, I. G. Farben, the giant German industrial combine, needed slave labor to make synthetic rubber. Our job was to build the factory.

On the night of our arrival, the Nazis needed workers, but normally, once the daily "worker" quota was filled, those not chosen were immediately sent to be gassed. It was just the luck of the draw. On days when slaves weren't needed, all new arrivals "went up the chimney."

Auschwitz. We had to find the strength to survive. Our first meal was served. Soup. It came in great vats and each of us got half a bowl. That was it. Nothing else. I wolfed it down and discovered a few potato peels in the bottom of my bowl.

On the next page is a copy of an original Nazi document listing the transports that arrived in Auschwitz from February 15, 1943, to March 3, 1943, including the transports' origins. It includes the numbers that were tattooed on those selected for work.

Jahr 1943	Nummern - Serie	Herkunft des Transportes
15.2.43	1o2 350 - 1o2 492	RSHA, Drancy
16.2.43	1o2 493 - 1o2 525	RSHA, Kattowitz
16.2.43	1o2 526 - 1o3 504	Krakau - Tarnów
17.2.43	1o3 505 - 1o3 514	Sammeltransport
18.2.43	1o3 515 - 1o3 714	RSHA, Westerbork
19.2.43	1o3 715 - 1o3 766	Sammeltransport
2o.2.43	1o3 767 - 1o3 795	Sammeltransport
7.2.43	1o3 796 - 1o3 797	Lemberg Institut Weigl
2o.2.43	1o3 798 - 1o3 937	RSHA, Berlin
22.2.43	1o3 938 - 1o3 95o	Sammeltransport
22.2.43	1o3 951 - -	Bialystok
22.2.43	1o3 952 - 1o3 961	Sammeltransport
2o.2.43	1o3 962 - -	Kattowitz
23.2.43	1o3 963 - 1o3 974	Kattowitz
23.2.43	1o3 975 - 1o4 o26	Krakau
23.2.43	1o4 o27 - 1o4 o32	RSHA, Breslau
25.2.43	1o4 o33 - 1o4 o89	RSHA, Westerbork
25.2.43	1o4 o9o - 1o4 124	Sammeltransport
26.2.43	1o4 125 - 1o4 152	KL Niederhagen
26.2.43	1o4 153 - 1o4 172	Krakau
26.2.43	1o4 173 - 1o4 188	Krakau
4.3.43	1o4 189 - -	Radom
26.2.43	1o4 19o - 1o4 235	Krakau
26.2.43	1o4 236 - 1o4 322	Prag
26.2.43	1o4 323 - 1o4 325	Kattowitz
27.2.43	1o4 326 - 1o4 373	Sammeltransport
27.2.43	1o4 374 - 1o4 529	RSHA, Berlin
1.3.43	1o4 53o - 1o4 563	Sammeltransport
4.3.43	1o4 564 - -	Radom
2.3.43	1o4 565 - 1o4 592	Krakau
2.3.43	1o4 593 - 1o4 597	Kattowitz
2.3.43	1o4 598 - 1o4 739	RSHA, Berlin
2.3.43	1o4 74o - 1o4 889	RSHA, Berlin
3.3.43	1o4 89o - 1o5 424	RSHA, Berlin
4.3.43	1o5 425 - 1o5 456	KL Flossenbürg
3.3.43	1o5 457 - 1o5 5o6	RSHA, Berlin

This document is one of the most astonishing, descriptive pieces of evidence of the Nazi attempt to wipe out the Jewish people. It was discovered in Auschwitz after it was liberated by the Russian Army, ten days after the Nazis evacuated the camp on January 18, 1945. It is written in German and is page 39 of a document dealing with the arrival of transposrts in Auschwitz. The word *nummern* refers to the numbers of those who were chosen for slave labor. *Herkunft der Transporters* means origin of the transports. *Sammel Transport* means smaller transports were grouped together.

The document shows that in 1943, during the seventeen days between February 15 and March 3, thirty-six transports arrived at Auschwitz. Each transport consisted of 15–25 cattle cars. Between 60–100 men, women, and children were packed in each car. The duration of their trip was, depending on the origin of the cattle car, between two and five days. No food or water was distributed. The total number of all Jews arriving during that seventeen-day period can only be guessed, but it is estimated that the total number was between 40–50,000. I was among them.

Each transport was assigned a set of numbers. These corresponded to the inmates selected for slave labor, who were tattooed on their left arms with that number. On 3/3/43, the transport I was on arrived at Auschwitz. From this transport, 534 men were selected for slave labor. Compared to the other transports, this was by far the largest group of slave laborers selected. I was on this transport by sheer luck, and was tattooed with the number 104995. Others were not as lucky. For example, the transport arriving on 7/2/43 was assigned the numbers 103796–103797. From this entire transport, only two men were selected as slaves. All the others were killed were immediately gassed.

The total number of Jews selected for slave labor during that seventeen-day period was 1,844—1½ to 2 percent of the estimated 40–50,000 who arrived during that period. All the others, approximately 98 percent, were never counted. They were immediately sent to the gas chamber.

On days when no slave labor was needed, everyone was immediately taken on foot or by truck the short distance to the gas chambers. I was lucky that day. I. G. Farben needed slaves. Otherwise, I wouldn't be here.

How I survived that period, I will never understand. Normal life expectancy in Auschwitz was four to six months. By then, you were skin and bones, and you almost didn't care. Somehow or other, I never gave up hope. Some of us must survive. I promised myself that if I survived, I would tell what had happened.

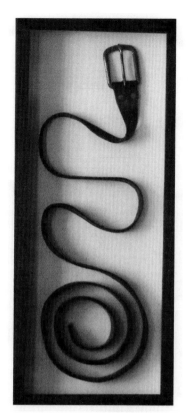

This is the belt I wore in Auschwitz, one of the two items I brought back from the concentration camps. The other item was a pair of grey and blue striped pants. (*see chapter 17, page 122*)

These are the pants I wore in Auschwitz. They are now in the Holocaust Museum and Education Center in Skokie, Illinois. (*see chapter 5, page 39*)

The yellow star that had to be worn by all Jews on the left side of their clothing. (*see chapter 4, page 28*)

Auschwitz Birkenau: the twenty remaining barracks. In the background are all that remains of the approximately 300 barracks: their chimneys. Each barrack was "home" to 300–500 inmates.

Lotte and my parents in 1938, the night before she was sent across the border to France. She was eleven years old. (*see chapter 2, page 19*)

The interior of the Mannheim synagogue after *Kristallnacht*, November 9–10, 1938. I took this photograph. (*see chapter 1, page 9*)

Suitcases brought by Jews to Auschwitz. They are now in the Auschwitz Museum. (*see chapter 6, page 50*)

Before the selection. Men and women divided into separate queues, awaiting word from the S.S. troops.

Jews, wearing the yellow star all Jews were forced to display on their clothing, after exiting the cattle cars visible in the background.

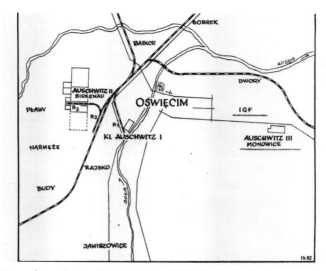

Map of Auschwitz (Oswiecim) and the three Auschwitz camps:
KZ Auschwitz I—The Main Camp
KZ Auschwitz II—Birkenau (the extermination camp)
KZ Auschwitz III—Auschwitz Monowicz (Buna)

In Auschwitz Birkenau. In the background is the entrance gate through which the cattle cars carrying Jews arrived. It is estimated that 1,500,000 Jews were killed here.

My sister Lotte and I in 1955, at her kibbutz, Kibbutz Ein Hanaziv, in Israel. This was our first meeting since she was sent to France at age eleven, in May 1939, before the outbreak of World War II.

Kibbutz Ein Hanaziv in 1946. In the beginning, my sister's kibbutz was a village of tents. Now, it is a modern village with eight hundred members. In the background is Jordan. Lotte is one of the founders of the kibbutz and still lives there today. (*see chapter 20, page 154*)

On my first return to Auschwitz, July 1983, in front of the Auschwitz Buna monument. Auschwitz Buna was totally dismantled by the Russians and does not exist anymore. (*see chapter 27, page 212*)

6

A "NORMAL" DAY IN AUSCHWITZ

Wake-up call came at 4:30 A.M. We were often three in a bunk because there were not enough bunks available for each inmate to have his own. Breakfast was a cup of boiled water with a coffee substitute. There was no place to wash up. No towels. No faucets.

Then came roll call. Twice a day, in the morning and evening, all inmates had to assemble for the count. The sick and dying inmates had to be carried to the assembly place. Summer, winter—we often stood for hours because the count had to be accurate. Next, the march to the Buna factory, somewhere between three and five miles away, I don't remember exactly. We passed by an orchestra composed of inmates who had been musicians in their previous lives, playing Viennese waltzes. We marched five men in a row. To our left and right were SS men with their guns drawn. No talk was allowed. For the amusement of the SS men, every once in a while one took the cap of an inmate, threw it away, then shot him as he tried to retrieve it, calling it "Another escape attempt!"

Tired and hungry, we arrived at the Buna factory. It was hard construction work; eight to ten hours a day carrying heavy cement sacks, wood, steel, anything. It was all done by hand. "*Schnell, schnell,* lazy Jews!" was the constant SS order.

We had to ask for permission to relieve ourselves, except there was no place to go. We were guarded all the time.

At noon there was a whistle and we had our big meal of the day— potato soup, but there were hardly any potatoes in the pot. Even line-up took effort. You tried to place yourself so that you were not among the first when the soup was ladled out. If you were lucky to get soup from the bottom, there was a chance that there was some vegetable or maybe even a potato. It just depended on which individual dished out the soup. Your life literally depended on that.

Each of us had been given a bowl. Losing the bowl was a death sentence.

In the evening, after eight hours of exhausting work, we walked back the same distance to the camp for roll call. Rain, snow, or shine. Again, standing for an hour, often more.

We dragged ourselves back to the block to lie down. Each one of us received 300 grams of bread, sometimes accompanied by 25 grams of sausage or margarine or a tablespoon of marmalade. Often the food was moldy or spoiled. Our total calorie intake was approximately 800 per day. Many inmates committed suicide. They simply couldn't take it anymore. We could never wash up. You just existed, waiting for the day when you knew it was your number going up the chimney. We all knew it. It was just a matter of time.

That was a normal day in Auschwitz. We worked six days, Monday through Saturday. The only reason we didn't work the seventh day was that the Polish workers at the building site kept Sunday as a holiday.

The three camps of the Auschwitz complex were built very close to the Polish town of Oswiecim. The town had an original population of 12,000, and 7,000 were Jews. Today's population is 40,000. No Jews live there any more. The complex was built in 1941 on the orders of the SS, the elite Nazi troops who ran the camp.

The main camp, Auschwitz I, was originally a Polish army garrison. It was also the headquarters of the SS leadership who ran the camps. It was here where most of the medical experiments were conducted by Dr. Josef Mengele.

The largest of the three, Auschwitz-Birkenau was built in the early 1940s, solely for the purpose of exterminating human beings, primarily Jews. Its four gas chambers and five crematoria were in use around the clock. It was the greatest extermination center in all of history, built for the exclusive purpose of murdering men, women, and children. It was divided into two separate parts, one for men and one for women. There were 300 wooden barracks; some 25 are still standing. Each barrack had three rows of three-tier bunks and housed approximately 500 inmates. The total number of inmates in Auschwitz-Birkenau was approximately 100,000.

There were no benches, no tables, no chairs—only wooden bunks. There was no water, no toilet. At the single entry door to each barrack was an empty pail. If it was full, the last person had to carry it out and dump it in the cesspool near the barrack.

For 24 hours a day, inmates in their blue and grey striped clothing, called members of the *Sonder Kommando*, had to carry the bodies from the gas chambers to the crematoria to be burned. My parents died that way. Members of the *Kommando* were regularly replaced and suffered the same fate as those they carried away.

The third Auschwitz camp, Auschwitz-Buna or Auschwitz-Monowitz, was named after the nearby town. It was built on the specific order of the German chemical giant, I. G. Farben, the largest chemical company in Europe. That was where I spent almost 22 months.

At the Nuremberg War Crimes trial, which, as you will read in chapter 16, I covered for the German news agency DANA in 1945 and 1946, Rudolf Hoess, the Kommadant of Auschwitz, appeared as a witness for the prosecution. A small, inconspicuous individual in an ill-fitting suit, he read a prepared a statement. Here are excerpts of his sworn testimony:

> I am 46 years old and a member of the Nazi party since 1922 and since 1934 a member of the SS. Since 1934 I have been in the administration of the concentration camps. On May 1, 1940, I was appointed Kommandant of Auschwitz. I estimate that at least 2,500,000 victims were gassed and exterminated, a minimum of another 500,000 died of hunger and illness, for a total of 3 million. This number is approximately 70 to 80 percent of all prisoners sent to Auschwitz.

Three million! Has ever another individual in history been able to claim credit for the murder of three million?

Hoess exaggerated. He seemed proud of that incredible statement. Yet the total number of those killed in the gas chamber was only 1.5 million, not 2.5 million as he had stated.

The huge headquarters of I. G. Farben was in Frankfurt. It was here where detailed plans were developed to build the largest factory in Europe for the purpose of producing Buna, artificial rubber. Since Germany had no access to rubber, I. G. Farben scientists created Buna. They were guaranteed cheap labor: Jews.

Of the three camps, Auschwitz I and Auschwitz-Birkenau today remain just as they were in January 1945, when they were liberated by the Soviet Army. Before the Nazis left, they blew up the gas chambers and crematoria. They remain today as they were found—in ruins. The Auschwitz-Buna camp was demolished by the Russians. Auschwitz today is a museum, the largest tourist attraction in Poland. In an average year, over a million visitors from all over the world visit Auschwitz. The museum shows the suitcases brought by doomed arrivals. Shoes, hair shorn from men and women, utensils, prayer shawls, clothing, personal items, family photos. The parking lot is full of buses and cars. There is even a flower shop, a snack bar, and a bookstore.

7

MY LIFE IS SAVED BY CALLIGRAPHY

I t was Passover, 1943. A few of us from Paderborn—Gerd, Onny (he had worked the sewers with Gerd and me), and Piese, who arrived at Buna a few months before we did, were discussing the implications of Passover. We had no matzoh, traditionally known as the bread of affliction. We had no wine, just water potato soup. Elijah's cup was a battered tin bowl.

Passover, Pesach. The time of our liberation. We remembered traditional feasts and family gatherings. We also remembered the endemic Passover pogroms and false accusations called "blood libels." We had been slaves in Egypt, led out of bondage to build a nation and a way of life that would endure. We were slaves in Auschwitz and we too would endure. We dreamed and talked of freedom. We played a game of "What if?"

"What if the Americans came and liberated us?"

"What if we could have anything we wanted to eat?"

"We have no seder, we should think about the service."

"Well, then, next year in Jerusalem."

"You're crazy," someone said. "We'll never get out of here."

"If we do, we should get together. Why not?"

"Sometime, someplace."

"If we survive."

"If we live."

"If we don't go up the chimney."

Sometime that summer I caught a vicious blow to the head with the butt of a gun. The SS guard who hit me was biting into a meat sandwich. I was thinking about Buna soup and he must have caught me looking at him.

"You lazy Jew!" he yelled, just before the blow landed. "Get to work!"

He hit me so hard, I fell and lost consciousness. When I came to, I was bleeding profusely and had a splitting headache. A few days later the wound became infected and I developed a fever. It got so bad, I could hardly keep up at work and, although my friends tried to protect me, I knew that unless I did something, I wouldn't last. My physical condition was rapidly deteriorating. I didn't need a mirror or a scale to tell me I looked like a "Muselman," the label used for those ready to go up the chimney.

Under normal Auschwitz conditions, you could last four to six months. After that you were so weak, SS officers picked you for the short journey to the gas chamber. That was a fact of life. We were driven to hang on for another day, another week. We wouldn't give up. Something might happen. We would finagle an extra piece of bread or soup from the bottom of the canister, and we would last a big longer.

Nobody wanted to go to the KB, the *Krankenbau*, the camp hospital, until they had no choice. Word got around. Regular or random selection at the KB increased your chances of being gassed. Many went. Few came back.

I could hardly walk. I couldn't eat. I was afraid the SS would pick me out at the gate. I told my friends I was going to the hospital only to get the wound cleaned and bandaged. I wouldn't stay overnight and run the risk of a selection the next morning. I took the short, scary walk to the gate separating the regular camp from the KB.

A guard told me to go to the barracks where injuries were being treated by prisoner-doctors. I later learned that some of these were world-famous specialists, transported to Auschwitz like everyone else. Dozens of prisoners had very serious injuries, mostly from beatings and work-related accidents. Compared to them, I was in good shape, but I wanted to get the wound cleaned up and return to my barracks. I waited for more than an hour.

Abruptly, an apparently important prisoner wearing the KB armband strode into the room, carrying lists.

"Does anyone here have decent handwriting?" Nobody moved.

It was probably a trick. You never knew what they were up to.

On impulse, just as he was turning around to leave the room, I raised my hand. What did I have to lose? Maybe I could earn an extra piece of bread.

"I do."

He stared at me for a moment. "I studied calligraphy at home."

"Follow me," he directed.

I got up and followed him into the next room. He handed me a pen and some paper.

"Here, write. Name, Auschwitz number. Then add: *Koerperschwaeche*, 'weak of body.' Go ahead."

I sat down, remembering how my father—it seemed a lifetime ago—persuaded me to learn calligraphy and how I protested. For a few moments I forgot my pain and discomfort. I took the pen and started to write. I couldn't remember the last time I held a pen. Slowly it came back to me and I wrote *"Koerperschwaeche"* next to the prisoner's name and number. I still didn't know who the KB official was or the meaning of the exercise. He stood behind me, watching. After a minute, he stopped me.

"Fine. You'll do."

I looked up, dizzy from the unaccustomed effort. "Can I get this taken care of?" I said, pointing to my infected head wound.

"Sure. Wait here."

A moment later, another prisoner in his forties, probably a doctor, entered the room. I showed him my injury.

"I'll take care of it." His accent was Eastern European. In a few minutes my wound was cleaned and bandaged. I began to feel better, although I was still very weak. I spent the next two hours writing the same words over and over again. It didn't take me long to figure out what I was doing. The list contained the names of those who were shipped to Birkenau and the gas chamber. The Nazis, with their usual efficiency and attention to detail, kept records of all inmates sent to be gassed. Except that nobody died by being gassed to death; they all died by being "weak of body"—*Koerperschwaeche*—or from *Herzanschlag*—heart attack.

Every once in a while the prisoner who had given me the job came by to see how I was doing. Satisfied, he left me alone. I later learned that his name was Stefan Heyman, chief registrar, or *schreiber*, of the KB—a Communist and longtime camp inmate. After the war Heyman became the first minister of the interior for the East German government. He was one of the most decent inmates in Buna and saved many Jewish lives.

When I finished, he offered me two bowls of bottom-thick Buna soup as compensation. Never, in all my time at Buna, had I struck it lucky and gotten soup from the bottom of the canister. My joy lasted a moment—the first spoonful was so salty, it was inedible. Somehow the salt had settled to the bottom, along with the potatoes. I gagged, unable to get it down. It was a low blow. The last straw. I was so fed up, I wouldn't have cared if they took me to Birkenau right then and there.

When Heyman came back with more lists and learned why I didn't eat the soup, he made up for it by getting me two slices of bread with margarine. I had not eaten that well since…I couldn't remember when.

"Your handwriting is good," Heyman complimented me as I wolfed down the bread. "Stay here overnight and work on other lists tomorrow. You'll get some rest and something extra to eat." Looking me up and down, he added, "You can use it."

I hesitated. After all, I didn't know Heyman and I was afraid of a "selection," the picking out of prisoners for the gas chambers. He sensed my concern and addressed it right away. "You don't have to worry. I'll protect you if there's a selection. You will be listed as a convalescent who will go back to work in a few days. In the meantime, you'll work on the lists." Somehow, I trusted him and agreed to stay. It turned out to be the best decision I could have made. The job as the assistant registrar led to a permanent position as an orderly on the KB staff. Eventually I learned to handle the injured and sick.

For the first few weeks, they listed me as a patient soon to be discharged. I learned the KB routine and continued writing lists. Tallies were kept of those headed for the gas chamber and regular prisoners who came to the KB. Some came for a short stay, many were sent to Birkenau. Most who came were in serious condition. Otherwise they wouldn't have risked visiting our compound.

For a few days I worked for Dr. George Kovacz, a Jew from Slovakia. He offered me the job as a permanent orderly and I quickly accepted. There is no doubt in my mind that Stefan Heyman and Dr. Kovacz saved my life. I never could have made it without them.

The KB consisted of five barracks, each with its own staff of prisoners, from the Blockaelteste to the head doctor, his assistant, and the orderlies. There were three or four of us in each barracks. The head of the SS was in charge of the entire operation. The Lageraelteste, the prisoner in charge, was a Pole named Dr. Bujaczek. The SS liaison officer was SS Oberscharfuehrer Neubert, and there were the ever-present SS guards.

If you did your job (and there was plenty to do), they usually left you alone. We took the responsibility of caring for the seriously sick. We needed to get those on their way to recovery out of the KB as quickly as possible, for obvious reasons. We dreaded the regular selection process.

Every morning SS Oberscharfuehrer Neubert, accompanied by Dr. Bujaczek and a guard, entered the barracks. We orderlies stood at the entrance.

"*Muetzen ab*! Hats off!" Heinz Lippman, the barracks leader (a Communist from Berlin) would yell. We took off our caps and stood at attention.

"At ease."

"Infection Barracks: 165 men, 22 corpses. All accounted for!" Lippman reported.

I was assigned to the barracks for infectious diseases. Under our minimal hygienic conditions, almost everyone had lice, and lice led to outbreaks of typhus. Those suffering from that dreaded illness were immediately sent to the gas chambers.

Slowly Dr. Bujaczek, Lippman, Neubert, and Dr. Kovacz made the "rounds." There was always an ominous silence. They hardly spoke as they went by the patients. Neubert, although not a doctor, knew who was sick just by looking at the men in their bunks. Every so often he would ask Dr. Kovacz for an explanation. Decisions were made very quickly. A brief nod, the number was noted on the pad, and we knew that one more man would be on the next truck to Birkenau. Many prisoners were so far gone that they didn't react, but every once in a while someone would plead for mercy. Seldom was it granted. Dr. Kovacz was in a tough spot. He knew that if he protested Neubert's decisions too often, his own role would be jeopardized.

I met two young men who became my closest friends and comrades. They were Honzo Munk from Prague, Czechoslovakia, who had been in Auschwitz since 1942, and Felix Schwartz from Vienna. We became inseparable and depended on each other throughout the trials and tribulations of camp life. We shared everything. Together we worked to save what lives we could.

Honzo was 21, bright and energetic, and had inventive solutions to every problem; he taught me a lot. He also saved my life when I caught typhus in 1944. I had a high fever and was often delirious, but Honzo washed me several times a day, kept my temperature down, and hid me from the daily selections. Felix was a year younger; tall, brash and camp-smart. If there was a shortcut, Felix knew it and put it to good use.

The worst part of our work was the disposal of the bodies. In our barracks alone, dozens died daily. Hunger, disease, diarrhea, and the results of heavy beatings took their toll. We took the corpses to a special storage room attached to the barracks. We carried thousands of bodies during my stay in the KB, first to storage and then, on the same afternoon, to the trucks which took them to the crematoria. Most of the adults were skin and bones on bodies weighing less than 80 pounds. There were also children ten and twelve years old.

One young boy was from France. Every night I would watch him search through the Buna soup for a piece of potato. He would eat the liquid, saving the potato for last. He would look at the potato for a while, examining it from all sides, and then would eat it, bite by tiny bite. For his birthday, we decided to give him a present. When our soup was distributed, we all looked for a piece of potato and held it aside. We put 40 to 50 pieces of potato into one tin cup and gave it to him. He didn't know what to say or do. He sat there looking at the bowl of potatoes and at us. Then he got up and, with tears in his eyes, told us it was the most beautiful birthday present he ever received.

8

MY FRIEND WALTER

A few weeks after my appointment as a regular KB orderly, I received permission to visit my old block. The wound had healed and I had gained a few pounds. I carried with me a few slices of bread for my friends.

When I suddenly appeared, as if out of nowhere, my Paderborn comrades thought I was a ghost. I wanted to find Walter. I hadn't seen him since I had left for the KB. He came to Buna a few days after I did, and I missed him. He was the only link to my life in Mannheim.

"Who's the stranger?" they wondered. "Who's this guy in a clean uniform? How come his ribs aren't showing?" their faces seemed to be saying. Slowly, they realized who it was.

"Ernst! Ernst Michel! What happened to you? We were sure you went up the chimney!" I calmed them down. "I'm all right. I'm an orderly in the KB diarrhea block."

Other inmates came over—familiar faces and new ones. The familiar ones looked at me in disbelief. "They told us you weren't in the barracks for the injured. We were sure you were gone for good. What happened?"

I reassured them all, watching the mixed feelings on their face—relief, concern, maybe a little envy. I looked around. There was one face missing.

"Where's Walter?"

"He's in his bunk," they told me. "He was kicked hard by one of the SS. In the ribs, in the stomach. Over and over again. It happened a few days after you left. Since then he's not the same. Go, let him see you alive. It will be good for him."

I walked the few steps to our old bunk and climbed up to the third tier. There he was, my old friend from Mannheim. The change in him was frightening. He had lost weight. He was skin and bones. His eyes were closed. I shook him gently. "Walter, it's me." Slowly he opened his eyes, grabbed me.

"Ernst! You? Is it really you? I am not dreaming? You are not… They didn't send you to the…?"

"No, Walter. I'm real."

With effort, he raised himself on an elbow. His face had the look of a man about to give up the struggle. I told him how my fortunes had changed at the hospital. I tried to make it exciting, to convince him that there was hope. He didn't respond.

"Are you getting lazy?"

No answer. The look in his eyes was easy to read. It was clear that he wasn't fit to get up and go to work. He would collapse. Unless he could get some medical help, he wouldn't survive the next 36 hours. He coughed and turned away. I could see that he was hiding something from me.

Walter, who was always so open, had withdrawn into himself. Walter, who was always so strong, was so weak that he had reached the point of helplessness. Walter, who was always so ready to laugh and bring smiles to others, was tight-lipped and grim as death.

I needed to help him. He had helped me, just a few short weeks earlier, when I was in a bad way. Now our roles were reversed. I didn't have to do the heavy work, I didn't have to line up for roll call. But how could I help Walter?

"Walter, tomorrow morning, come to the KB. Be there early. I'll be at the gate to take you in. Don't worry about a thing, do you hear? Everything will be all right."

He tried his best to look relieved, to sound hopeful. "Are you sure you can do that?"

"Yes, I'm sure. Just leave it to me." His face was still full of questions. I didn't give him a chance to say a word. I climbed off the bunk and told him I was going back to work. "If I'm late—who knows—maybe they'll fire me and throw me out of the camp!"

"Ernst, thanks."

"Oh, shut up. Don't thank me."

"I'll be there early tomorrow."

"Keep your spirits up, Walter. You're going to be just fine."

I put confidence in those words, but deep down I wasn't so sure I could help him. He seemed too far gone. I had to talk with Dr. Kovacs and Heinz, our Blockaelteste, the prisoner in charge of my barracks, the diarrhea block.

Dr. Kovacs had been transferred to another block. His place was taken by a recent arrival from a Greek transport, Dr. Samuel Samuelides. He was a small, wiry, energetic and very efficient individual who encouraged us to keep up our spirits and held us together as a working team. He was an excellent doctor, a warm human being, and an inspiration to many of us.

It took some doing, but we managed to get Walter assigned to fixing the lights in all the hospital barracks. He received a special pass and had time to rest during the day. I also got him extra soup and bread. The trouble was, he had no appetite.

The next day he told me the truth. "Ernst, I can't keep it to myself any longer. I'm spitting blood. I thought it would stop, but it's getting worse." I knew it. Tuberculosis.

Walter's job was temporary. If we kept him around much longer, Neubert would become suspicious and all of us would be in trouble. I met with Izzy and the remaining Paderborners. How could we help Walter?

Izzy, dependable Izzy, managed to get Walter transferred to the garbage Kommando. He had more to eat, but found it harder and harder to keep food down. Things got worse. He developed severe diarrhea and constantly had to go to the toilet. In the camp, that was not easy. More than once, he didn't make it in time. I managed to get some medicine to stop it. Izzy—I don't know how—got him some soft food.

Despite our efforts, Walter continued to weaken. Worse, his face had the telltale look of a Muselman; he gave up, lost the will to fight.

How many times had I seen that look? Every time I saw it, death was near. Why couldn't I get used to it? This was Walter, and I would never get used it.

There was only one option left, one we hesitated to use. We admitted Walter to the KB as a patient. If the SS Untersturmbannfuerher, Dr. Koenig, saw him on his regular selection tour, he would be the first passenger on the short truck ride to Birkenau. I arranged to have him admitted to my barracks, so I could keep an eye on him.

Walter didn't resist. He was more lethargic than ever. Not a trace of energy was left in that once robust, joyous body. He was a skeleton. To hell with regulations. I managed to get some of our friends to visit him. It was *Streng Verboten*, but they came for Walter.

I was able to obtain bread, even some margarine, but Walter made no effort to eat. I sat with him, fed him; there was some improvement. I changed his KB report to indicate that he was getting better. Dr. Koenig passed by, saw the report, and left him alone. After two weeks, we had to discharge him. We had taken too many chances.

"Walter, how is the blood?" I asked.

"Much better. Really. I haven't seen any blood for several days. I feel better. Really."

Was he telling the truth? His face looked just as hopeless, his eyes just as resigned.

"Can you manage cleanup *Kommando*?"

"Sure I can." He knew, and I knew, that he was dying.

I saw him a few days later. He was carrying garbage, barely able to stay on his feet. The next day he collapsed at the feet of an SS officer.

"Get up!"

"I can't."

"You won't. You're another lousy, lazy Jew!" And he kicked him. Once. Twice. Walter tried to get up. It was obvious, even to the SS man, that he was in great pain. The officer turned away. Walter crawled away to the toilet. Izzy found him there, holding his stomach, and brought him to the KB.

When I saw him, I knew it was over. His face had no color. Deep shadows were under his eyes.

"Ernst, it's no use. I can't go on. I'm finished." He lurched past me to the toilet. I found him there, tears streaming down his face.

"What have I done, that they beat me and torture me? I want to get away. Far, far away. I want to rest, to sleep. Help me."

I couldn't do anything. What could I say? I carried him to one of the cots and arranged to have him officially readmitted. I got him a bowl so he wouldn't have to keep running to the toilet.

One night, one of our barracks friends showed up with two small flowers for Walter. Flowers in Auschwitz! I wondered where they came from.

The next morning, as I cleaned him up, I saw blood. A lab report confirmed the diagnosis, "Advanced status of TB." If this appeared on his chart, it would be over. I threw out the card and started a new one every few days. If they had caught me, they would have thrown me out of the KB and taken me for a truck ride. I didn't care. I wouldn't let Walter be sent to Birkenau.

He needed butter, milk, nourishment. He needed the sun, a sanitarium. Instead, he was in the stinking diarrhea barracks of Auschwitz with death all around him. He ate watery soup and sawdust bread. Once in a while, he would have a piece of margarine. It was the best we could do.

It wasn't easy, but time and again we managed to get Walter past the Birkenau selections with help from Heinz, our Blockaelteste, who usually accompanied Dr. Koenig on his selection rounds. Without him it wouldn't have worked.

The routine was always the same. Dr. Koenig entered the barracks. We stood at attention. Heinz reported. Dr. Koenig nodded, always elegant in his long leather coat, hands folded behind him. Accompanied by the Polish prison doctor, Bujaczek, he walked slowly and deliberately through the barracks. Honzo, Felix, and I stood at attention, not moving a muscle, our caps in our hands.

He stopped at some beds to look at the patients and the written reports, pointed quickly, and went on. An hour later the truck came by and we loaded it with those he had pointed to. Most of them were silent and resigned, too weak to care. An SS man with a drawn machine gun stood next to the truck. When he was gone, I carefully noted the new count. It was down to 146. But Walter was still with us.

Dr. Samuelides told me Walter wouldn't last much longer. I knew he was right. I had seen enough men in his condition. Nobody had ever stayed in the KB as long as Walter. He just lay there. We moved him to a corner, out of sight of the endless stream of dead bodies going out the door, as many as twenty a day. Many were new-comers—Frenchmen, Dutchmen, Greeks, Hungarians—Jews from all over Europe.

One evening, as I was feeding Walter, he stopped me. "Ernst, do me a favor." He looked me straight in the eye. "Ask all our friends who are still around if they would come to see me tomorrow."

He knew. I could see it in his eyes. "I will," was all I could answer.

He touched my hand with his gaunt and bony one. The following night Izzy, Peter, Horst, Onny, Gerd, the remaining Paderborners, came to the barracks. He tried to shake their hands and nodded to each of them. Their greetings sounded hollow. "You don't look so bad. How about coming to work again? We could use you. Lazy guy, Look at him…"

He smiled wanly, then waved his hand. He looked from one to the other, his eyes lingering a moment on each face. "I know how much you have helped me. I want to thank you. Don't…"

He fell back, then struggled and tried again. "I know it's only a matter of time. If some of you survive—or only one of you—don't forget me." One after another, wordlessly, each man touched Walter's hand and left.

Two days later, Friday morning, Walter lost consciousness and went into a coma. That night, after my tour of duty, I sat on his cot. Dr. Samuelides told me to stay as long as I had to. Just before midnight, I saw it was over. I sat there for hours, looking at my dead friend. I closed his eyes, then slowly picked him up—he hardly weighed any-thing—and placed him in the adjacent hall with the other corpses. I swore on that day that I would tell his story.

I've kept my promise, Walter.

9

WITNESS TO DR. MENGELE'S MEDICAL EXPERIMENTS

N ext to the entrance of the KB in the first barracks, was a special room with a locked door. Days earlier, we saw a truck deliver equipment, but nobody knew what it was for. There was an unusual amount of tension among the SS.

One morning the door was open and I caught a glimpse of the inside of the room. There were electrical wires, a special high table, and some strange objects with all kinds of buttons and levers. The door was closed quickly and I went on my way. It wasn't healthy to see too much, but the guessing game was on. What were they up to? The SS head doctor was often seen coming and going. One day a Red Cross truck drove up to the KB and stopped out front. It was different from the trucks used to pick up the bodies of those destined for Birkenau.

One of the aides accompanying the truck motioned to us. "Come over here. We need blankets, at least a dozen or so. On the double! Bring them here! Right away!"

As I listened to him, I saw first one, then another, then a third, and then more women climb out of the truck. I couldn't believe my eyes. They were assisted by a woman orderly wearing a KB armband. She was a prisoner like us. It couldn't be. In Buna? I hadn't seen a woman since our arrival. A far as I knew, no woman had ever come into Buna. Now they sent in a truckload. I couldn't figure out why they looked so strange.

"Get going! Stop staring! Get the blankets!"

I ran to my barracks, looking for Honzo. "Honzo!" I grabbed him coming out of the morgue. "There are women in the KB. A whole group of them. Maybe six. Maybe more. What's going on? They want us to bring blankets! Right away!"

He hesitated for a moment, but he knew from my voice that I wasn't joking. We took a dozen blankets—they were so thin anyway—and went back to the first barracks. The truck was still there.

"Here are the blankets," I told the officer guarding the entrance. "We're supposed to take them inside." When he saw our KB armbands, he let us in. The room was empty except for a row of cots. There were eight of them. We were spreading the blankets out when the door opened. An SS doctor unfamiliar to us stood there. He ordered, "Help her down from the table."

Honzo and I went inside. There were a number of SS doctors standing around, among them the notorious Dr. Joseph Mengele. I remembered him from the first day of our arrival, during the selection at the tracks. I went cold with fear. Mengele! The chief doctor of Auschwitz handled the selections and directed the medical experiments. Mengele, the Death Doctor himself, was right in front of me.

Experiments! That was it! They were conducting medical experiments on women! I put two and two together. It explained the look on those women's faces. They were mentally disturbed. Now I understood their strange looks and strange behavior. Just as quickly I realized what the machine was for—the wires, the box with buttons and the switches. Electricity!

A young girl lay on the high table. She couldn't have been more than sixteen. Her eyes were closed. Her chest was heaving. She was strapped down by her ankles and her arms. Her teeth were clenched around a roll of paper, and sweat poured down her face. Mengele and the other doctors were standing in the corner and we could hear snatches of conversation.

"Expected more dead…considering the voltage…more the next…"

Honzo and I lifted the young girl from the table and placed her carefully on a stretcher. Her arms were rigid. Her breath was coming in short spurts; her eyes were still closed. We took the stretcher to the next room and put her on one of the cots.

Even in her agitated state I could see that she was beautiful. She had short black hair and clear skin. There were scratches on her arms. What had happened to her? Who was she? I thought of Ruth and the night we arrived in Auschwitz. I remembered holding her one last time as they ordered the women to the side, to the gas chambers. I shook my head.

"Don't think of it. It's no use. Stay strong. Live for each day, then the next. Some of us will come out alive and tell the world what happened here."

Inside the next room I could hear the voices. "More...More..."

When I looked at the girl again, she had relaxed a bit and looked around, obviously disoriented. Her big dark eyes looked at me and Honzo, helpless and totally confused. The roll of paper was still in her mouth and I sensed it bothered her. I gently removed it. "Hello, beautiful." I didn't know what else to say. What language did she speak? Where did she come from?

The door to the room where the experiments took place opened again. Two other orderlies brought out another woman. She didn't look well. Her face was frozen in a grimace and she wasn't moving. She was stone cold, dead.

"Couldn't take it," one of the orderlies said, nodding at her. "They gave her too much." One of the doctors appeared, and looked at her again to make sure.

"One less. No problem. There are enough of them!"

Is that what had happened to "my" young girl? I dreaded to think about it. I went back to her. "How do you feel?" She looked at me uncomprehendingly.

Honzo tried to speak to her in Czech. There was no reply. On a hunch I pointed to her. "Budapest?"

The young girl suddenly clapped her hands together and began to laugh. "Budapest. Budapest."

Woman number three was older, in her thirties. Her skirt was torn, and it was pitiful to see what was left of a once-attractive woman. It was difficult enough to watch men and boys waste away day after day. But women? Why were the Nazis treating us this way? What had we done to deserve such inhumane punishment? I bit my teeth together so I wouldn't scream; I knew there were no answers. In the meantime, I was more determined than ever to hang on to life as long as possible.

Other doctors and SS men came through, quickly looking at the women lying on the cots. They did the experiments with eight women. Three were dead. The others were in various stages of stupor or agitation. One of them tried to move her upper body as if she were dancing. Anytime someone came near her, she screamed and wouldn't let anyone touch her.

Dr. Koenig and Dr. Mengele, having evidently completed the experiments, entered the room and exchanged observations.

"On the next trip I think we should increase the voltage," one of them said as they left the room. They didn't give us so much as a glance. We didn't exist.

An SS guard ordered us to take the women to the truck and clean up the rooms. I quickly moved over to "my" girl and, with Honzo's help, carried her carefully outside to the truck.

"Goodbye, my friend from Budapest," I said quietly, although I'm sure she had no idea what I was saying. "Come back." And then I quickly corrected myself. "No, don't come back. Just get well." I felt she had no chance at all.

Honzo and I cleaned up without a word, each caught up in our own thoughts. I was despairing. It couldn't last forever.

A few days later they brought the women back. We were put on alert by Heinz and told to be ready to help. My thoughts were focused on the young girl from Budapest. Was she with them? If so, what condition was she in?

Honzo and I rushed out, took the blankets, and assisted the women. Most were ambulatory. Mengele and company were already there.

I looked for her, and I almost didn't recognize her as she stepped out of the truck. In a few days, she had aged years. She was sick. There was an empty expression in her eyes and she was obviously disturbed, walking as if she were in a trance. Her clothes were ripped and dirty. This time the experiments were much more severe, and it showed. Those who survived never recovered consciousness. Among them was "my" young girl. The female orderly from the Women's Camp who accompanied them told me the young Hungarian girl's story.

"Her name is Diana. She came to Auschwitz from Hungary two months ago, together with her whole family. It was one of those busy days when there were no selections. The gas chamber worked full blast. Her whole family was immediately taken away. One of the high SS officers, taken by the exquisite beauty of the girl, pulled her out and took her to his barracks. You can imagine what happened.

"When the SS officer was through with her, he assigned her to one of the most horrible jobs in the camp. Diana took little children away from their parents and brought them to the gas chamber. The children would follow her more easily and without a fuss. She had no choice. She brought them to the place with the sign 'Bath and Disinfection.'

"One day she recognized a cousin of hers, a four-year-old boy. It was the last straw. She attacked the SS officer running the operation with her bare hands and began to laugh with a horrible, angry expression on her face.

"They brought her to the KB. We tried to help her but she didn't have a chance. She became more and more agitated and confused, and Dr. Koenig selected her for the electric shock experiments. The rest you know. You've seen her. She'll never come back. On the outside maybe. Not here."

I don't know how long I stood there, in shock. I could see her as she opened her eyes and I heard her say: "Budapest."

"Hey you! Don't just stand there!" It was an SS man. "There are still some women inside—get them out!" I pulled myself together and went back into the barracks to help the other women.

I will never forget Diana.

10

A FOILED ESCAPE FROM AUSCHWITZ

Whenever something needed fixing in Buna, the call would go out for the *"Beton Kommando"*: Chaim, Janek, and Leo. They were old-timers, and everyone knew who they were and liked them for their resourcefulness and willingness to help. The three men exemplified camaraderie and friendship. I knew Leo because his brother, Freddy, was a friend of mine.

A few days before they had fixed the door to our barracks. Now they were in solitary confinement, in the "Bunker." Word spread through the camp like wildfire. "The special *Kommando* is in solitary."

No one could believe it, and rumors immediately began to circulate. Everyone heard a different version. Sabotage? Talking back to an SS officer? Smuggling? They tried to escape? Escape from Auschwitz? Impossible! We were surrounded by barbed wire, guarded by the SS with machine guns. It couldn't be.

Eventually the story emerged. Chaim, Janek, and Leo had indeed attempted the impossible. The true story was known only to a few, but I managed to piece together the information from those frightening days. We can only guess at some parts of the story.

The three, because of their extraordinary know-how and ability, were often asked to handle special jobs at the SS barracks. They even did repairs on the electrically charged barbed wire which fenced in the entire camp. Their knowledge of the camp and its surroundings, the easy access they had both inside and out, must have given them reason to believe they could in fact escape.

They managed to steal civilian clothing and arranged for outside work on the day chosen for the actual escape. Their plan was to hide in one of the many sheds on the construction site until nightfall and then make their way into the countryside. Once away, they hoped to join up with Polish partisans. They knew they had time until the evening roll call before they would be missed. By then the three would be gone.

It didn't work out that way. They forgot to factor in the German shepherds sometimes used by the SS. On that particular day the dogs were deployed, and even before all the *Kommandos* returned to the camp, Chaim, Janek, and Leo were caught.

They were taken to the punishment hole, 3 feet by 3 feet, which wasn't big enough to stand up in or lie down. They were charged with attempted escape, and their sentence was death by hanging. Camp Commander SS Hauptsturmfuehrer Schwarz, his deputy, Obersturm-fuerher Schoette and two other SS officers, Traute and Wiszorek, used the escape attempt to punish the entire camp. We were called to the Appellplatz, the roll call assembly place, where the entire camp spent the night out in the open—standing at attention. Nobody was permitted to sit down. Those who could not stand were taken out by the SS and shot. In the morning, just as the sun was rising, Schwarz, accompanied by his entourage of SS officers, made an announcement.

"The three camp inmates," and he read out the numbers of Chaim, Janek, and Leo, "are sentenced to death by hanging as punishment for their escape attempt. The sentence will be carried out tomorrow in front of the entire camp. Let this be a warning to all of you. As further punishment, all rations will be cut in half for the rest of the week. Dismissed for work!"

We found out later that our friends were tortured until they confessed, then were thrown back in the punishment cell, where they stayed without food or drink. The mood was tense. The SS guards knew it. Guards at all posts were doubled and the dogs were always in view. One wrong move and the situation could lead to a massacre.

Although we all lived with death every minute of the day and although we witnessed cold-blooded murder every day, this was the first time the entire camp would be forced to witness a hanging. It was especially repugnant because the three were popular.

It was a bleak Saturday morning in October. We gathered at the Appellplatz. There were three gallows at the spot where the camp commander was customarily given the result of roll call. The orchestra, comprised of prisoners, some of the best musicians in Europe, was playing, "Do not cry, yes, do not cry..."

We had never seen so many guards, and their machine guns were pointed directly at us. The place was beginning to fill, as *Kommando* after *Kommando* reported to the SS officer on duty. "*Kommando* 12 with 42 prisoners. All accounted for. Hats off!"

It took more than an hour for the entire camp to assemble. Hardly a word was spoken. The tension grew.

Even we, the orderlies from the *Krankenbau*, were ordered to line up. Heinz, our Blockaelteste, told us that because our barracks was where all the corpses were gathered before being shipped to the crematoria, after the hanging we were going to take down the bodies of Chaim, Janek, and Leo and move them to the morgue. There was nothing we could do. Somebody had to do it. Honzo and I were given the job.

From where we stood, we could see them being brought in, one by one, their hands tied behind their backs. They were surrounded by SS men in uniform and marched to the front of the entire camp. There were between 12,000 and 15,000 people present.

The entire SS hierarchy was assembled from Schwarz down. I recognized Koenig and Mengele among the officers. It was deadly quiet. No one spoke a word. Only the voices of the SS broke the silence. The three stood in front of the gallows. They wore their regular prison uniforms. Their faces were blank. Three comrades. Three of us.

Chaim was on the left. Janek was in the middle. Leo was on the right. Wiszorek, in his dark gray long leather coat and officer's cap, came forward and read the official death sentence.

"In the name of the Fuehrer and Chief of the SS, it is my duty to inform you..." and then he read the details. The tension grew stronger. Fingers on hair-triggers made us nervous. One wrong move by an inmate and there would be a bloodbath unlike anything we had ever known. Fight them? With what? Bare hands?

We stood at attention, some of us with tears in our eyes, as we watched the ghastly proceedings. Wiszorek finished reading the sentence. Two SS officers took Chaim up the few steps to the gallows. One of them threw the rope around his neck. His hands were tied. Just before the SS officer kicked the stool out from under him, he yelled as loud as he could, "Farewell, comrades!" And then Chaim's body swung and he was no more.

As Janek reached the gallows, his voice reverberated over the entire assembly. "We are the last!"

It was now Leo's turn. Before they fastened the rope around his neck, he too raised his voice. "Long live freedom! Don't forget us!" It sounded like an echo bouncing off the barracks. "We are the last!"

We stood, taking it all in, never to forget the moment three of our best were killed. Killed for what? Because they wanted to live as free men. The orchestra resumed playing as, one after the other, the Kommandos dispersed.

Honzo and I moved forward to cut down the bodies. We placed them carefully in a cart and wheeled them to the morgue next to our barracks. Silently, almost reverently, we carried their still warm bodies into the cold room where other bodies were lying in a heap. The day's toll: those who died of malnutrition, disease, or murder by the SS. We placed our friends side by side, away from the others, and then stood with our heads bowed.

Chaim, Janek, and Leo. Three of our best.

11

THE RUSSIANS
ARE COMING

"I t can't last much longer. The Americans have penetrated the German border. From there to Cologne isn't very far. Once they cross the Rhine they'll break through. It's only a matter of time."

As 1944 came to a close, this was the main theme, the only theme, in Auschwitz. You could feel it. It wasn't going to last much longer. The important thing was to stay alive. If the rumors were true, Germany sooner or later would have to capitulate. It would be suicidal for the Germans to keep fighting. We had to hold out.

The news from the Eastern Front was that the Russians had reached Warsaw, then Tarnow. One rumor was that the Red army had captured Lublin and was moving west. How long would it be before they reached Krakow and then Oswiecim-Auschwitz? How long before they got here?

Here we were, the remnants of the millions who had come in on the trains to Birkenau. We were the survivors, about 60,000 of us, in the three camps called Auschwitz.

What would the SS do with us? Would they let the Russians march in without a fight? What would happen? Would they let the Russians see the murder factory, the gas chambers, the crematoria, the emaciated corpses?

None of us, even the most optimistic, believed that the SS leadership would simply give up and turn us over to the Russians. So what would they do? Kill us all? Why not? They had done it before.

Come on, you Russians. Come fast, while there is still some hope. Free us! Liberate us! Can't you hear our silent prayers? Come! Soon!

Those were our thoughts, hopes, prayers during those cold, bitter winter days and nights. December turned to January. It was 1945, five years and four months since my arrest in Mannheim.

One of the men who frequently went to Birkenau said the gassing had stopped. We heard that the gas chambers and crematoria were dynamited by the Germans. That made sense. The selections, too, came to a halt. The flow of bodies stopped. The transports from the KB to Birkenau stopped. The trains also finally stopped coming.

More new rumors.

"The SS plans to move us to Germany before the Russians get here!"

"Impossible!"

"How can they ship fifty to sixty thousand inmates on trains to the West? There aren't enough cattle cars. Even if they shove eighty of us into each car, they would need over six hundred cars!"

That's how it went. The rumor mill was going full blast. Every day, every hour. We worked halfheartedly. Even the SS men became less vicious. There were fewer beatings, and the killings stopped.

Someone claimed to have seen a German newspaper that confirmed what we already knew. The Germans were retreating en masse. Cologne was taken by the Americans…Goering had been shot…Hitler fled…gas war…what was true? What was rumor? The only thing we knew for sure was that one way or the other, something was going to happen—soon.

The thermometer hovered between 30 to 40 below zero at night. The patients were restless. We tried to allay their fears as much as we could and assured them that the transfers to Birkenau were over. There were no new admissions. The sick and injured avoided the KB for as long as they could.

On January 15 a new rumor swept the camp. The Russians had broken through and were on their way to liberate Auschwitz. Later that night the rumor was confirmed.

Gerd, who had special privileges as a kapo, came to see me at the hospital.

"Ernst, it's true. They broke through. In a week we'll be either dead or free. The chief engineer at the plant told me he heard it on the radio." He grabbed my shoulder. "We'll make it. We will!"

I was skeptical. I knew all about false hope.

"Gerd, be sensible. Do you believe the SS will surrender without a fight? Do you think they'll turn us over to the Russians just like that? After everything we know about this place?"

Were we to be liberated or murdered?

We continued to follow the daily routine. The *Kommandos* went to the factory and the work on enlarging the camp went on. The orders were always the same. "Move! Move!"

At noon one day all the barracks commanders were ordered to meet at the Appellplatz. For a change, even the Blockaelteste, of the hospital barracks was included. "Something big is happening," Heinz Lippman, our Blockaelteste, told us. He put on his cap and buttoned up his jacket. "It also means our worst fears won't come true. They won't kill us. Otherwise why would they assemble the barracks heads?" He walked off.

In less than half an hour he was back. We met him in the hallway, desperate to hear what he had to say.

"We're all being evacuated. We leave tomorrow or the day after."

"How?"

"On foot."

"On foot?!" We looked at each other in disbelief.

"That's the order."

"Where to?"

"They won't say."

"How about the patients who can't walk or are too weak? What will happen to them?"

Heinz's eyes hardened. "Orders from the SS. Those who can walk, walk. The others will remain."

I looked at Heinz.

"What does that mean?"

He looked me in the eye. "I don't know. We asked that question. They ignored it. My feeling is they don't care. They have other problems.

They can't worry about a few hundred sick prisoners."

Now we knew. Evacuation on foot. The waiting was over, the uncertainty gone.

"Listen carefully," Heinz said after we had a few minutes to let the news sink in. "All patients must be carefully evaluated. No one is to say a word about evacuation. Anyone who can walk will be discharged as quickly as possible. Those who can't will be fed before we go. Try to leave enough food and water so that they can help themselves when we're gone."

We went to work, immediately. "Are you well enough to get out of the hospital? Yes or no? Can you walk?"

There was no other way. We had to let those who had a chance know the options. We all knew what it meant to march in the dead of winter, with no socks, in wooden shoes, without coats or sweaters, in snow and ice. No one could know how long we would last and where we were being taken.

"What will happen to me if I stay?" was the question most often asked. I told the truth. "Honestly, I don't know."

We left the decision to each individual. Most of those who could, decided to get out. There were some heartbreaking scenes as brothers, fathers, sons faced the most agonizing decision. Stay or go? Was there a right answer? It would be hard for a healthy man to march in below zero weather; how could a sick person possibly manage? What chance did he have? How long could he last?

Come on, you Russkies! Hurry up! Save those who stay behind!

In the middle of the night, our last in Auschwitz, a tremendous blast woke us from a fitful sleep. A second one followed. Then a third. In the distance we could hear the sound of airplanes. Russian? German?

One explosion after another shook the camp. All the lights went out. Even the guard towers were blacked out. The sound of the plane engines soon faded.

In the morning we discovered that Russian bombers had destroyed the railroad tracks leading to Auschwitz and that the Russian troops captured Krakow, 30 miles away. The hope spread that they would arrive before we were marched away. No such luck.

Immediately after roll call, the order was given. "Prepare for the march! All barracks march as one. Hospital barracks last. Anyone who tries to flee will be executed on the spot!"

One hour later SS Obersturmbannfuehrer Dr. Koenig arrived at the KB. "We are leaving. Anyone who can walk, walks." That made it official.

In the afternoon, the first of the inmates of Auschwitz-Buna shuffled through the gate. We each were given two pounds of bread. That was all. We were told it had to last for five days. No other food would be distributed. Anyone who could, stormed the kitchen to take whatever food was there. Others raced to the clothing storage to grab coats, caps, shoes—anything they could get their hands on. We needed to keep warm for the march.

With the SS guards gone, chaos reigned. The camp had become a place of anarchy. Prisoners ran from one block to the next. They came to the hospital to search for friends and relatives. There was no one to stop them. They entered the quarantine area, where those suffering from infectious diseases were housed. Honzo, Felix, and I prepared for the worst. We had two jackets each. Even better, we had heavy paper to stuff under our clothes. Paper gives good protection from the cold.

Dr. Samuelides, our barracks doctor, worked until the end to ease the suffering of those most seriously ill. He left medicine behind, hoping it would last until the Russians came. He hoped at least some of the inmates would live long enough to be liberated and cared for.

The departure took longer than the Nazis anticipated. All three camps were being evacuated at once. This meant nearly 60,000 inmates began the march that day. Barracks group after barracks group marched out the gate. We were among the last.

I took a final walk through "my" barracks and tried to comfort those who had to stay behind. "It won't be long until the Russians come. They're close. You're better off than those of us who have to march." I shook hands with some of my patients, wondering who would survive to greet the Russians.

"*Krankenbau*—March!"

That was us. We left the hospital compound for the last time. I remembered the first time I came through those gates and how lucky I was to survive for the last 22 months. Without my father's calligraphy course, I would have died a few weeks after the SS officer slammed me in the head with the butt of his gun. That was July 1943. It was now January 1945.

How many bodies did I carry during those months? Thousands. Among them were Walter and some of my closest friends from Paderborn. Ludwig, Guenther, and all the others, all those nameless ones. They came from all the corners of Europe and spoke different languages. They were individuals, each one once part of a family and having a future. Then they became numbers, tattoo marks on an arm. Who would remember their names?

Of the 100 Paderborners who arrived almost two years before, eleven were left. Of the 3,000 who arrived on our transport, fewer than 150 survived. Our endurance quotient was higher than that of some of the others. We passed the Appellplatz and Barracks 10, where I spent my first night of horror an eternity ago.

Late in the afternoon of Thursday, January 18, 1945, I marched through that gate for the last time.

I had lived through 674 days in a manmade hell.

Six hundred seventy-four endless days and nights.

Six hundred seventy-four nights in the abyss.

And so the march began.

12

THE DEATH MARCH OF 60,000 INMATES FROM AUSCHWITZ, JANUARY 1943

"**K**eep going! Pull yourself together!"
"It can't be much farther to the rest stop."
"If you give up now, you're dead!"

Tired and weak, we encouraged each other to keep going. Honzo, Felix, and I stuck together. We were a team with one goal—survival.

We marched for 15 hours straight, without rest. Those who couldn't keep up littered the roadside—living corpses. Earlier, the Nazis had shot stragglers. Now even they were too weary to care. They simply left them to fall onto the ground where they would certainly freeze to death in the snow. Some prisoners feigned exhaustion and dropped. They probably hoped to meet up with Polish partisans in the area.

When the SS guards showed signs of fatigue, they climbed onto carts drawn by inmates. We dragged ourselves through villages and along main roads. We made a ghoulish panorama—tens of thousands of prisoners in striped prison suits, guarded by the SS, dragging themselves trailing through snow and ice. It took hours for our columns to pass. The Polish men and women along the way stared at the spectacle but rarely said a word. They looked at us without pity and just shook their heads.

Prisoners began collapsing in droves. They lay helpless in the snow, unable to continue. Thousands were dying from exposure. At first we tried to help them up and get them going, but we weren't effective. We realized that we needed to preserve our own energy reserves, now badly depleted. The cold was numbing, despite the heavy paper and

our extra jackets. For three snowy and icy days, we shuffled and staggered over Polish roads. It was death by attrition.

We spent the first night in a huge brick factory, crowding together
to keep warm. The second night we were in Gleiwitz, where, rumors
had it, we would be boarding trains to Germany. By day three we
would be out of bread. We reached the train station just outside the
city of Gleiwitz and we were crammed into open cattle cars. The last
time I was herded into one was almost two years before, when we left
Paderborn for Auschwitz.

The train ride took five days and nights. On the second day some
bread was thrown into the car. Lack of water was a major problem,
but the snow saved us. Our ranks shrank as dead bodies were tossed
out of the car. We had lost half of those who began the march, almost
30,000 people.

The SS had a very simple disposal system. They ordered us to stack
the corpses in the first car. Then they filled the second car: those still
able to move were transferred to boxcars with those of us who were
still alive. The Nazis obviously didn't want to discard the bodies in the
villages, so we all rode together, the living and the dead.

Something amazing happened on the way, near Prague. As the
open train and its skeletal passengers passed by a factory, we were recognized by the workers, undoubtedly because of our striped prison
clothing. Within moments they bombarded us with anything useful
they could get their hands on. Sandwiches, sausages, shirts, hats—
whatever they could find was thrown into the open cars and quickly
grabbed by those of us who were lucky. It was a rare outbreak of spontaneous compassion from people who didn't have much and reached
out to those who had nothing. Thank you, Czechs. We've never forgotten you.

It was a bitter, cold day when we arrived. Eight days had passed
since we left Auschwitz. We marched into KZ Buchenwald, through
the gate inscribed, "Right or Wrong—My Country." Directly under-
neath were the words, "To Each His Own."

Buchenwald was in the heart of Germany, located near Weimar,
the city of Goethe. It was being used as the dumping ground for prison-

ers from camps in danger of being overrun by the Allies. The camp was jammed beyond capacity, and new transports were arriving steadily.

That night we were put in Barracks 58, in the so-called "small camp." A thousand of us were trying to find a place to sleep in a barracks designed to hold no more than 300. I don't know which was worse, the hunger, the dirt, the fatigue, or the lice. It was quite a combination. There were no blankets, no mattresses, not even straw. All we had were barren wood planks. The three of us decided to take turns lying down so we could all get some sleep.

There were major differences between Auschwitz and Buchenwald. First of all, there was absolutely nothing to do. We stood around all day waiting for one of two meals: a breakfast of sawdust bread in the morning and thin soup at night. The death *Kommando* made rounds through the barracks each morning to collect the bodies. There were no washing facilities. Toilets, if you could call the holes that, were filthy and disease-laden. Many who had survived the march died at Buchenwald.

The second major difference was the way we were treated by those in charge of the barracks. Most were old-time prisoners. There were no beatings, no unnecessary harassment. Their attitude was to maintain the status quo and not increase the distress factor.

There was one more thing. Twice each day, loudspeakers in the barracks would broadcast the latest official German news. And despite the fact that they continued to claim victory as they reported the heroic battles of the German armies, the cities they named made it clear that the Allied armies were slowly but surely advancing on all fronts.

We could hardly wait for the newscasts. They gave us the incentive to hang on. Without them, Felix, Honzo, and I would not have had the courage to fight to stay alive.

Later, after the war, I learned what happened to those we left behind in Buna. Auschwitz was liberated by the Russian army on January 27. The inmates who survived the five days between the time we left and the Russians arrived were cared for by Russian doctors. I met some of the survivors after the war.

Meanwhile I continued to wonder what would happen to us. My

friends' faces had changed. We were all skin and bones. Felix looked like a walking skeleton. Honzo didn't look any better. Did I look like them? How long could we go on?

One day I witnessed cannibalism. Some of the barely alive prisoners were eating the flesh of those newly dead. It was a horror that is still etched in my mind.

13

ESCAPE

For days, the sound of artillery fire could be heard in the distance. Although we had heard news of the German retreat, we waited for something to happen. The SS were hardly visible. Food was scarce and there was nothing to do. So we waited and hoped.

There was a roll call every morning and every night. Then word of transfers trickled through the ranks. Fear and tension increased and our optimism soured. One morning, the Blockaelteste read names off his transport list. Honzo and I were to be sent to another camp, two hours away. Felix wasn't listed, so we begged the kapo to allow Felix to join us and he agreed. The three of us, with 40 other prisoners, were loaded into a truck and transported to the sub-camp Berga, which held 1,500 prisoners. Here, for the first time, we encountered American POWs.

We were put to work digging tunnels for underground munitions factories. The Americans were working right next to us, forced to do the same hard work. We observed their leather shoes and their wristwatches. We had seen neither in years. When I tried to speak to them in German, some, to my total surprise, replied in Yiddish. They were Jews—American Jews! American Jewish prisoners of war!

During our meager lunch break, we learned that they had been captured and taken to a POW camp, where the commandant tried to separate the Jews from the non-Jews. The non-Jewish POWs wouldn't let him do it and ordered their comrades not to move. Some, afraid of being singled out, threw away their dog tags, which bore a telltale "H" for "Hebrew." When no one stepped forward, the camp commandant announced that they had 24 hours to change their minds. The prisoners were told that unless the Jews identified themselves voluntarily, they would be found out and killed. Those who had agreed to hide them would be executed as well.

The next morning, Jewish POWs, unwilling to let their comrades die in retribution, stepped forward. They were separated from the rest and wound up in a POW camp near Berga, where they lived under miserable conditions, receiving the same bad food and bad treatment that we did.

Unable to withstand the conditions—sickness, starvation, and lice infestation—many American-Jewish POWs succumbed. Between early March and the liberation of the camp in the spring, 70 out of 200 died. The rest were reduced to skeletons and were saved only when the camp was finally liberated in April 1945. One of the soldiers was so desperate that he offered to trade his gold watch for a few potatoes. I don't know if he lived long enough to be liberated.

The SS guards were nervous. They knew that it was only a matter of time until the war was over. Their demeanor showed it. They were less brutal, perhaps because they hoped to buy some "protection insurance" by behaving almost civilly toward us. The sound of the battles raging west of us seemed to come ever closer, and they heard the guns as clearly as we did.

"Any day now. Let's hold out. Let's not do anything to provoke the guards," we kept repeating to each other.

Once again, our hopes for liberation were shattered. The SS announced it would evacuate the entire camp. The date was April 11. We were told to take along one blanket and our tin bowls. We assembled early in the morning and began another march.

"Where do you think we're going now?" I really didn't expect an answer. Felix and Honzo knew as much as I did. Nothing.

"Rows of five. Line up! Quick!" the officer barked. Within minutes, Berga was behind us. Each of us had one piece of bread in our pockets. That was all. The SS guards, with their weapons ready, were marching at our side. We trekked along small country roads, avoiding farms and villages. The pace was leisurely. The sounds of battle faded.

We didn't talk much trying to conserve our energy. There was little yelling and no hitting. The guards too were obviously aware the end was near. And for them, as for us, the future was unknown.

In the evening we stopped at an old factory, ate part of our chunk of bread, and drank some cold ersatz coffee. Dead tired, using our blankets together, we huddled close and tried to get some sleep.

Early the next morning, when we lined up, we were hit with a surprise announcement: "*Achtung!* I have important news." The SS officer, using his megaphone, stood on a large rock at the edge of the forest. "The American warmonger, President Roosevelt, is dead!"

It was another one of those moments that remain with me, etched in space and time. I remember Honzo's expression, the dazed look in his eyes, his mouth open, his hand reaching out to me. "It can't be! Not Roosevelt!"

Ever since I could remember, in my early days at school, the American President, Franklin D. Roosevelt in a wheelchair, was a symbol of everything we hoped for and did not have—freedom, stability, democracy, and full acceptance as Jews. We knew Roosevelt opposed Hitler and choreographed America's entrance into the war, the creation of the Allied Forces, and finally, the landing in Europe on D-Day in June, 1944. The only other person whose name mattered as much to us was General Dwight D. Eisenhower, the commander of the Allied Forces. The survivors stirred restlessly.

"Listen!" the officer shouted. "This is the turning point of the war! Germany will throw the Allies back! The Fuehrer will succeed. And now, form your rows. March!" In shock, we regrouped and the march continued. The march to nowhere. On the third night, after watching a random incident, the three of us decided to escape.

Several men were pulled from the transport, taken to a clearing, and in full view of all of us, summarily executed. The pretext, according to the SS officer's warning, was that they had tried to steal some food from a farm during the night.

"Let this be a warning to all of you!" he yelled after the men had been shot. "We will not permit this. You are still camp inmates. My responsibility is to deliver all of you, and I mean all of you, to our destination. We expect to be there in a few days."

I don't remember which of the three of us first uttered the word "escape." We tried to weigh our chances carefully. How could we do it? When could we do it? Should we organize a mass escape and take the chance of a large number of us being killed? Should we try to overwhelm the SS men? We quickly discarded that last idea. The SS were positioned so that there was always a backup with machine gun at the ready. Any attempt to overpower them would result in a bloodbath with few survivors.

Honzo closed the discussion, whispering quietly as we curled up in our thin blankets out in the woods, "Look, I didn't survive three years of concentration camps, hunger, murder, dirt, and lice to get shot within the sound of the Allied armies. They'll be here in a matter of weeks, maybe days. Mass escape is out of the question."

He was right. "We must think of a better way. Think about it and give me some ideas." It took a long time to fall asleep. Escape. How?

Our chance came on the sixth day. The SS chose a young forest for us to spend the night in. They positioned themselves around us and took turns on the watch. At night a smaller force was on the alert. They were either sitting down or slowly making their rounds.

Felix came up with a plan. "The only time we'd have is at night. No daylight attempt would work. The transport consists of fifteen hundred men. We march in rows of five. That makes three hundred rows, stretching out over a total length of one thousand meters, or three thousand feet. It's a long column. The SS has several hundred men with machine guns. Each SS man, walking on the outside, keeps his eyes on a few rows."

"So?"

Felix spoke with intensity. "Instead of marching in the same row, we position ourselves on the outside, a few rows apart, just behind an SS officer with his gun. Once we reach a spot, in the evening, near dusk, just before we usually camp down, when we go through a few bends in the road, I'll give a signal. Each of us, positioned behind an SS man, kicks him in the back and we immediately run zigzag into the woods. But we need a young forest, thick with trees. Otherwise we'll be shot."

Honzo and I listened attentively. "Not bad." I said. "What are our chances?"

Honzo said, "Not great. But what are they if we don't try something?"

The more I thought about it, the better I liked it. With one exception. We were concerned about what would happen to all the others. They would have no idea what was happening and we couldn't afford to share our plans with too many of them. They were at a disadvantage and many of them could get shot. This was a major flaw. There had to be another way.

They both looked at me. Nobody said a word. I tried to pick Felix's plan apart. Would it work? Would the guards recover quickly and take aim at us before we reached the safety of the woods? What about all the others? What would happen to them? Would there be reprisals? Would some of them get away? Without advance notice, their chances might be less than ours. If we weren't careful, we would ensure the massacre we all feared.

But Honzo was right. We had to get away. Otherwise death was almost certain.

Late in the afternoon of April 18, just as it was getting dark, the three of us slowly walked a few steps into the woods and pulled down our pants as if we were following a call of nature. We weren't the only ones. Others were doing the same thing. The difference was that we kept going, slowly sneaking deeper and deeper into the woods.

My heart was pounding so loudly, I thought I could hear it. I was scarcely able to breathe. Honzo was 30 feet to my left; Felix was ahead of me, about the same distance to my right. We moved further into the woods, putting a considerable distance between ourselves and the group. Faintly we heard the Nazis order the columns to march. We ran through the trees. I looked around and couldn't see anyone but Honzo and Felix.

Totally out of breath, I fell in the middle of the forest, tears streaming down my cheeks.

I was free. Free! Free!

For the first time in many years I wasn't surrounded by guards, dogs, wire fences, or machine guns. There was no one to order me around, no one to tell us what to do. There was nothing but utter silence. I was overwhelmed, and a feeling of exhilaration, a kind I never experienced before or since, swept over me. I was alive!

We moved through the forest westward towards the Allied troops. We walked at night, sleeping in the daytime. We avoided roads and listened for anything unusual. Felix found a few rotten potatoes and devoured them. We took water from a pond. Our only other food was grass, tree bark from young trees, and corn left in a field.

On the second night, while crossing a road, we heard voices.

"Down! Quiet!" Honzo pushed me behind a bush. Felix, a few feet away, pressed his to the ground. Twenty yards away, a group of German soldiers walked by. We stopped breathing. If one of them glanced in our direction, we were done for. Hour-long minutes passed and then they were gone. We lay on the ground, catching our breath. We pulled ourselves together and moved on, more carefully than ever.

On the third day we saw a barn that looked deserted. We decided to spend the day under its roof and try to find something to eat. We were climbing through an opening when we heard faint whispers from the other end of the barn. Were they women's voices? We called out to them and discovered that we had come upon a small group of Jewish women from another transport. Like us, they had escaped and found shelter in the barn.

"Where are you from?" Felix whispered in Yiddish. Someone replied, in a whisper, "Wilna."

"What camp were you in?"

They named several camps and ghettos in Poland. We wished each other good luck. Exhausted, the three of us slept.

When daylight came, we were ready to move on, and they were gone. Hunger gnawed at our guts. Somehow we had to get some food.

We decided to look for an isolated farm, where we would pretend to be foreign laborers and offer to work for food and lodging. It was April, time for spring planting, and farmers could use all the help they could get. We found one in a valley. After watching it for hours, we approached the farmhouse. Since I spoke fluent German, I became spokesman. Dogs barked as we neared the farmyard, and a heavyset woman came out to meet us.

"Hello," I said, as she looked us over suspiciously. "We are three forced laborers. We were separated from our transport after an air attack and are looking for work. We will do anything in exchange for food and lodging."

She didn't say a word. She just stared. I realized that I was speaking to a German woman for the first time in a long time. "We are hungry. We need some food. Any kind of food. We'll work for it."

"Stay here! I'll ask my husband." She spoke with a heavy Saxonian dialect which I found difficult to understand.

I nodded. "Yes, ma'am. We'll wait. But please, if we could get a piece of bread, we would be grateful. We haven't had any food for days."

Wordlessly, she walked into her house and came back a few minutes later, laden with a pitcher of milk, a loaf of bread, and some butter.

"Wait here!"

Milk, bread, and butter! No food ever tasted that good. We devoured it.

"Let me warn you." Honzo said after we had wolfed down everything. "Our stomachs aren't used to this kind of food. As much as we need and want it, we have to get used to it slowly."

Honzo's warning was on the mark. After the liberation I heard stories about former camp inmates who were fed bars of chocolate by well-meaning G.I.s. Their stomachs couldn't digest the fats and sugar and they died shortly thereafter.

The farmer came from the barn, looked us over, and told us that we could work only if we received permission from the local authorities.

"Who's that?" I asked.

"The Buergermeister."

"Where do we find him?"

"It's about a half hour from here. He's there now."

"If we get a permit, will you give us work?"

"If he gives you the papers, yes. At least one of you. The others can go to another farm."

It didn't take us long to find the little office of the Buergermeister. If he was a Nazi, we were in trouble, but we had to take the chance. We used the same story we had told the farmer and it seemed to work. We kept our jackets on to hide our Auschwitz numbers.

The Buergermeister was "our" farmer's cousin. He accepted our story and didn't ask questions, since the farmers needed help in the fields as much as we needed food and shelter. He wrote our names on a piece of Nazi stationery and stamped it. These were our working papers. He made one request, which, after a silent conversation with our eyes, we had to accept. We had to separate, to work on different farms in the little village.

We started our new lives working, but apart. We were fed and, in a few days, became regular members of our respective households. My farmer and his family didn't ask questions. They seemed satisfied to have an extra hand around for the planting season.

Honzo, Felix, and I met every other evening. We knew how lucky we were. In this small hamlet time seemed to have stopped somewhere in the nineteenth century. There was no evidence of war, no soldiers. Remembering Honzo's warning about eating, I ate slowly and felt some of my strength coming back. The work was hard, but the food made all the difference.

We had been farmhands for just over two weeks and I was helping the farmer repair a fence in the field when we saw his wife hurrying toward us. I assumed she was bringing our lunch. I can still see her in her formless green dress, a kerchief covering her head, coming to us in her heavy boots.

"The war is over. It's on the radio. Germany has surrendered!"

I stood there with a 2 by 4 in my hand. I didn't know whether to cry, laugh, scream, or run. Against all odds, I had survived it. It was over.

The farmer acted as though the news didn't concern him. He went on with his work. His wife went back to the house. I stood transfixed, allowing reality to sink in, until the farmer gave me a shove, "Come. Work must go on."

The moment I had been praying for since 1933 had finally arrived. The Nazis were vanquished. The killing was over. The war was over.

As a Jew, I wanted to celebrate. I reached for my 2 by 4 and went back to work.

When Felix, Honzo, and I got together that night, we were exuberant but still not totally able to shed our disbelief.

"What do we do now?" Felix asked.

"You know what?" I said as much to myself as to my two friends "I never really thought about what life would be like afterwards. We concentrated on survival. Now we're free, and we really have to decide what to do and where to go. The future we never thought we'd have is ours."

"I know what I'm going to do," Honzo declared. "I'm leaving tomorrow morning to go to Prague."

Felix was less sure. "I can't see myself going back to Vienna. But I can't see staying here, that's for sure."

Honzo and Felix left the next day. Our farewells were difficult. We had been inseparable for almost two years. We had shared food, helped each other through very tough times and some perilous moments, and had often depended on each other for our lives. Would we ever see each other again? Where? When? I didn't have an address. I had no home. Where would I be next week? Next month? How does one say goodbye under such conditions? For a few minutes we sat quietly, each absorbed in his own thoughts. Then we embraced, trying, unsuccessfully, to hold back our tears.

Honzo's hair was beginning to grow back. His farmer had given him some work pants and an old jacket. Felix and I wore the same outfits in which we had escaped. Just before he left, Honzo gave me his old address in Prague. I gave him mine in Mannheim, not knowing if I would ever get there and, if I did, what I would find. We hugged one last time, and then they were gone. I was alone.

I went back to my farmer. I was all alone, really alone, for the first time in my life. It was a strange feeling.

Lindenau, the little hamlet where we had found refuge, was in the only part of Germany never occupied or overrun by either the Russian army or the Allies. Nobody bothered; the place was just too unimportant. Its future was uncertain. And so was mine.

Work went on as before. My farmer asked if I would remain. With the war over, he offered to pay me. I told him I would stay until I made up my mind about what to do. "Why not stay?" I asked myself.

I even toyed with the idea of changing my identity, using a new name, pretending to be a non-Jew, and making a new life for myself. Ever since I was a kid, I had been persecuted for being a Jew. I had lost my youth, my family, everything but my life. Why not change everything and let go of the past?

But Mutti's voice on that morning in Mannheim whispered in my head. "Be a good Jewish boy" were her last words to me. Did I survive the horror of the camps, the endless years of disease, death, and hunger to live the simple life of a farmer? What about the promises I had made to bear witness, to tell the world what I had seen and experienced?

We now had Allied broadcasts that spoke of dramatic changes. Germany was under total Allied occupation. Hitler's "New Germany" was in ruins. All German newspapers were shut down. Radio was run by the occupation forces. And here I was, wracked with indecision. I performed my daily farm chores. I gained weight and puzzled about what to do next.

14

COMING "HOME"

In early June, nearly one month after the war ended, I made my decision. I would return to Mannheim, to learn what I could about my family. I was 22 years old. I had no job, no education, no possessions. Nothing. The only thing I knew was how to survive in concentration and labor camps. I had no idea how far this knowledge would get me in the real world.

My farmer's wife, trying to persuade me to change my mind, packed what seemed to be a month's supply of food and bade me farewell. The family had been good to me. Although I was still much below my normal weight, I felt better and my strength was coming back.

On a beautiful summer morning I left the farm, heading west toward what I assumed would be the Americans. I walked through small villages. I met refugees coming the other way. At night I slept in barns. Nobody bothered me.

On the third day, coming around a bend in the road, I was stopped by a black American soldier in uniform! I had never in my life seen a black person before. He was carrying a rifle and ordered me to stop. He didn't speak German, and my English obviously made little sense to him. He motioned me to the side of the road, where I joined a group of other men, about twenty or so, most of them German soldiers. I thought it best not to say very much and to keep to myself.

A few hours later a truck showed up and we were told to get in. I wound up in yet another camp, this one a German prisoner-of-war camp. So, after weeks of freedom, I was once again behind barbed wire. My attempts to speak to the Americans brought the reply, "You'll have your turn! Wait."

Indeed, my turn did come. One by one we were interrogated by a German-speaking American soldier who sat at a small table and took down all pertinent information. He hardly looked up from his papers.

"Name?"

"Michel."

"First name?"

"Ernst."

"Age?"

"Twenty-two."

"Place of birth?"

"Mannheim."

"Were you ever a member of the SS?" I couldn't help but laugh.

"No."

"What army outfit did you serve in?"

"None!"

"Come! I haven't time for games. What was your army unit?"

"I wasn't in the army. I was in camps."

He looked up for the first time. An American soldier wearing glasses, clean-shaven, speaking German without an accent, obviously born in Germany.

"What do you mean, you were in camps?"

I looked at him, wondering how to say it, how to answer. "I've been in camps since 1939. The last one was Buchenwald. Before that I was in Auschwitz."

He stared at me. "You were in Auschwitz?"

"Yes."

"You have a number?"

"Yes—104995." I showed him the tattoo.

"What are you doing here? This is a prisoner-of-war camp."

"I've been trying to get someone's attention but I was told to wait."

Then: "Are you Jewish?"

"Yes."

The young American got up from his chair and grabbed me by the arm. "Come with me!" he urged. Turning to the others standing in line waiting their turn, he said, "Wait. I'll be back."

He led me to what seemed to be the officers' barrack. "Sit here." He left and came back minutes later with two officers. They stared at me as if I were a visitor from another planet.

For the next hour I had to tell the story of what happened to me in the camps, beginning with *Kristallnacht* in 1938 until the escape. My words were interpreted by the young soldier, who, he told me later, was born in Berlin and emigrated with his family to the States in 1936.

The trio listened attentively. I was the first camp survivor they had met. That night I was fed a scrumptious dinner. I slept in a real bed in the officers' barracks. After a great night's sleep, the young soldier who had separated me from the German POWs asked me about my plans. I told him I wanted to get back to Mannheim. "I don't know where else to go."

"How will you get there?"

"I'll walk."

"Do you know how far it is?"

"Well, all I've got is time. Nobody's waiting for me."

He thought for a moment. "Have you ever ridden a motorcycle?"

"No, why?"

"You can't walk to Mannheim. Too difficult. Too dangerous. You're alone. There's a curfew in effect and no way for you to get there."

"So how do I get a motorcycle? I have no money."

He laughed. "That's not a problem. We've confiscated hundreds from the German army. All kinds, big and small."

The next day I was the owner of a motorcycle. It took me another day to get the hang of it.

My new American friend provided an official document for me stating that I was a concentration camp survivor, that the vehicle was given to me by the U.S. army, that I was on my way to Mannheim, and finally, most important, that I was to be given all possible assistance by U.S. army personnel.

The letter worked like a charm.

After thanking my benefactor, I began my journey to my hometown, a city I had last seem in September 1939. When I needed gasoline or food, I stopped at an army installation, showed my papers, and, bingo, I was taken care of.

The destruction I saw on the way to Mannheim is difficult to describe. Whole cities were destroyed and the main roads were often impassable. Only the countryside was peaceful and serene. I saw trains and trucks full of refugees being transported by the U.S. army to different destinations. Every city was under Allied control. There was no German government.

I remember one particular stopover. Since there was a 9:00 P.M. curfew, I needed to find an army post before that hour. I was in a small village outside of Frankfurt when I had a mechanical problem with my motorcycle. I was unable to find a place to stay. As time ran out, I knocked at a house and asked if I could stay for the night.

The family turned out to be one in which one of the parents was of Jewish descent. They had been able to hide during the war and survived intact. The family consisted of parents and two daughters in their early twenties. I told them a little bit about myself and spent a very warm, pleasant evening with them. It was the first time I had found myself in a private home since the last night I spent with my parents. The girls entertained me and taught me how to dance to the latest American hits. I heard, "You are my sunshine, my only sunshine..." It's still one of my favorite songs.

Two days later I reached Mannheim. By coincidence, it was my twenty-second birthday, July 1, 1945.

What a homecoming. The city was in total ruin, with hardly a building left standing. I rode through streets I remembered from my childhood, but I was often unable to recognize the neighborhood. The place where the synagogue had stood, the school I went to, the center of town—all were rubble. The few people walking around seemed to be in a trance-like state. All the shops were closed. Finally, with some trepidation, I drove to what used to be our apartment building, 26 Richard-Wagnerstrasse.

Only the lower floor, where our family had lived, was left standing. The street number, 26, could still be seen. I stopped, turned off the motor, and walked to the door. Nobody lived there. Nobody was on the street. Everything was rubble. I stood there, transfixed by my thoughts, when a jeep marked "Military Police" braked to a halt. The MP officer called me over. He spoke broken German.

"Don't you know it's curfew? You have to be off the street."

"I have no place to go. This used to be my home," I said, pointing to the destruction behind me.

"I'm sorry. You can't be on the street. You have to find a place to stay overnight."

I tried to explain to the MP that I had been in a camp. I showed him my army paper, which he studied carefully. Then he turned and whispered to the other soldiers. "Follow us," he said to me.

I got on my motorcycle and followed them. I had no idea where they were taking me. It turned out to be the Mannheim jail. It was, ironically, one of the few buildings in the city that was somewhat habitable. An American officer, speaking German, motioned me to sit down.

"You were in a concentration camp?"

"Yes. Several of them."

"You were born in this city?"

"Yes. We lived here till I was deported. My parents were deported a year later."

"What happened to them?"

"I don't know. I came back to find out."

"Where did you think you would stay?"

"I don't know. I didn't plan."

The American shook his head. "I really don't know what to do with you. You can't stay on the street." He ran his fingers through his hair. "I'm afraid you'll have to spend the night here. There are military rules and I can't let you run around town. Tomorrow go to the Military Government Headquarters, DP section. They'll take care of you."

"What is DP section?"

"Displaced Persons. People who were deported and have no place to go."

I spent the night of my twenty-second birthday in jail. It was indeed a strange homecoming. I hadn't known what to expect, but I certainly hadn't anticipated that I would spend time in the Mannheim jail.

In the morning I rode over to the Military Government Headquarters, parked the motorcycle, locked it, and walked in. The building used to be a school but it was now occupied by the U.S. Military Government. There were officers wearing various insignias on their lapels. As I looked closer, I noticed one particular officer with an unusual patch. It looked to me like the tablets of the Ten Commandments. The man was talking to another officer, but I kept staring at him, rudely, because I couldn't figure out what the strange patch on his uniform meant. After a while, he noticed me and came over.

"Why are you staring at me?"

He was clean-shaven, wore glasses, was rather short, and looked at me with a friendly smile. He spoke broken German.

"Your uniform has tablets on the collar. I've never seen that before."

"Do you know what it means?"

"No, but I know what it stands for."

"Are you Jewish?"

"Yes. Are you?"

"I am a Jewish chaplain with the United States army. I am a Rabbi."

I kept staring at him. "You are a Rabbi?"

"Yes. I am Chaplain Abraham Haselkorn, attached the U.S. Third Army. Who are you?"

Briefly I told the chaplain who I was and how I got there. He shook his head. "I can't believe it. I've been looking for Jewish people in this town and have found only some half-Jews." Then he asked me to go with him.

"I want you to meet the DP officer. He'll be surprised!"

I went with him to another building, and we climbed up to the second floor. On the door was a sign, "Albert A. Hutler, Lt. U.S. Army Displaced Persons Section."

"Wait here a moment."

He walked into what was evidently the office of the Displaced Persons officer. A sergeant and another G.I. were busy interrogating a

German. They hardly looked at me. I just stood there, waiting. After a few minutes, the chaplain came back.

"Come in. Lieutenant Hutler wants to talk to you."

I followed him into the small, spartan office. I had no idea how profoundly this meeting would affect the rest of my life. Lieutenant Hutler was in his thirties, with dark hair. He wasn't tall but was solidly built, with warm, friendly eyes. Chaplain Haselkorn did the translations. The lieutenant shook my hand and asked me to sit down.

"I understand from Chaplain Haselkorn that you were born in Mannheim."

"Yes. In 1923."

"You are Jewish?"

"Yes."

"And you spent the war years in Nazi concentration camps?"

"Yes. Auschwitz, Birkenau, Buchenwald."

"You have a number?"

"Yes." I rolled up my left sleeve and showed him my tattoo.

He looked at it, as did the chaplain, shaking their heads.

For the next hour or so I told Lieutenant Hutler and the chaplain what had happened to me since the deportation. I told them about my family, the forced labor camps, Auschwitz, the selection process, life in the camps, the escape, and my arrival in Mannheim the day before. Both men hardly interrupted as I told them my story.

"And so you came back to where you were born and spent the first night in jail?"

I nodded.

"Do you know that you are the first Jew from Mannheim who has come back?"

"No. I didn't know, but I'm not surprised."

The two men talked to each other. I couldn't understand what they were saying. "What are your plans now?" Lieutenant Hutler asked.

"I really don't know. I thought I might get some idea here. I would like to find out about my parents and my sister."

"You don't have a place to stay, do you?" he asked almost rhetorically.

"No."

Taking his military cap, he motioned the chaplain and me to follow him. He turned to the G.I.s in the outer room, who had obviously been waiting for him.

"Take care of the store. We're going for a ride."

"But, Lieutenant, you have to meet with the colonel in half an hour!" one of them protested.

"Make an excuse. I'm busy. See you later."

With that, the chaplain and I followed him to the parking lot and his jeep. In less than half an hour we were on the outskirts of Mannheim in an area which was surprisingly undamaged.

He turned to me. "Which house do you like?"

I didn't understand.

"Just tell me which of these houses you would like to live in." I was puzzled by what he had in mind.

"I don't know. All of them look fine to me."

He stopped the jeep in front of a pleasant house with a small garden, jumped out, and knocked on the door. A man answered, well dressed, tall, a German.

"By order of the Military Government in Mannheim this house is being taken over. You have ten minutes to vacate."

When the man protested, Lieutenant Hutler answered, "You have nine minutes. This is an order!"

He attached an official-looking document to the front door, stating that this house was now occupied by the U.S. Military Government for an unspecified period.

That's how I found my first place to live. Later, Lieutenant Hutler asked me to work as an interpreter and personal aide. I got to know the rest of his staff: Sergeant Harold Weiss; P.F.C. Andrew Sikora; and Paul Vennekor, a Dutch DP who had been a forced laborer in a factory near Mannheim.

The Displaced Persons Section, under Lieutenant Hutler's command, was responsible for the lives of literally hundreds of thousands of DPs of all nationalities in the area. During the months I worked with him, we repatriated Russian, French, Polish, Dutch, and others who had been forced to work in German industry and were now ready to go home.

Shortly after beginning my job at Military Government, I had an extraordinary experience. An American G.I. came to our Displaced Persons section. He was Heinz Kuhn, my childhood friend who had lived around the corner, one of the boys I had played soccer with. I don't know who was more shocked, he or I, as we stared at each other. "Ernst, what are you doing here? What happened to you?" He could not get over seeing me in the office.

Heinz, now Staff Sergeant Henry Kuhn, had come to Mannheim to look for any friends or relatives who might have survived. He was told to come to the Displaced Persons section, and I was the first person he met. It took a while for both of us to get over the shock. We spent the evening together catching up on what had happened to us. Henry got out of Germany in 1938 and was now living in Chicago. He gave me his address and I promised to get in touch with him if I ever came to America.

During that initial period of adjustment to normal life, I first learned about the Joint Distribution Committee, an American-Jewish organization concerned primarily with the thousands of Jews from all over Europe. They helped us find housing, family members, and work and offered medical care and financial assistance to those, like me, who found themselves stranded in Germany, waiting for an opportunity to pick up their lives.

We were the remnants, the lucky ones. But the question loomed large. What now? I knew that my work with Lieutenant Hutler could not last forever and that eventually I would have to decide what to do with my life. All efforts to learn the fate of my parents or my sister were unsuccessful. Wherever I turned, I ran into a stone wall.

I assumed they were all dead, that I was the only surviving member of my family.

15

I AM A REPORTER AT THE FIRST NUREMBERG WAR CRIMES TRIAL

S ome time during the early fall of 1945, Lieutenant Hutler received his orders to return home to civilian life. I was sad to see him go, but I realized that my work with the Displaced Persons Section of Military Government would come to an end sooner or later.

Watching him work on a daily basis, and being part of the small team of Americans responsible for the orderly repatriation of the thousands of DPs, taught me to respect him greatly. He seldom lost his temper under pressure. He made life-and-death decisions, always keeping in mind the welfare of those who future was in his hands, and he had a special feeling for "his" Jews.

I suppose I symbolized the survivors for him, since I was the first Jew from Mannheim to come back. There were other survivors who found themselves under Hutler's wing, most of them Polish, Hungarian, or Rumanian. A few of them shared "my" house, but none of them wanted to return to the countries of their birth—most of them wanted to go to Palestine.

There were rumors of an underground group, organized by American servicemen and members of the Jewish Brigade, that was said to be smuggling people from country to country and then onto ships bound for Palestine. It was a risky trip. Many survivors were caught and arrested as illegal immigrants. I often thought about making the trip but somehow took no action.

One afternoon, Lieutenant Hutler asked me to come to his office. Standing near his desk were two young officers with a Magen David insignia and the letters "Palestine Brigade" on their jacket sleeves. I had heard they existed, but this was the first time I saw a "Jewish" soldier.

"Lieutenant Hutler, you wanted to see me?"

"Yes, indeed." He turned to one of the members of the Brigade and introduced me.

"This is Ernst Michel."

I wondered what was happening. What did the Palestine Brigade want of me?

The officer approached me slowly. "You are Ernst Michel?"

"Yes."

He took something out of his pocket. "You are born in Mannheim?"

"Yes."

"I have a letter for you."

A letter? I couldn't believe it! Who would write to me from Palestine? Who knew I came back? The envelope was addressed to "Ernst Michel, Mannheim. No Address." I didn't recognize the handwriting.

"You'd better sit down. This may shock you."

I wasn't hearing him. I was oblivious to everything but the letter. I looked at the bottom of the page, at the signature.

Lotte! My sister Lotte! How could that be? Was this a trick to test me somehow? I raced through the contents of the letter, and I still remember how it began:

"My dear, beloved brother Ernst. I don't know if you are alive or if this letter will reach you. But I want to do everything to find out if you survived."

I sobbed and then I began to cry. The letter really was from Lotte. She was in Palestine. She had made it! She had gotten out! The letter wasn't very long.

"Lieutenant Hutler," I cried, "Lieutenant. It's from my sister! From Lotte! She's alive!" Tears streamed down my face, blurring everything. The men in the office, Lieutenant Hutler, they were all crying too. I sobbed, I laughed. I didn't know what to do first. Lotte was alive!

She skipped details. She had heard that a few Jews came back to Mannheim from the camps, so she wrote, hoping that I was one of them. She had nothing to lose. She had been through difficult times;

she was hidden by Catholic nuns and eventually arrived in Palestine on a Youth-Aliyah transport in 1944. She wrote about our parents, who were deported from Gurs in 1942. Lotte wasn't sure, but she believed their final destination was Auschwitz. Now I was sure of their fate.

I felt like I was reconnected to the past.

Lieutenant Hutler hugged me. "Ernst, we're happy for you. We're privileged to share this moment with you."

After I calmed down, the officer from the Palestine Brigade told me that he was carrying letters from people in Palestine who heard that some of their relatives survived and were living in various DP camps. He described himself as a delivery boy who hoped he could reunite lost family members. As he wiped his eyes, he told me that no one could ever repay him for the joy he felt when families were brought back together. He offered to arrange for my response to be delivered to Lotte, who would have it in a month's time.

Before Lieutenant Hutler left Mannheim, he thanked me for being so helpful and handed me a slip of paper. "This is my address in Chicago. Let me know what you'll do. I'm sure you'll find your way. You're an unusual young man and I'm honored to know you. If you ever come to the United States, my family and I would be happy to see you."

I was touched and told him how much I was in his debt. I had no idea what an important role he was going to play in my life.

Around that time, I received an interesting visit from an American Military Government officer, Captain Picard. I met him during his visits to Mannheim to meet with Lieutenant Hutler. He worked on German rehabilitation, a subject of much concern to the American occupying forces. How you do you deal with a country of 60 million people that, for all practical purposes, had no government?

He told me that the Military Government intended to let proven non-Nazis publish daily papers in some German cities. At that moment only one newspaper existed for all of Germany, published by the Military Occupation Force.

"One of the first papers will be published in Heidelberg. The editor will be Theodor Huess. He was ostracized by the Nazis and lived in seclusion during the war. I told him about you and he would like to meet you."

With my job with the DPs coming to an end, I thought about what to do next. It was late summer. I had discarded my dirty camp clothing weeks earlier and felt ready to move on. I climbed onto my motorcycle and rode to Heidelberg. It was only a short distance from Mannheim but, oddly, had not been touched by the war at all.

Dr. Heuss welcomed me graciously. A conservative, soft-spoken, gray-haired man, he introduced me to his associate editor, Dr. Rudolf Agricola, and told me how pleased he was that I was joining his small staff.

A few days later, I began my career as a newspaperman. I had always enjoyed writing and, despite my lack of formal education, I had no problem covering some local stories for the Rhein-Neckar-Zeitung.

Gradually, as other newspapers received permission to publish, the Allies created a news agency, DANA, to distribute international, national, and local news.

One of the major breaking news stories at that time was the approaching Nuremberg War Crimes Trial, where top Nazis—Goering, Keitel, Ribbentrop, Von Papen, Kaltenbrunner and others—were to be tried by an Allied Military Tribunal. Twenty-two Nazi leaders were scheduled to go on trial in late November.

I wanted that assignment.

I spoke with Dr. Heuss about it and he agreed to recommend me. With his support, I got the job. After several days of briefings, I received press credentials as a special correspondent to the trials. Bill Stricker, a German-born American, was in charge of the news team and our Nuremberg stories were dispatched by DANA to all the newly licensed German papers. There were now approximately 50 of them, and more were joining the syndicate each day.

My colleagues were all young Germans carefully chosen by the Military Government. I was the only Jew among them. They regarded me with something close to awe when they learned of my background. Though I was Jewish, I didn't parade that fact before them, because I didn't want it to get in the way of our working together. I couldn't have concealed it long, because in addition to my regular assignments, Bill Stricker asked me to write some personal stories under the byline "Special correspondent and Auschwitz survivor, #104995, Ernst Michel."

I wrote some personal reflections, which were published in all the German papers. It threw me back into the twilight zone. Less than six months before, I was an inmate in a Nazi concentration camp, and now I sat in the courtroom at the Nuremberg Hall of Justice. The scum who were responsible for the greatest crimes against humanity sat less than 25 feet away from me, on trial for their lives.

I had an assigned seat in the press section and I followed the proceedings via the simultaneous interpretation system, which was used for the first time at the trials. (It is now standard at the United Nations and all multilingual conferences.) To my right were the eight judges, two each from the United States, the Soviet Union, France, and England. On the left were two rows with the 21 defendants, including Goering. Their defense counsel sat in front of them and MPs guarded them from the rear.

I was the only Holocaust survivor to serve as a reporter at the trials, and many American and British newsmen wanted my reactions. One interview with an American reporter appeared in papers throughout the United States and found its way to Israel, where my sister saw it. Even if that member of the Palestine Brigade had not found me, Lotte would have learned about my survival from the interview.

I pinched myself every morning as I entered the courtroom, to make sure I wasn't dreaming. There sat Julius Streicher, editor of the anti-Semitic hate sheet *"Der Stürmer,"* who had incited the German people against Jews with his lurid propaganda and imaginary atrocities.

There sat Ernst Kaltenbrunner, who was among the higher echelon who ran the death camps. He, with Himmler, was responsible for the systematic slaughter of our people in the concentration camps. His attitude was one of disdain.

There sat Von Papen, the patrician, elegant head of the Reichsbank, which became the depository for the billions of dollars' worth of Jewish property confiscated by the Nazis.

There sat Rudolf Hess, the Deputy Fuehrer, who flew to England during the war in an abortive effort to end it. He seemed the strangest of all the defendants and behaved as if he didn't belong there.

I stared at the lot. I couldn't keep my eyes off them. These were the men who were determined to wipe out the Jews of Europe. If they had won the war, they had plans to murder all the Jews in the rest of the world. They were responsible too for the suffering and deaths of millions of others, including people of conscience, Jehovah's Witnesses, homosexuals, gypsies, and Communists.

Sometimes I wanted to jump from the press gallery to shake their shoulders and yell in their faces, "Why did you do this to us? Why did you kill my friend Walter? Why did you hang Leo, Janek, and Chaim? Why? Why?"

The trial proceedings were conducted in an almost antiseptic atmosphere. Documents were presented. "Is this your signature, sir?" "Objection, your honor!" "May it please the court?" It was all very civil. It wasn't easy to keep my personal feelings separated from my job as a reporter, but fortunately, in addition to my regular assignments, I was given the opportunity to write a few feature stories, in which I could vent some of my emotion.

After one particularly harrowing day in the courtroom, when evidence about the death camps was presented to the court, I wrote the following story, in English, for *Stars and Stripes*:

AUSCHWITZ PICTURES TELL A STORY

By Ernst Michel, DANA Staff Correspondent

(Formerly prisoner No. 104995 at Auschwitz concentration camp)

Nuremberg, February 20 (GNS)—

I have a book in front of me. A picture book. But not a picture book for children. A book which in Russian carries the title "International Military Tribunal, Nuremberg" and on the middle of the binding says "Auschwitz Camp." The last two words are underlined.

The book has no preface at all and very little text. As I said it is a picture book, but a picture book of reality. And it is simply "exhibit No. such and such." Nothing more. And the Russian prosecutor who introduced it in court doesn't say much about it.

In fact, that isn't necessary at all, for these pictures speak for themselves. They speak of the life—or rather the death—of the prisoners at the Auschwitz concentration camp, which was the largest of all German concentration camps.

Three miles from Auschwitz there was Birkenau. A nice name, giving the impression of a birch wood, an opening in it and a small, quiet village. But that was not the Birkenau that I am speaking of. The Birkenau near Auschwitz was something different. It was a camp where about 100,000 prisoners were quartered—one can't say "were living."

And behind this Birkenau camp there were five large smoke-stacks, which were smoking steadily. These were the five giant crematoria and the giant gas chambers of Birkenau, which were working day and night, where not tens of thousands, not hundreds of thousands, but over a million human beings were gassed to death. That was Birkenau.

And my glance rests again on the little picture book with the title "Auschwitz Camp."

There is the electrified double-barbed wire fence with the sign "danger" and the death's head, the wire into which 20 of my co-prisoners were driven in one night.

I am leafing through the book and see another picture showing a large blackboard. This blackboard used to hang in the SS headquarters at Auschwitz-Buna and listed the daily changes in the numbers of prisoners. The board in the picture is dated Jan. 16, 1945, the last day it was used. The number of prisoners that day was 10,224. And the next day 60,000 of us began to march along the icy roads of Upper Silesia, "fleeing" from the advancing columns of the Red Army. The remainder was left behind—they couldn't march any longer.

When we arrived at Buchenwald after three days of marching and five days of travel in open freight cars in blizzard weather, there were about half of us left.

The book is finished. It is again in front of me. I pick it up. It doesn't weigh much. But it is the history of millions of my co-prisoners, and today, here at the Nuremberg trial, where the bill is to be paid, it weighs much, very much.

Shortly after this article appeared in the press, I was asked to meet General Rudenko, the chief Russian prosecutor. By agreement, the Russians presented the evidence of the atrocities committed in the concentration camps. They had lost the largest numbers during the war, and it was felt they had that right. I met with General Rudenko in his office at the Palace of Justice with an interpreter present. He had heard through the grapevine that I was an eyewitness to the medical experiments Dr. Mengele conducted in Auschwitz and he wanted details.

"When did these experiments take place?" he asked.

"In Auschwitz-Buna in 1944."

"Was Dr. Mengele present when these experiments were conducted?"

"Yes."

"Did you see him?"

"Yes, I did."

"Did he conduct the experiments?"

"Yes."

General Rudenko was the first person who asked me about the electric shock experiments Honzo and I had witnessed. I thought of Diana.

The General scribbled as I talked and then asked me if I would be willing to appear as a witness for the Russian prosecution on the subject of medical experiments. Of course I would. I would be keeping the promise I made in Auschwitz to Walter and the others, the promise to bear witness. I also thought about the story angle, the reporter in me always at work. "Reporter Is Witness at Nuremberg Trials."

Nothing came of it. I waited in vain for the date of my court appearance, and as the prosecution prepared to rest its case, I contacted the general and asked for an explanation. His staff was very evasive. Finally a junior staff member took me aside and told me the truth.

"It's because you're German," he told me.

"Me? German? Yes, I was born in Germany, but I'm Jewish and that's why I spent almost six years in the camps!"

"Our government's policy is not to call on any German witnesses, regardless of their religion. The one exception is Field Marshall von Paulus, who was the general in charge of the German army at Stalingrad. There is nothing we can do to change this."

As a goodwill gesture, he handed me a copy of the official document presented by the prosecution, which unrelentingly gave the graphic details of the atrocities and horrors of Auschwitz, including the medical experiments.

One of the photos in the document was taken by a Russian army photographer in Auschwitz-Buna a few days after the Russians moved in. It showed the official count of our camp on January 18, 1945, the day we were evacuated, which listed the categories of prisoners: Jews, criminals, gypsies, political prisoners, homosexuals, and so forth. I had the picture enlarged and framed with my other memorabilia from the camp. Eventually it will all become part of the permanent exhibit at the New York Holocaust Museum.

As part of my journalistic assignment, I was to interview some of the defense lawyers to get comments on and reactions to the proceedings. Dr. Stahmer, Goering's chief defense counsel, followed the reports in the German press with special interest, as did the other defense lawyers. Goering's secretary arranged several interviews with me and Dr. Stahmer. I found him to be a very able defense attorney who was fighting a lost cause. He used every legal means at his disposal to defend his client.

One afternoon, at the end of the proceedings, he took me to the sparse prison cell where Hermann Goering passed his time. There was a bed, a small table which held a photo of his wife, and a chair. That was all. It was a far cry from the opulent palace where the high-living Reichsmarshall threw his famous parties.

The meeting was arranged under the condition that it remain off the record. This is the first time that I feel free to write about it. I was nervous. What should I say? Should I shake hands? Ask questions?

Since I couldn't write about it, why did I want to go through such a painful experience?

Goering stood up when Dr. Stahmer and I entered his cell, which was constantly under guard. "This is the young reporter you asked me about," Dr. Stahmer said, motioning to me. Goering looked at me, started to reach out to shake hands and, sensing my reaction, turned away for a moment. I stood frozen.

What the hell am I doing here? How can I possibly be in the same room with this monster and carry on a conversation? How could I talk logically, unemotionally?

Mr. Goering, how does it feel to be here? What do you think of the proceedings? Are they treating you well? Should I shout at him, tell him that he was responsible for my six years in the camps? Should I blame him for my lost childhood? For the death of my parents?

I did nothing of the sort. I stood there and stared while Dr. Stahmer discussed the next day's proceedings. Then, on an impulse, I bolted for the door and asked the MP to let me out. I couldn't take it. I couldn't remain. I had to get away. There was no discussion, not a word was exchanged, no comments or statements were made. I was there, and then I was gone. Period.

I regret the incident to this day. I regret agreeing to meet him, and I regret standing there silently and then running out. It was irrational. But as I look back at that period of adjustment in my life, I realize that I was overwhelmed by the experiences crashing in on me, by my survival and my role as eyewitness. Standing with Goering in his cell was more than I could handle.

Toward the end of the trial, on April 11, 1946, I had the opportunity to witness, and then report on, the incredible appearance of Ernst Kaltenbrunner, the former chief of internal Nazi security and one of the leading architects of "the Final Solution." He had agreed to appear in his own defense, and my fellow reporters, as well as the judges and the prosecution, were eager to hear from the one individual who knew more details about the Nazi killing machine than any of the other defendants.

We were in for a surprise. Kaltenbrunner, 6 feet, 6 inches tall, entered the witness stand at 10:45 A.M., dressed in a dark blue suit, and repeated the oath in his broad Austrian dialect. He swore "to tell the truth, to hide nothing and to add nothing."

His testimony was incredible. He denied any complicity in or knowledge of the activities in the concentration camps and went so far as to say that he had been responsible for the rescue of Jewish camp inmates. He recounted how, in 1944, at the behest of Himmler, he arranged for the transfer of 1,200 Jews from Theresienstadt to Switzerland.

"What was your reason for this act?" his defense counsel asked.

"To obtain favorable headlines in the American press for Himmler."

What Kaltenbrunner didn't mention was brought out in cross-examination. An American Jewish organization paid one million dollars for this "humanitarian" gesture. The prosecutor then elicited astonishing replies from the defendant.

"How many concentration camps were there?"

"To the best of my recollection, I knew of three camps. At the end of the war there were a total of twelve. In addition, there was a camp for the SS. That was all. I never created a concentration camp. That was done by Himmler."

From the trial records, the transcripts quote his words:

"I never saw a gas chamber and did not even know they existed."

"The meaning of the Auschwitz camps was not known to me."

"I am convinced that it was only due to my intervention that the persecution of the Jews came to an end in October 1944."

"I never knew that atrocities were committed in the concentration camps."

"Only a handful of men, Himmler, Glueck, Pohl, et cetera, dealt with the camps. I never heard about deaths in the extermination camps."

These replies came from the man responsible for running the camps. Then, under cross-examination by Colonel Amen of the American staff, Kaltenbrunner was shown a damaging document carrying his own signature. "This is not my signature!" Kaltenbrunner yelled at the unbelieving prosecutor. Even the judges showed astonishment.

It was, to me, a remarkable coincidence that Kaltenbrunner's appearance on the witness stand took place on the exact day when, one year before, we began the forced march from Berga which led to my escape.

16

AN INVITATION FROM THE GERMAN GOVERNMENT

The envelope read "Brigette Zypries, Bundesministerin Der Justiz, Berlin." This was the letter:

Berlin, May 27, 2005

Dear Mr. Michel,

This coming November, we will commemorate the 60th anniversary of the beginning of the Nuremberg Tribunals, a date which also marks the beginning of an effort to enforce the rule of law with respect to nation states and those individuals acting on their behalf. The German Federal Ministry of Justice plans to pay tribute to that date with an event in Berlin on 21 November 2005. Please allow me to ask you whether you would be willing to appear at the planned event as a contemporary witness to relate your experiences as a reporter at the Nuremberg Tribunals. Quite possibly, the dimension of the developments initiated by the Nuremberg Tribunals becomes comprehensible only by attaining a clear view of their origins in Nuremberg in 1945. Not least, I would like to offer this opportunity to younger German lawyers who have no direct experiential link to the events of that time. This is another reason why we would so much appreciate the opportunity to share your knowledge and experiences.

Brigette Zypries

I could not believe it. An invitation from the German Minister of Justice to come to Berlin and speak on the sixtieth anniversary of the opening of the Nuremberg International War Crimes Trial!

Sixty years to the day after I entered the press gallery in room 600 of the Palace of Justice. Sixty years after I saw for the first time Hermann Goering and the remaining top 21 leaders of the Nazi government being brought to trial. Sixty years and seven months after my escape from the final death march on April 18, 1945.

That is how on November 21, 2005—the actual date in 1945 was November 20—I found myself in Berlin at the German Ministry of Justice, addressing a select group of government officials, judges, prosecutors, lawyers, and foreign dignitaries invited to commemorate the opening of the Nuremberg Trial.

How times had changed. Sixty years before, Germany was in rubble. Many major German cities were totally destroyed. Hitler had committed suicide as the Russians entered Berlin. There was no German government, no radio, no newspapers, hardly any food—everything was run by the Allied forces. In the twelve years from the time the Nazis took power in 1943 and Hitler declared the beginning of the "1,000 Year Reich," until Germany capitulated in 1945, 55 million people had died. Europe was in ruins. One out of three Jews in the world had been killed.

I will never forget the moment I entered the press gallery at the Palace of Justice in 1945. I remember looking at Hermann Goering sitting in the first row in the defendants bench. I will always remember the film Auschwitz being shown in the courtroom, showing the camp where I had suffered. I remember Rudolf Hoess, the Kommandant of Auschwitz, on the witness stand, being asked how many victims were killed in Auschwitz and replying "2.5 million, mostly Jews."

There was an unbelievable contrast between then and now. I was in Nuremberg not only as a reporter but also as a survivor, thinking of my parents and all those millions who did not survive. It was incongruous. I often had to pinch myself to make sure I was not dreaming, that this was really happening.

I walked the streets of Berlin, visited the newly rebuilt Reischstag. I went to the train tracks, now a Holocaust Memorial, from which tens of thousands of German Jews were deported to their deaths in the east, including my friend Norbert.

It was not easy for me to sit there day after day listening to the proceedings as the remaining top Nazis were on trial for their lives.

I did not know it at the time, but I learned many years later that among the observers at Nuremberg was a lawyer and Polish Jew named Rafael Lemkin. He was the man who coined the word "genocide," which eventually led to the United Nations adoption of the "Convention on Genocide." Today it is part of international law. It is far from perfect, but it is the first time in history that crimes against humanity, the killing of innocent victims, is now punishable by international law. Lemkin's efforts led to the creation of the International Criminal Court, or the ICC, headquartered in The Hague, Holland. In 2007 for the first time, sixty years after Nuremberg, those responsible for committing genocide are now facing an International Criminal Court. That was the lesson of Nuremberg. I had the privilege of being there as one who had been marked to be a victim of genocide but was lucky to survive it.

17

LIEUTENANT ALBERT HUTLER— MY AMERICAN FAMILY

The Nuremberg Trials ended in April 1946. By then I was a bona fide journalist with a solid reputation based on my work at the trials. I had a lucrative offer to run one of DANA's regional offices.

Perhaps because I was one of the few Jewish survivors who was becoming widely known in Germany, I met people who would later play key roles in the emergence of a democratic German government.

Dr. Heuss, the newspaper publisher in Heidelberg, was being mentioned as a possible future president. I also met Konrad Adenauer, who had read my articles on the Nuremberg Trials. He told me he was pleased that someone with my background was writing for a German news agency.

Despite my satisfaction with my growing career and the acceptance I experienced in a totally new German environment, I couldn't escape feelings of discomfort from living in the country of my birth. Every time I met a German, I couldn't stop asking myself where were they when I was in Auschwitz. Were they SS? Did they kill Jews? What did they do on *Kristallnacht*?

I was 22 years old, it was less than a year after my escape, and I often had to pinch myself to make sure the life I was living was real, that I wasn't dreaming. My world was certainly changing.

I spent a great deal of my time working with Abe Laskove, director of the Joint Distribution Committee in Germany. I knew about the "Joint," as we called it, because they had helped rescue Lotte in France. I learned even more while I was working with Lieutenant Hutler at the DP section in Mannheim. I saw how much the Joint was doing to rehabilitate and relocate the survivors. There were tens of thousands of survivors living in DP camps all over Germany and Austria, hoping to go to Palestine. The illegal immigration, which was later depicted in the book *Exodus* by Leon Uris, was in full swing. Although I had a job and didn't live in a DP camp, Abe Laskove told me that thousands of DPs would be permitted to emigrate to the United States under a special DP quota.

I had three choices. I could remain in Germany, with the almost certain assurance of a promising career in journalism; I could join the thousands of former camp inmates on their way to Palestine, who hoped to create a Jewish state—or I could go to America.

The only person I was able to talk to about my dilemma was Abe Laskove, who became my friend. I respected his opinions and valued his judgment. He filled me in on his organization's history, and that's when I first head of the United Jewish Appeal. Although Abe in no way influenced my eventual decision to come to the United States, he planted the seed that was to flower into my involvement in the Jewish community and eventual full-time career with the UJA. The other person who steered me in that direction was Al Hutler, but I'm getting ahead of myself.

It was an agonizing decision for me to make, because I was on my own. I asked for advice, but deep down I realized I couldn't depend on anyone but myself. I eliminated the first option very quickly. A promising future and being comfortable in my mother tongue weren't enough. I simply couldn't stay in the country that had caused me so much agony and was soaked with the blood of all those dear to me.

The final decision, then was between Palestine and America.

I had always admired and envied the way people lived in the United States. It was the power in the postwar world, and I was more and more convinced that it would provide greater opportunities for me. And so, in June 1946 I was among the first Jewish DPs who boarded the U.S.S. *Marine Flasher* in Bremerhaven for the voyage to the United States.

I carried a small suitcase with a few personal belongings, including one item I kept from the camps—the belt I wore in Paderborn,

Auschwitz, and Buchenwald. It didn't fit anymore, but I kept it as a memento. Today it hangs in my office, behind my desk. Eventually it, and other items I kept from the camps and the postwar era, will be part of the exhibit in the New York Holocaust Museum.

The thing I remember best about the journey was the food. We were served delicacies I hadn't tasted since I was a child. Though the ocean tossed us around a bit, it didn't stop me from eating. There was Spam, jams, jellies, eggs, and more.

Halfway across the Atlantic, JDC representatives gave us permission to send a cable to the States. I decided to send mine to Lieutenant Hutler in Chicago, certain that he would remember me. I remember the cable:

> *Lieutenant Albert A. Hutler*
> *4721 Greenwood Avenue*
> *Chicago, Illinois*
> *Just wanted you to know that I am coming to America with the U.S.S.* Marine Flasher. *Hope to see you someday. Best regards to you and your family.*

All of us assembled on deck as the ship approached New York. We had heard so much about the Statue of Liberty and were eager to see her, but our first sighting of the New World was a place called Brooklyn. Our disappointment was forgotten as soon as we saw the majestic Lady standing in the harbor with the New York skyline behind her. We fell silent, each of us wrapped in our own thoughts.

What would the future bring in this strange, powerful country? Although the streets were rumored to be paved with gold, I had few illusions. I knew that it wouldn't be easy to adjust to a new and strange environment, where I didn't speak the language.

The voice from the loudspeaker scattered my thoughts. "Please have your papers and identification cards ready as you proceed through immigration." And then: "Would Ernst Michel please identify himself? You have someone waiting for you at the gate."

I was bewildered. Who knew I was arriving? I hadn't informed my relatives, because I preferred to contact them after I arrived. So who was waiting for me? The mystery was solved when I reported to the official from the Joint.

"I'm Ernst Michel."

He looked at my papers. "Okay, there are two ladies looking for you."

"Two ladies? Who are they?"

"I don't know. They asked for you."

I was escorted to two well-dressed ladies in their sixties. One asked if I was Ernst Michel.

"Yes. Are you sure you are looking for me?"

"My son told me to expect a young boy. I'm Al Hutler's mother, and this is my cousin. Al called me from Chicago and asked me to meet a young Jewish refugee who was arriving on the *Marine Flasher*. He also asked me to bring you to my apartment."

I stood there with my mouth open. Lieutenant Hutler got the cable I sent from the ship! That's what happened! How did he find out where and when I was arriving? I would never have sent the telegram if I thought he would go to the trouble of having someone greet me at the pier. I was embarrassed. Al Hutler's mom was nonplussed, too. The little boy she had come to meet was a grown man.

A representative of the National Refugee Service who had brought me to these wonderful women stood nearby. He suggested I join the other DPs. I said goodbye to them and promised to visit. Then, we were bused to one of several hotels for processing, consultation, and counseling. I wound up at the Hotel Marseille, just off Broadway.

As I was settling in for the night, there was a phone call for me. It was Lieutenant Hutler in Chicago, and he was welcoming me to the United States. He had just come back from San Diego, where he was being interviewed for the top position at the Jewish Federation. When I called him Lieutenant, he told me to call him Al. When I began to apologize for imposing on his family, he cut me off and insisted that I come to Chicago and stay with his family. They had a room for me. How should I respond to this generous offer? What would I do after a few days? And where was Chicago?

In the morning I met with the social worker from the NRS. I told him about Lieutenant Hutler and his invitation to Chicago.

"What will happen if I stay here?" I asked.

"Well, you rest at the hotel for a few days. Then we'll help you find a job and a room. We'll help you with some financial support for a reasonable amount of time, until you can take care of yourself."

"And if I go to Chicago?"

"In that case you will be pretty much on your own. We'll give you a train ticket to Chicago and a few dollars pocket money. When you get to Chicago, contact the Jewish Federation office. They'll help you."

I phoned Al the next day to accept his invitation. I searched out my relatives in New York, an uncle and cousins who had left Germany just before America entered the war. They were all struggling to make a living, and there was no way I would impose on them. They were very nice, but when I told them I was going to Chicago, I am sure they were relieved.

My first days in New York were unforgettable. Photos and movies were one thing. Manhattan was fantastic. The traffic, the skyscrapers, the different ethnic faces from all over the world—it was almost too much. But more than all of that, the one impression that overrode the others was the one left by supermarkets. I had never seen so many shelves filled with fruits, vegetables, meat, cakes, ice cream, whatever your heart desired. Just looking made my mouth water. Could Americans understand what it meant to subsist on a piece of bread and a bowl of soup? I promised myself that I would never, ever, take anything for granted.

I carefully counted the money the social worker gave me and headed for the first restaurant I could find. It had linen tablecloths, and the tables were set with fine china. I sat down and ordered 25 cents worth of whipped cream. I had dreamed about whipped cream in the camps. To me, whipped cream was the ultimate dining experience.

"That's all you want?" The waiter looked at me incredulously.

"Yes. That's all. I've had dreams about whipped cream for years. When I was in one of those camps in Europe, all I could think about was whipped cream."

He stared at me for a moment. "You were in a concentration camp?"
"Yes."

A few minutes later, he came back with three pieces of cake, each topped with a generous portion of whipped cream.

"I read about what happened to you people," he told me. "I'm Irish. My people were also persecuted, a long time ago. I know how you feel. Enjoy. No charge. It's on the house."

It was the first time I had been in a restaurant since I was a child, when my parents took Lotte and me for a treat. All I could think of as I gobbled down the cake and whipped cream was that rotten potato that Honzo, Felix, and I had shared in the woods after our escape. It was a highlight of my brief stay in New York.

Two days later I was in Chicago, and the Hutlers were at the train station to greet me. Al looked different in civilian clothes, but he had the same open smile and warmth I remembered from Mannheim. I met Lee, his wife, and their two daughters, Suzie and Frankee. They quickly made me feel at home and welcomed me as a member of their family. I felt awkward calling the Lieutenant Al and his wife by their first name, but I got used to it. The girls called me Ernie, and that's the way it's been ever since.

The Hutlers lived on Chicago's South Side. Al was an executive with the Jewish Federation in Chicago, and just before I arrived, he had accepted a position as the Executive Director of the Jewish Federation in San Diego. The whole family was looking forward to the move to California and was making exciting plans to buy a house and preparing for the change in their lives. We all spent evenings talking about the future.

"Well, Ernie, now that you're beginning to get a feel for America, what do you want to do?"

Al began what I knew would be an important discussion.

"Before you answer, there are a few things you should consider. Ever since Rabbi Haselkorn brought you to my office in Mannheim, I've looked at you like a younger brother. We've accepted you fully and we know that you too feel at home with us. You're an unusual young man who's come through a horrible experience. I could never have lived through what you went through. Despite all that, you're healthy, you've got a great attitude, and I have no doubt you'll be a success in America."

Lee nodded her head every once in a while, and I listened carefully.

"The way I see it, these are your options. You can stay with us as long as you want. You can take a night job and go to school and we'll pay the tuition. Consider it a loan. Your English isn't bad; it's lots better than my German. After a while we'll help you find a place to live. I can even help you find a job through the Federation. Your other option is to come with us to San Diego and we'll help you get started there. But first decide what you would like to do."

I was overwhelmed by their warmth and generosity. They had taken me in as if it was the most natural thing to do. I visited Al in his office at the Federation and learned something about his work. I discovered that he knew Abe Laskove through their common work with the DPs in Germany. Al had earned his law degree and decided to go into social work in the Jewish community, and his army assignment in Germany turned out to be natural.

Through Al I learned how funds were raised in the Jewish community, how they were spent to help the Holocaust survivors, and how they were used for the maintenance and development of Jewish institutions at home. More than once Al would say, "With your background you could make a valuable contribution to the Jewish community. But first you have to finish your education and improve your English."

During these discussions, which continued on and off for several days, I'm sure the seeds were sown for my eventual professional career in UJA-Federation. I've often felt, subconsciously, I suppose, that there must have been a reason for my survival. It would be natural for me to go into Jewish community service and contribute in some way toward Jewish continuity and survival. It would be one approach to guarantee that what happened to us in Europe would never happen again.

But first I needed a job, any job. And I needed to improve my English.

There was one bizarre encounter I will never forget. Remember my childhood buddy, Henry (Heinz) Kuhn, who found me in Al Hutler's office in Mannheim in July 1945? He now lived in Chicago too, and I called him after I moved in with the Hutlers. He took me to his home, and when I admired his brand new car, he asked me if I knew how to drive.

"Of course I know how to drive. What a question!" I retorted, despite the fact that I had never driven an automobile in my life. I didn't think it was going to be tough.

"Do you want to take it for a ride?" he asked.

A few minutes later I was sitting in the driver's seat trying to find the starter button. Henry sat next to me. When the car started, I shifted gears. Instantly the car careened backward across the street, knocked over a fence, uprooted a few bushes, and was abruptly intercepted by a neighbor's stoop, where it stalled. The whole adventure lasted less than thirty seconds. Henry was as shocked as I was.

"I thought you knew how to drive," he glared at me. I was too scared to say anything.

Within moments, the police hauled us into the paddy wagon and we were on our way to the local precinct house. I was so stunned and upset, I could hardly talk. Here I was, less than a week in the United States, with no driver's license and no papers, on my way to jail. I had visions of being deported.

Henry was engrossed in conversation with one of the officers and I saw him reach into his pocket and take out some bills. The driver pulled over and we were ordered out of the vehicle with a warning.

Henry and I walked back to the house, and I stood there while he apologized to his neighbor and promised to pay for all the damages.

Despite the expensive driving lesson, Henry is still one of my closest friends and has never allowed me to repay him.

18

MY FIRST JOB
IN AMERICA

"A ticket to Port Huron, Michigan, please."

"One way or round trip?" the teller at the Greyhound station in Chicago asked.

"One way."

"You'll have an hour to change in Detroit," he said, handing me the ticket.

Three days before, I had never heard of the place. Now I was setting out on my own, taking responsibility for myself.

When I arrived in Port Huron in the early evening, I immediately looked for the Times Herald building. The place was practically deserted. The publisher was gone for the day, but he would be back in the morning, and there was nothing for me to do but find a place to sleep.

It was a warm August night in 1946, and I spent it sleeping on a bench at the bus station in Port Huron. I had ten dollars in my pocket, the change left from the purchase of my ticket to this little midwestern town, population 30,000, located on the shores of Lake Huron, 60 miles northeast of Detroit.

I was job hunting, and so far I had struck out—and had been rejected by every newspaper in Chicago. I finally stood my ground at United Press and forced my way into the office of the Midwest Regional Bureau Chief, Mims Thomason. I told him that I wouldn't leave until I got work. He stared at me as if I had fallen from Mars. In fractured English, I asked him for a job. He was the first person who took the time to listen to my story. Then, after a half hour of discussion, he suggested I apply for a job at a small-town newspaper, where I could improve my English as I learned about America.

The next morning, my bones aching from a few hours of fitful napping on a bench, I washed up in the station's washroom. I looked at myself in the grimy mirror in the dim light and wondered if it really was such a good idea to show up in a strange town on the basis of a conversation with a man I barely knew. The scrap of paper in my pocket was my only security—it was a letter of reference from Thomason to Mr. Louis A. Weil, publisher of the *Port Huron Times Herald*.

I presented myself at the receptionist's desk and told her that Mims Thomason had sent me to see Mr. Weil. In a few minutes I was ushered into his office.

"What can I do for you?" Mr. Weil was a tall, distinguished man in his seventies with white hair and friendly blue eyes.

"Mims Thomason of the UCP in Chicago told me I might find a job here. He gave me this letter for you," I said, as I handed it to him.

Weil looked at me with some surprise, but he took it, opened the envelope, and read it. I stood waiting.

"How long have you been in this country?"

"Five weeks, sir. I arrived in New York in early July."

"And you want to get a job on our paper?"

"Yes, sir. I want to become a reporter."

"Sit down, young man," he said in a friendly voice. "Tell me about yourself."

And so I told him my story. I told him about Germany, my life in the camps, the escape, my work at the Nuremberg Trials, and my arrival in the United States. When I finished, he asked me questions about Germany, the war, and my family. His reaction was quite different from that of most people I had met. I did not sense that he felt sorry for me. I tried several times to lead the conversation back to the purpose of my visit, but he refused to be hurried along. An hour went by.

"Well, Ernest, that's quite a story. We read about these events, but you lived through them." He paused for a moment. "Now, about the job."

My hands were shaking and I tried to keep them under control.

"Your English isn't bad, considering the fact that you've only been here a few weeks, but it's clearly not good enough for me to hire you as a reporter."

I was waiting for the ax to fall. No job.

"And we can't afford a specialist on German affairs. But…"

I held my breath.

"…we can use a copyboy. That way you can improve your English and learn how a small-town newspaper works. We'll pay you twenty-five dollars a week. It's not much, but it's a start."

I had to restrain myself from jumping out of the chair and throwing my arms around him.

"You mean I've got a job?" I couldn't believe it.

"Yes. You have a job."

I danced, more than walked out of the office. Twenty-five dollars a week. My first job in America and on a newspaper!

It didn't take long to find a place to live. Mrs. Low, the tall, white-haired widow of a World War I veteran, had an upstairs room for rent for $5 a week. It included use of the refrigerator in her kitchen. She was a bit standoffish but checked with the paper and then accepted my $3 deposit. Now I had my own place, my own bed, my own job, for the first time since 1939. I was on my way, and I was thrilled.

That evening, I strolled down Main Street, past the movie theater, the bank, the five and dime store, the corner drugstore. I was part of America.

At eight o'clock the following morning I presented myself to the city editor. He told me my duties and introduced me to the other members of the staff. Nobody asked me any questions, and if my accent surprised them, they did not comment.

My job was easy, and in time I became familiar with the reporters, the editors, and the men in the printshop. I started out by being formal, calling people by their last names. It didn't take long, though, before we were all on a first-name basis and they called me Ernie, a nickname that has become part of my very being.

For the first time since coming to the States, I was forced to speak English all day. In New York, and even in Chicago, I could always lapse into German when I found myself looking for words. Now that safety net was gone. If I couldn't think of the right word, I had to find a substitute or make myself understood in some other way. This situation forced me to learn fast—faster than if I had stayed in New York or Chicago.

Lunchtime was my nightmare. I dreaded the moment when the reporters who had completed their morning assignments would unwrap their sandwiches and discuss some of their activities. These sessions were fascinating and stimulating to me, but I felt awkward for not eating. I couldn't afford to buy a sandwich. I needed to stretch my $5-a-week food budget, which allowed me only breakfast and a skimpy dinner. When the men invited me to join them for lunch, I decided to skip breakfast and eat lunch instead.

Those hours were an informal seminar on American life. I learned about the New York Yankees and the Detroit Tigers, about local primaries, the news from the police beat and the City Council, the Junior Chamber of Commerce. I learned about Li'l Abner, Dick Tracy, and Orphan Annie. Whenever something came up that was new to me, I would ask questions, but mostly I listened. Some of the staff were war veterans who had seen action in Germany, and so we had something to talk about. The nicest thing about my co-workers was that they were eager for me to feel at home and went out of their way to help me in every way they could.

They couldn't believe I chose Port Huron as my first home in America. I didn't know anyone there. I took a risk looking for a job. Mostly, they couldn't believe that I survived eleven camps. When one of them happened to notice the tattoo on my arm, he looked at me as if I had come from a different world.

On the sixth day, my money ran out. The next day was payday and I received my first pay envelope. My first salary in America! It was an exhilarating moment, and no compensation I received since, regardless of the amount, has ever meant quite as much to me. My net pay, after my first donation to the Internal Revenue Service, was $19.75. That evening I splurged on a steak and treated myself to a movie. I was really living!

I read each issue of the newspaper from cover to cover. In my second week, Ed Snover, the city editor, took me aside. "Ernie, I've got an assignment for you. We have a daily feature on the paper," he continued, "called 'Events of Yesteryear.' It recalls major events of general interest—ten, twenty-five and fifty years ago, locally, nationally, and internationally. So take a look at that column for the last few days, then read the papers in the morgue and let me see what you come up with."

And so I was given a chance to learn about America and its past. I had always loved reading old newspapers, and I read contemporaneous accounts of Prohibition, the Teapot Dome scandal, the fight over U.S. membership in the League of Nations. I read about Presidents Wilson, Hoover, and the assassination of President McKinley. I read about Babe Ruth and the Four Horsemen of Notre Dame. Local and regional events became familiar to me. I learned about the Rotary Club and who spoke there, the proposed changes in the city charter, and the local high school referendum. I became acquainted with the bond issue to build a new sewer system and many issues concerning life in Port Huron. I was enjoying myself, loving every day.

But there were sad and very lonely moments, too. I spent most of my evenings at the library, or I went to the movies. When I came back to my little room, I'd sit there and listen to the radio.

As time went by, I made a few friends. Sometimes a reporter would invite me for dinner with his family. I accepted eagerly, not just to avoid an evening alone but because I enjoyed the discussions with my colleagues and, realized more and more how vastly different their lives were from mine. I specifically remember the utter bewilderment of one of the reporters when I tried to explain—I'm sure unsuccessfully—that Hitler's only reason for the extermination of 6 million Jews in Europe, including my parents, was that there were Jews. It seemed so far-fetched, so beyond belief, that I knew he accepted it with some skepticism.

The fall of 1946 saw the beginning of the Cold War. With the fighting over, friction began to develop between the United States and the Soviet Union. British Prime Minister Winston Churchill delivered his famous speech about the "Iron Curtain" descending on Eastern Europe.

I knew and lived with many Russian POWs in the camps, and they were often treated as badly as the Jews. I found it difficult to understand why, only a year after Hitler's defeat by the Allied Forces and a great sacrifice on the part of the Russians, there would now be a serious rift between the former Allies. After giving it some thought, I sat down and wrote about the Russians I had known, about their suffering during the war. I must admit today that I was a bit naïve, but I felt strongly about the subject and wanted to express my point of view.

On the spur of the moment, convinced that I had written a masterpiece, I sent it with a brief note to Mr. Weil. When I didn't receive an acknowledgment, I assumed it had found its way into the wastebasket.

When I opened the paper the following Sunday, I was stunned. Mr. Weil ran a weekly column entitled, "Between You and Me." That week he described how a young man had come to Port Huron a few weeks before, looking for a job on the paper. It gave some of my background and then—I couldn't believe my eyes—he quoted my Russian piece word for word, even to the point of leaving in all the mistakes I had made.

My friends congratulated me when I came to work on Monday, and I was proud of my first published piece. The next day a student from the local junior college called.

"Mr. Michel, I'm president of the Foreign Relations Club at Port Huron Junior College. My friends and I read about you in the *Times Herald*. We had no idea that someone with your background lived in Port Huron."

We chatted a bit and then he asked me if I would speak about my experiences at the next meeting of the Foreign Relations Club. I protested, "But my English isn't good enough to speak at a college."

"We only have about a dozen members," he told me. "It's no big deal. Just tell us a bit about yourself, your experiences during the war and the Nuremberg Trials. Then we'll ask questions. It's all very informal."

I let him talk me into it and for days I prepared notes, rehearsing for the meeting.

If I was stunned when the paper published my article, you can imagine how shocked I was when I was greeted by an auditorium full of people, standing room only. The young student who had invited me apologized. In addition to the brief announcement in the *Times*

Herald, the campus newspaper ran announcements which advertised the talk as: "From the Gas Chambers in Auschwitz to the Nuremberg Trials—An Eyewitness Report!"

"The demand was so great, we needed to change the venue." He did not seem at all unhappy.

I was petrified. I didn't know what to say or to do. My first inclination was to run like hell for the exit. I hoped for an earthquake, but they never happened in Port Huron. There was not much hope for that. As I literally shook in my boots, I followed the young student into the packed auditorium. I don't remember how I got to the microphone.

I was facing hundreds of young Americans. Youth was the only thing we had in common. They grew up in normal surroundings, protected by their parents, free to enjoy their lives, their freedom, and their education. At 14 I had been thrown out of school, subjected to hatred and discrimination. While those guys worried about making the cut on the football team and who they would date for the prom, I was taking care of Walter in Buna, watching Ruth shuffling down the line toward the gas chamber, seeing Diana's torment. While they hung out at the soda shop, I was scrounging for potatoes and sharing one thin blanket with two inmates who never made it. While they studied biology, I witnessed Mengele's murderous experiments.

True, many of these students were war veterans, had experienced hardships and faced death, but at least they had weapons to fight back with and knew how to defend themselves. All we could do to was stand by helplessly, surrounded by electrically charged barbed wire and SS guards with machine guns, watching the systematic slaughter of people all around us.

Undoubtedly, these thoughts spilled over into my remarks. I discarded my notes and talked about what happened to me as a young boy growing up in Germany, what it felt like being kicked out of school because I was Jewish. I talked of the slow, methodical enslavement of millions of people in Europe, of life in the camps, of the constant hope of survival which died a thousand times, and how liberation finally came to the few who managed somehow to stay alive.

My words tumbled in an uncontrollable stream. Even in my poor

English, it became a catharsis. I lost all track of time. In the middle of a sentence, I stopped. My throat was dry. I couldn't go on.

There were no questions, no applause. The students filed out quietly. I was totally spent. The students who had invited me came over to shake my hand, looked at me, didn't say a word and left. I was sure I had laid an egg.

The next afternoon Mr. Weil asked me to come into his office. It was the first time I was in his office since the day he gave me the job. I wondered if he was going to fire me.

"I heard you gave quite a speech last night," he greeted me.

I stood there silently.

"Well, Ernie. It must have been quite a talk because I had a number of calls from parents of students who heard you. Now, what do you know about the Rotary Club?"

What did I know? After reading through old newspapers for days, I knew about the Rotary Club and also about the Lions, the Exchange, and a number of other clubs, as well.

"I want to invite you to come as my guest and talk to our members. I want you to tell them about some of your experiences. But I have one request, Ernie—no more than 25 minutes. Not like last night." He smiled.

"How long did I speak?"

"More than an hour and a half!"

When Mr. Weil introduced me at the following week's Rotary Club meeting, I was as proud as I had ever been in my life. He described me as "the newest member of the *Port Huron Times Herald* staff who, despite his young age, has seen more of life than most of us do in a lifetime."

Little did I realize then that I was rehearsing for an even more important job—a job that would fulfill all the promises I made to those who perished in the camps.

Before long, my reputation as a guest speaker in Port Huron began to spread. Pretty soon I was receiving a steady stream of invitations to speak.

One request rather baffled me. A lady phoned and introduced herself as a member of the Daughters of the American Revolution. She invited me to address their monthly tea, but I had never heard of them and was reluctant to accept. After all, I had been in the country only a short time and wanted nothing to do with revolutionaries. Later, the full significance of the request hit me. I accepted.

A few months later Mr. Weil spoke to me about my work, my new life, and the progress I made since I first arrived. Then he came to the point.

"Ernie, how would you like to write a daily column for the paper?"

I floated out of Weil's office on Cloud Nine. My daily column was called "My New Home." I wrote about anything that struck me as unusual about America in general, and Port Huron in particular. I also received a raise. I was more thrilled with the recognition I was getting. Now I was a legitimate newspaperman.

And so began another new phase in my life. I wrote about all the things that happened to me as a newcomer. Some incidents were humorous, others serious, but all pointed to the vast differences between life in a free country and my life in Europe. Fan mail arrived at the paper, most of it sympathetic and encouraging, but there was also a sprinkling of poison pen letters—all of them unsigned.

I was introduced to that strange phenomenon of American life, the blind date. The reporter on the paper who initiated me into this experience explained, in reply to my startled inquiry, that the young lady in question was perfectly able to see. He gave me some pointers as to what to do and what not to do, but he omitted one vital factor which to him was so obvious, that he never mentioned it to me. I had never dated anyone before and I knew nothing about dating etiquette.

I picked her up at the appointed hour, and we decided to see a movie. At the box office I bought a ticket for myself and waited for her to do the same. She just stood there, until I finally realized something wasn't quite right, much to the amusement of the cashier and doorman. It took me a while to get it. I was supposed to pay for both of us! Embarrassment is a good teacher. I chalked it up as another lesson in the customs and mores of America.

It took a few weeks, but soon anyone who needed a speaker knew where to find me. A few weeks after my column first appeared, a minister from one of the largest churches in town invited me to address his congregation at the Sunday morning service. I asked him whether he really wanted me, a Jew, to speak in his church. He assured me that he and his parishioners were eager to hear what I had to say. He reminded me that others, in addition to the Jews, also suffered in the camps.

That's how, one Sunday morning, I found myself standing in the pulpit of the First Methodist Church in Port Huron, speaking to the congregation about the true meaning of religious freedom. I told the listeners how miserable I was as a child because I was born a Jew and was persecuted for it. I tried to describe a world that accepted hatred for and discrimination against Jews.

I explained that as Jews we were prohibited from carrying on normal relationships with persons of different faiths, that we had experienced savage hatred directed against us by non-Jews, and how that experience, in turn, isolated us. I tried to explain how drastically and dramatically my attitude had changed in the few months since I had come to Port Huron.

I stressed that I was Jewish but it seemed not to matter to anyone, except me. Being Jewish validated my experiences, and people wanted to hear about them. I never understood the meaning of religious tolerance and the real meaning of American democracy—its goal of equality for all people—as forcefully as I did in those moments I spent standing in the pulpit of that church.

The most indelible memory I have of my stay in Port Huron took place that summer. Once again I was summoned to Mr. Weil's office, this time to meet the principal of Port Huron High School. After complimenting me on my column, he looked me in the eye and said, "Mr. Michel, on behalf of the faculty and members of the student body of Port Huron High School, I have the pleasure to invite you to deliver the commencement address at the graduation exercises of the senior class of 1947."

I didn't know what to say and looked from the principal to Mr. Weil. He just stood there and smiled. I was very moved and delighted to accept.

On graduation day I put on my new suit and went to the high school auditorium. I saw many of my colleagues and friends at the *Times Herald*—some were parents of graduating children—but others came to hear me speak. It was the first ceremony of this kind that I had ever witnessed. I was tremendously impressed with the pomp and circumstance, the choir, the procession, the dignity of the occasion, the presentation of the scholarships, the valedictorian address—everything that makes this such a meaningful event.

I sat on the platform between the high school principal and a city official and watched the students slowly march down the aisle to receive their diplomas. And as I sat there, I thought about my own parents, who were denied the happiness of seeing their children grow up.

The points I made during my address were designed to impress the students with the blessings of freedom they were privileged to enjoy. I tried to explain how the denial of those freedoms meant denial of life itself. I explained that millions of people in many parts of the world live under repressive and totalitarian regimes and do not know what it means to live in a democracy.

"Don't ever take these freedoms for granted," I told them. "Be aware what these freedoms mean. Enjoy them, but at the same time cherish them and work for them as part of the responsibility you carry as Americans and as free men and women."

I was accepted and made to feel completely at home in a community where, only a few short months before, I arrived as a stranger, unknown and unfamiliar with the fabric of American society. Port Huron had, in the real sense of the word, become my hometown. I firmly believe that the luckiest break of my new life was the privilege of spending my first year in this small and friendly midwestern city. I learned the meaning of living as a free man.

As time passed, I joined the Junior Chamber of Commerce. My social life was active and I made a number of friends. My financial situation too was improved. My salary was substantially higher than when I had started as a copy boy. Although I never asked for any compensation for my speaking engagements, many clubs and organizations added an honorarium to the customary letter of thanks. I owned three suits, moved to my own small apartment, and contemplated buying a car. My English had vastly improved, and I had begun to think in English, not in German.

I was an avid radio fan, and one day, in response to a promotion by a shaving cream company, I decided to enter a contest called "My Closest Shave." I wrote about my escape and mailed it in. I realized that there must have been thousands of entries, and my story had a small chance of winning. After a few weeks, the advertising agency sent me a notice suggesting that I listen to the radio at a certain hour on a certain evening, when the winners would be announced.

That evening I was glued to the radio as the announcer read the winning entry. I don't remember the story, but I remember that the first prize was a trip for two to Hawaii. Then they announced the second prize winner. I could hardly believe my ears when the announcer said, "Second prize in the contest goes to Ernest W. Michel of Port Huron, Michigan" and read my story on the air. I had won a new car. It was better than Hawaii, because I would have had no one to take with me. A few weeks later I received the sponsor's official letter telling me to pick up my car at the local dealer, that I could choose the color but that I had to pay for all the extras and would be liable for any taxes. I ordered a tan four-door Ford V8.

After one of my speeches in one of the Michigan communities, a man came to talk to me and introduced himself as the chairman of the local United Jewish Appeal campaign.

"Mr. Michel," he said, "our annual United Jewish Appeal drive is being held this evening. It would be a privilege if you would stay over and speak to us about some of the things you talked about during your address this noon. I know it would have a profound effect on all those coming to our meeting."

I accepted. After the meeting the professional representative of the organization asked me whether I would be willing to address some other functions of the organization in the area and maybe even in other parts of the United States. He felt that, with my background, I would make an excellent addition to their roster of speakers.

I was willing, but I told him that it would depend on whether Mr. Weil would allow me leave of absence. The next day Mr. Weil and I discussed the offer. He readily agreed but added one condition.

"I have no problem with your accepting these invitations as long as you continue to write your daily column. You will have some interesting experiences traveling around the country, experiences our readers will want to hear about. They enjoy your column and look forward to reading it."

The national office of the United Jewish Appeal in New York called to tell me, "We'd like you to come to New York to discuss it. Could you be here next Monday?"

Thus began my new career. One invitation followed another. I went to Texas, to Louisiana, to the northwest, and eventually to California. I wired my column to the newsroom from wherever I was, and it was printed the following day. I described my travels and my experiences. One day I even sent in a column from jail—I had car trouble, no motels were available, and the local sheriff allowed me to spend the night in his hoosegow as a gesture of his hospitality.

I had been in Port Huron for more than a year and now I felt that the time had come to move on. It was a difficult decision to make and I wrestled with it long and hard. I was dating a young Irish girl. Her family was very nice to me, but, I knew my religion was an issue. That was another reason I felt it was time to move on.

My car was ready, and I took that as a sign from Providence. Mr. Weil, one of the finest and most understanding bosses anyone could ever wish to work for, wholeheartedly approved of my decision. He regretted my departure, but he understood and encouraged me to get on with my life. The time had come for me to say goodbye to "my hometown."

My last week there was a difficult one. As I wrote my final column, I felt sadness and a genuine sense of gratitude toward the people of Port Huron. They had made me feel as if I belonged. I wrote:

This will be the last column of "My New Home."

I wanted you—the American people—to see through the eyes of a newcomer, what a great place this country is and how everyone should appreciate that he can live in this country. I did not just want to tell you some stories or to entertain you—my boss would not have allowed the space for that anyway—but I wanted to show you in little examples how other people in other parts of the world used to live and still do. I wanted to tell you how I hoped for a chance to live again and how I found it.

And more than all, I wanted to show to you how much I appreciate that I was given the opportunity to start life all over again in this country.

Fourteen months of life in America have made a new human being out of me. I have been given a new lease on life. The horrible experiences of six years in concentration camps in Europe are fading away. Sometimes I don't believe that they were true. It seems like a terrible dream to me.

In three years and ten months I will be an American.

I will wait and work for that day when I really can call it MY HOME.

It wasn't easy to say goodbye to my colleagues at the *Times Herald*, and to the friends I made in Port Huron. At the farewell luncheon, I read genuine regret in their eyes about my decision to leave, and I felt like I was leaving home. Mr. Weil gave me a farewell gift, a token of respect and friendship from him and my colleagues, which I have always treasured. Then, slowly, with tears in my eyes, I walked down the stairs of the newspaper for the last time.

A year before, I had ascended these steps with fear and trepidation wondering if my decision to look for a job in an unknown town was foolish. I knew I couldn't have had a finer welcome to America.

I left Port Huron in my new car, with all my belongings packed in the trunk. I knew that the decision had been the right one. As I passed down Main Street for the last time, I remembered distinctly the fear and anxiety with which I had looked at it from the Greyhound bus the evening I arrived. The buildings and stores were familiar to me now and so were many of the people.

It was at that moment that I fully recognized how much I had changed during that first year. I was no longer isolated. I had shed the feelings of insecurity that haunted me from my childhood, whenever

I found myself in a non-Jewish society. The people of Port Huron offered me a home in the truest sense of the word. I will always be indebted to that town.

19

A VOICE SINGS FOR ITS LIFE

UJA kept me busy with speaking engagements on the West Coast, but I had never given up my dream of being a journalist, so I often spent time between trips at the UJA Federation office in Los Angeles. There I volunteered my services as a "newspaperman" to the Federation monthly. It gave me a chance to meet other people my age and develop a sense of community.

"Here's a story made for you," my editor said, pointing to an article from the *Los Angeles Times* on his paper-strewn desk. It announced the appearance of a young tenor by the name of Miklos Gafni, who was making his Los Angeles debut at the Philharmonic Auditorium.

"What makes you think this is a story for me?" I asked him.

"Good question, Ernie." He turned toward me and looked me straight in the eye. "It could be a great story but I'll let you decide. You might not want to do it."

I was intrigued. "Come on, give. What's the story about?"

"Did you read the whole story in the *Times*?" He emphasized the *whole*.

I admitted that I hadn't, although I had glanced at it, barely.

"Well, listen to this!" and he read me a paragraph. "'What makes Mr. Gafni's meteoric rise so astonishing is the fact that he barely survived the war, having spent time in a German concentration camp!'

"It could make an interesting feature, one camp survivor interviewing another survivor who has become an internationally acclaimed tenor. Take it from a personal angle, his background, how he survived—you know what I mean, human interest!"

I quickly found out where Gafni was staying, then I telephoned him for an appointment. He was receptive and we arranged to meet the following morning in his suite at the Biltmore Hotel. He spoke English well, but with a heavy Hungarian accent.

I spent the rest of the afternoon doing research on him. There wasn't much. He was discovered in Europe by an American impresario and had come to America just a few weeks ago. At his Carnegie Hall debut he was critically acclaimed as "a great find" and "the Hungarian Caruso." *Life* magazine devoted three pages to the young singer and mentioned that he had been an inmate in a Nazi concentration camp.

My curiosity was piqued. If he was as good as the critics said was, Miklos Gafni was on the verge of a great career.

The next morning, promptly at the appointed hour, I knocked on his door. I recognized Gafni from the pictures in *Life* magazine, but he was even heavier than he seemed in photos. He weighed at least 250 pounds.

"Come in," he said pleasantly as we shook hands. He seemed hesitant for a moment, looked at me with a quizzical expression, and asked, "Haven't we met before? You look vaguely familiar."

"I don't think so." Nothing about him seemed familiar.

He smiled, "Well, I must have made a mistake. You probably look like someone I know."

I began by asking him about his background. He told me that he was born in Hungary and had lost his family during the Holocaust. He had spent the war years in German concentration camps and had returned to Hungary after his liberation.

"Just a moment, Mr. Gafni, not so fast," I interrupted him. "This is the part of your story that will be of particular interest to our readers. I am referring to the time you spent in a German concentration camp. Incidentally," I added, "I too was in a concentration camp."

"How is that possible? You are American!"

"Now yes, almost, anyway, but not then. I was born in Germany and was sent to the camps by the Nazis shortly after the beginning of the war," I replied.

"You were! But you have almost no accent!" he exclaimed and added, "Which camps were you in?"

It was a strange interview. He was asking me the questions instead of the other way around. I named a few of the camps I was in. Then, in an effort to get the ball back, I put the same question to him.

"Auschwitz, Mauthausen," he replied.

"What year did you get to Auschwitz?" I continued.

"Nineteen forty-four."

"Nineteen forty-four! I was there the same year. I knew many Hungarians in Auschwitz-Buna, one of whom I remember particularly. His name was Miklos and he was..."

What followed then happened so fast that I don't remember the details. He probably recognized me a split second before I recognized him.

He jumped from his chair and grabbed me by the shoulders: "I knew I'd seen you someplace before! Auschwitz-Buna! The hospital!"

I stared at him, incredulous, my mouth wide open. This wasn't possible.

"Miklos! Miklos Weinstock! Buna! The soup!"

Too excited for words, tears running down our faces we fell into each other's arms. We couldn't speak. We just held each other, and shook our heads in disbelief.

Miklos Gafni was Miklos Weinstock, the young, emaciated camp inmate I met in Auschwitz-Buna in 1944. At the time he was one of the Muselman, a young man at the end of his rope, ready to run into the electrically charged barbed wire and end it all.

No wonder we didn't immediately recognize each other. When I first met Miklos, our heads were shaved, we were garbed in threadbare and faded prison uniforms, and he didn't weigh more than 90 pounds.

I remembered him well. He first came to my attention when he was admitted to the KB, the prisoner hospital, for a slight foot injury. After only three months in the camp, the hunger, brutality and generally harsh treatment were already beginning to show their effects. He had arrived with a Hungarian transport and was the only one left of his family. His parents, sister, and younger brother were gassed immediately upon arrival. He was all alone.

He was my age and I liked him, so I helped him with some extra food and a few day's rest to give him a chance to regain some of his strength. He left the hospital in a much better state, and with the determination to hold on. He asked if he could see me once in a while, even if it was from the other side of the wire fence which separated the main camp from the KB. Of course he could.

He regularly came to the gate, and I often smuggled over a piece of bread or an extra bowl of soup. We became friends, and I got to know him fairly well. We would fantasize about life after the camp and of a future we hardly believed in. He told me he wanted to be a singer but realized the chances were very slim.

"I know it doesn't make sense," he said, "but I won't let them kill my dream."

A few months went by. I hadn't seen Miklos for a while when he finally appeared at the gate one night. He looked awful and sounded worse. The left side of his face was swollen.

"An SS man hit me with a rifle," he said matter of factly. "I can't take it much longer. In my bunk, two men are dying. I'm hungry all the time and I know I can't last much longer."

I looked at him and I knew he was right. He had lost weight again. His cheekbones were sticking out and he had the dull look of a Muselman.

I always remembered our last conversation. We were two young men, both just 20 years old, and we were debating the right of a human being to take his own life. We were two young men without youth, with no knowledge of what youth could be like. We hadn't really lived, and we were talking about suicide.

I tried to convince Miklos not to give in but I couldn't do it convincingly. I saw he was at the breaking point.

"Come back tomorrow," I told him as he was ready to go back to his barracks. "I'll have something for you. Don't give up!"

He nodded. "I'll be here."

He didn't come the next night or the one after that. I felt I would not see him again.

"They were all shipped to Birkenau," I was told when I asked about Miklos's whereabouts.

That was that. It happened every day. There was only one destination for a transfer to Birkenau—the chimneys.

I slowly walked to my barracks, thinking of Miklos, a young man who dreamed of singing and would never get the chance. Now it all came back to me as I looked into Miklos Weinstock-Gafni's sparkling eyes. He was a man who was obviously enjoying life and was on the verge of a great future.

"So what happened? How did you survive? I looked for you and was told that you were shipped to Birkenau."

He shook his head and sat down. "It's a strange story. Sometimes I still don't believe it really happened. You remember that evening when I saw you at the fence at the hospital, when I was so low I wanted to kill myself?"

I nodded, remembering only too well.

"When I returned to my barracks that evening," he continued, "I felt that I had reached the end. Nothing mattered anymore. When our *Kommando* lined up for work the next morning, an SS officer pulled us aside; while the others went to work in the factory, we remained standing. After a while the SS announced that we would be transferred. We knew what that meant. Transfer! The end! The furnaces.

"Through the gate we went to what all of us knew would be our final destination. I was resigned. Better now than later.

"After a few minutes of marching, we were ordered to sing. 'Come on! Sing! You know how!' I was dumbfounded. Here we were, on our way to the gas, and he wanted us to sing. Most of us were so weak, we had trouble walking. And they expected us to break out in song!

"The German officer raised his gun 'Sing, I said.'

"I don't know what made me do it, probably that instinct for survival. I started to sing an old Hungarian folk song my mother taught me when I was a little boy. The scene was incredible. The SS officer walking on our left with his gun cocked and pointed at us, ready to shoot. Guards were all around us. The group, dirty, hungry, resigned to their fate, marched in silence, heads bent. And there I was, belting out a song as loudly as I could."

Miklos rose from his chair and stood near the window, looking out into the clear California sky, as if he could see the group marching down that lonely road in Poland, just four years ago.

"I didn't think I had that much strength left," he continued after a moment. "But for the last time, I wanted to hear my own voice. In the meantime, the *Kommando* came to a halt. I don't know whether the SS ordered us to stop or if it was spontaneous. I remember the SS officer as he stood before me with a perplexed expression on his face as he stared at me. At last I finished the song. The silence was overwhelming. Nobody said a word. We just stood there.

"'Another one!' the Nazi ordered.

"'What do you want me to sing?' I asked.

"'Anything!'

"So I sang a popular hit I remembered. Then another. The officer pulled me out of the line and, with the others grouped around me like a choir, I sang for my life. After the third song I told him that I could not go on. I had no strength left. He stared at me again, as if speculating what to do. Then he turned and whispered something to the other guards.

"'You stay here!' he said to me. 'The rest of you, fall back in formation. About face! Forward. March!'

"There was no chance for me to say anything to them. They fell back in formation, dragging their tired feet along the dirty road, and I watched them disappear in the distance on their way to death."

We both fell silent, caught in our memories of a time not so long ago.

"What happened then?" I asked. Miklos shook himself as if coming out of a bad dream and continued the story.

"The officer ordered me to follow him. We must have been quite a sight, the elegant SS officer leading the way and me dragging myself a few feet behind him. We took a side road to the SS barracks. Not a word was spoken. Then: 'Stay here! This may be the luckiest day of your life!' And he left.

"He returned accompanied by a high-ranking SS officer, who took one look at me, turned to the SS underling, and shouted as he pointed at me with disdain, 'You tell me that thing has a voice?' The junior officer ordered me to sing.

"It may well have been the strangest audition in history. I was a Jewish prisoner, weighing some 90 pounds, half starved, dirty, weakened beyond endurance, facing two immaculately dressed Nazi officers and singing a lullaby.

"With the last ounce of my energy I sang one more song. Strange lights danced before my eyes. My throat was parched and I shook all over. I must have collapsed, because the next thing I remember was coming to consciousness on a cot.

"I looked around. On a table beside me was the loveliest sight imaginable—two large sandwiches and a large glass of milk. I closed my eyes and opened them again, to make sure I wasn't hallucinating. Then I wolfed down the food. It was my first solid food since I arrived in Auschwitz. Nothing before or since has ever tasted so good.

"I spent the rest of the day in the room, with the exception of a brief walk to the washroom, where I was told to shower and change my dirty, ill-fitting prison uniform for a new one. In the evening I was given another delicious meal and told to get ready to sing.

"I was taken into the SS mess hall, where the guards were having their meal. While they ate, I sang. That's how I saved my life. Evenings, at noon, even in the middle of the night, whenever it struck the fancy of one of the guards to hear some music, I had to perform. Songs, arias, ballads—anything I remembered. The SS treated me well. I received ample food to slowly gain back some strength. I also did odd jobs around the barracks, but mostly they wanted me to sing. As far as I know, I was the only prisoner in the SS barracks.

"This lasted until Auschwitz was evacuated in January 1945. In the confusion of that day, when everyone was packing to leave, I managed to slip out and join the prisoner transport. Nobody asked questions. After three days and nights of marching in the bitter cold winter of 1945, we reached a railway station, where we boarded open cattle cars and, after a grueling ride, we arrived at Mauthausen. We all knew that the war would soon be over. It was simply a matter of holding on a while longer. A few weeks later, in May1945, our camp was liberated by American troops.

"I made my way back to Hungary, determined to become a singer. Having survived because of my voice, I knew I wanted to make this my life's work. Shortly before my first concert, my manager suggested changing my name from Weinstock to Gafni, and that's how I began my career. At one concert in Hungary, an American impresario came to the dressing room and offered me a tour of the United States. The rest you know."

Later that evening I sat in the first row orchestra in the Los Angeles Philharmonic Auditorium, and as I listened to the great voice of Miklos Gafni, I understood why even a German SS officer would be moved to spare his life.

Miki and I became good friends. I followed his career, which took him to concert halls and auditoriums all over the planet. His voice delighted audiences in Hong Kong, Sydney, New Delhi, Jerusalem, and the United States. He gave a concert for President Truman at the annual Jefferson Jackson Day Dinner, sang before the Queen of England at a Royal Command Performance, and entertained the Prime Minister of India. His records were enjoyed by music lovers all over the world, and one of his movies won an Academy Award for short subjects. Miklos Gafni went a long way since the day he thought he was hearing his voice for the last time.

Miki auditioned for the famous movie about Enrico Caruso, but the role went to Mario Lanza. For one reason or another, Miki never realized his full potential. He drifted into the record business and continued to make some recordings. He married and had two children, one of whom was born with a severe handicap and is confined to a wheelchair.

In 1981, as he was hurrying to a business meeting, my friend Miki suffered a massive heart attack and died. I miss him, and the recordings of his music comfort me to this day.

20

REUNION WITH MY SISTER LOTTE

It was 1955 and I was finally taking my first trip to Israel. As we left LaGuardia Airport in New York, word came that an El Al airliner was shot down for violating Bulgarian airspace. Mrs. Hahn, the wife of Rabbi Hugo Hahn, the spiritual leader of the German-Jewish congregation of Essen, was one of the passengers who died in the attack. I knew of him because my aunt's family had belonged to his congregation before the war. The news made us all very nervous, but I was determined to focus on the positive.

I could not wait to see Lotte. I hadn't seen her since that cold spring night in 1938, when Papi saw her off on the dangerous train ride to the German-French border. I wondered if I would recognize her now that she was 26 years old and the mother of two little girls. Our first fuel stop was Gander, and then we stopped in the Azores. It was going to take 24 hours to get to Tel Aviv, and the ride seemed endless.

Finally we crossed the Mediterranean Sea and I looked out at the coastline below, my heart bursting with pride. My thoughts went back to the Hachsharah camps I spent time at in 1941, when we believed we would be sent to Palestine. After Paderborn, Auschwitz, Buna, Buchenwald, and Berga, I would finally be setting my feet on Jewish soil. I thought of Mutti and Papi, of Oma and Lotte, of Walter and Ruth, of Diana, and all those I had carried in my arms.

The war had ended ten years before and only now was I able to weep. I cried like a baby when I saw the Jewish star, the Magen David, on the tails of the airplanes at Lod, which at the time was a ramshackle hut. If we had had a Jewish state in the 1930s, perhaps six million Jews would not have died.

The first few days in Israel passed in a haze. I remember that the road to Jerusalem was a narrow two-lane road. And we could not get to the Kotel (the Western Wall), because the Jordanian border was right behind the King David Hotel.

I traveled north to Haifa, full of joyful anticipation, to meet Lotte. I paced nervously in my room at the Zion Hotel as I waited for a knock on the door. Lotte and Sami, her husband, were taking the bus from Beit Shean, and we had arranged to meet at the hotel between 3:00 and 4:00 P.M. The minutes ticked slowly by. I looked at my watch again. Only two minutes had passed.

My image of Lotte was that of a little girl standing on the station platform with her suitcase and her knapsack, wearing her best coat, excited, afraid, saying goodbye to Mutti, who was trying to hide her tears.

There was a quick knock at the door, and then I was holding my little sister in my arms. Wordlessly, we cried for our parents, for Oma, for our childhoods and our friends. The little girl wasn't so little anymore.

"I never knew you had such blue eyes," were her first words to me.

"You're pregnant!" I crowed, as I looked at her bulging stomach.

"Number three! Maybe a boy this time!" We smiled through our tears.

We almost forgot my newfound brother-in-law, Sami. I liked him right away. He had an open face, a big grin, a firm handshake, and an embrace, and I felt I was finally reunited with my family.

We talked until the early hours of the morning, trying to catch up on two lifetimes of experience. Over and over we repeated the refrain, "If only our parents could know we survived…if they only could have died with that knowledge." Then we made arrangements to spend Shabbat together on the kibbutz where they lived, Ein Hanaziv, near the Jordanian border.

That Shabbat we settled down after dinner in Lotte and Sami's single, primitive but clean room at their kibbutz located near the ancient city of Beit Shean. It was a hot night in the Jordan Valley but I didn't feel it. I was too wrapped up in the excitement of being with my sister and tasting her delicious cake. The girls had long since gone to bed with the other children, and now Lotte told me her story.

"After Papi left me I was very scared," she began.

"I had only my German identity card. Papi told me over and over again what I should say at the border, but I had forgotten it. What if they did not let me get across? How would I get back? All my worries were for nothing. A German policeman winked at me as if he knew, then walked to the next car. Fifteen minutes later the train arrived at Strasbourg. I took my suitcase and my knapsack and waited on the platform.

"Our cousin Erna Fey came to fetch me, and laughing and crying, took me into her arms. She was in constant touch with the French Jewish relief organization and learned I was coming. Papi's letter had never reached her. So she waited at the train station day after day, hoping to find me."

After Lotte had spent a few days with our cousin, the relief organization farmed out the refugee children to various homes in Strasbourg. Lotte stayed with an Orthodox Jewish family, the Halfs—and she became Orthodox, because it gave her strength, even in the most difficult times. The Halfs were Swiss but lived in France until the Jews of Alsace-Lorraine were deported to the interior in the spring of 1940.

I sat there in bewilderment. My Lotte was a ten-year-old with short brown hair, full of mischief, and a pain in the neck. It did not feel real to be sitting in her kibbutz, in the Promised Land, in Israel. It didn't seem real to see Lotte as an attractive wife, the mother of two with another on the way.

Lotte continued her story. "When the order came for deportation in the spring of 1940, the Halfs decided to return to Switzerland with their own daughter and the six foster children they were caring for. We traveled for days by rail and foot to the border, but there they were turned away because they were caring for so many of us. Mr. and Mrs. Half went to the consulate to get the papers, and we were left together, a motley crew of seven children.

"After unsuccessfully trying to board a train to the French interior, our group was found, crying and totally desolate, by a young German soldier at the railway station. Alice Half, who was seventeen, told him we were separated from our parents and needed to get to a town just across the border from occupied France. "We just stood there and listened to the two of them. We had no idea what the young soldier would do. Did he know we were Jewish? He went to make inquiries, brought us some food, and told us that he had made arrangements for us to take a train to the border. I never knew his name, but if he is alive—and I hope he is—he has the eternal gratitude of seven young Jewish girls who owe him their survival."

Lotte went into many details since she has, as I do, almost total recall of the events of those unbelievably difficult and dangerous days. Travel was difficult in Occupied France because everyone demanded papers. Alice's father had given her Swiss francs, so they rented a room from a farmer. It took six months, but somehow Alice managed to get them permission to cross the border into unoccupied France to stay at a Jewish children's home near Perrigieux.

Then, when Lotte heard that the Jews of Mannheim had been shipped to Gurs on the French-Swiss border, she finagled permission to get there so she could find our parents. She arrived there on their twentieth wedding anniversary and found them, in filthy, unsanitary conditions.

"When they saw me, they couldn't believe their eyes. It was undoubtedly the most beautiful anniversary present they could have received."

"What did they look like? How did they live?" It was the first time I heard she had seen them in Gurs.

"They had lost weight and looked bewildered. Mud was everywhere. They had aged. Yet, they tried to make the best out of a miserable situation. Oma looked like a ghost. Her clothes were filthy, mere rags. She was eighty-seven years old, living in an unheated barrack in the cold winter. She did not recognize me and kept pleading, 'Give me a little piece of bread, a little piece of bread.' It was devastating."

Lotte stayed at Gurs almost a week, sleeping in a barn in a nearby village, and visited our parents every day. There was nothing to do for them. Several thousand Jews lived in that camp from May 1940 until deportation to Auschwitz in October 1942. Oma died a few weeks after Lotte saw her and is buried near Gurs. She was spared the final indignity and fate of those who arrived in Auschwitz.

"Did they know where I was?" I asked.

"The last they knew was that you were working in a labor camp."

Lotte, twelve years old, realized that this was probably the last time she would see our parents. She had to return to Perrigieux. Letters from them stopped coming in 1942. They had been deported to Drancy, and from there to Auschwitz.

We both fell silent, caught up in memories of our parents and the fate they suffered.

Lotte had spent the next three years in various orphanages. The children knew they were surviving on donations from American Jews. She didn't realize until later that I worked for the organization that kept her and thousands of other Jewish children alive. In 1943 there were selections, and the older girls were sent to Auschwitz. One morning five nuns appeared at the home and took charge of 24 girls, including Lotte.

I could only imagine the raggedy procession through the French countryside, drawing the stares of locals. Lotte found her new surroundings, filled with crosses and pictures of Jesus, very alien, but she is forever grateful to the Catholic nuns who snatched her from the hands of the Nazis. The girls were not pressured to convert. To the contrary, as much as possible, the dietary laws were observed and candles were lit on Friday night. In exchange, the girls helped the sisters with their work.

"In June 1944 Sister Jeanne Françoise told us to get ready to leave. The next morning, word came that our departure would be delayed. The Allied armies had invaded France."

A month later they were moved to Toulouse. By the time they reached the Pyrenees near the Spanish border, there were more than 100 boys and girls gathered, all about the same age. We later learned that the entire operation was organized with funds provided by the Joint Distribution Committee and handled by Sally Meyer, a Swiss silk merchant who negotiated with the Germans for the children's release.

Before the children began their difficult march over the mountains to Spain, Youth Aliyah took them under their wing, distributed rations to them, and led them through the treacherous Alpine passes. Soon they were out of food and had to discard what they brought with them. As the climb became tougher, Sami, another of the children, helped Lotte.

"I always tell Sami I couldn't make it without him, but really I was the one who took care of him!"

We agreed to call it a night. Lotte had prepared a small bunk in the hut next door. Despite my fatigue, it took me a long time to fall asleep. I was an American at the beginning of a professional career in the American Jewish community, and here was my sister, an Israeli kibbutz member, married with two children and a third on the way. Fifteen years ago we were two scared German-Jewish youngsters with no idea what the future had in store for us. Our parents were gone. It was up to us to build our own families and create a new future for ourselves.

After Shabbat was over, Lotte went on with her story. Her Alpine hike had lasted ten days until, exhausted and with only the clothes on their backs, the children reached Andorra and were taken by truck to Lerida, across the Spanish border. There they met other children who had also climbed the Pyrenees to safety. One group didn't make it; no one knew what had happened. They then went to Barcelona, then to Cadiz, where they boarded a small ship and arrived in Palestine in October 1944. Together with those who were with her on the journey, Lotte and Sami had built the kibbutz they lived on and created a home and family.

"We are now more than one hundred families and there are more than two hundred children. This is home, for Sami and me, our first real home. This is where we plan to live and to help to build this country so that what happened to us will never happen again. Then we were helpless victims. Today it is totally different."

Lotte's voice had taken on a new ring, one I had never heard from her. My sister had made up her mind to live here, far from any large city, in a desert, a mile away from the enemy. She was determined to build a life for herself and her family. I have enormous admiration for her.

21

THE LINDSAY FAMILY OF WILMINGTON, DELAWARE

PART II: YEARS LATER

When I was in Port Huron, in 1947, during my regular luncheon speeches to the service clubs of the Midwest, I ran into a man who asked me if I had ever been to Wilmington, Delaware.

Wilmington, Wilmington. Why did that sound so familiar? I wracked my brain...Wilmington...Lindsay...affidavit...

Wilmington! Of course! My pen pal Robert Lindsay! I hadn't thought of him in years. I remembered how I had came upon his father, lost in Mannheim, and how generous he was to get an affidavit for me. It certainly wasn't his fault it hadn't worked.

I went back to the office, stumped. For the life of me, I couldn't recall Mr. Lindsay's first name. I felt the compelling need to get in touch with him and let him know I was all right, that I had survived. I couldn't think of how I could begin my search for him, but resourceful newsman that I was, I soon had my hands on the Wilmington telephone directory.

Easier said than done. There was more than a full page of Lindsays, and calling all of them long distance would have been prohibitively expensive. I decided to use the local Wilmington newspaper to help me hunt for Mr. Lindsay. I wrote to the editor, briefly telling the story of how Mr. Lindsay had attempted to save my life by getting me an affidavit, and I sent it off with high hopes. Less than a week later I received a phone call.

"Is this Ernst Michel from Mannheim?"

"Yes. Why?"

"This is Herbert Lindsay."

"Mr. Lindsay! I'm so glad I found you!" I was so excited.

"So am I. So are all of us. You don't know how hard we tried to find news of you and your family after the war. It all came to nothing!"

It was really gratifying. He had never given up. He tried so hard to help, even though he hardly knew us.

"Mr. Lindsay, how is Bob? Is he home?"

"No, Ernst, Bob is in the Navy. He's a doctor, serving in the Pacific. Of our five children, three are in the service." We chatted for a long time. Mr. Lindsay told me the newspaper had printed my story on a prominent page and that he was thrilled when he saw it, thrilled I was alive and well. After I told him that my parents were deported to Auschwitz and that Lotte was living in Palestine, he made an astonishing offer.

"Listen, young man. My wife and I have been talking, and we want you to know that what I wrote to your father so many years ago still stands today."

I could hardly believe it.

"We want to open our home to you and give you a chance to get an education. Maybe you're a few years behind, but we want to send you to the university and help you to get the right start. What do you say?"

What could I say? This man was a Christian, in the true sense of the word. He hardly knew me, yet he was offering to spend thousands of dollars to send me to school. How could I respond?

I promised I would think about it and get back to him. He gave me Bob's address because I wanted to write to him immediately and tell him my story since my last letter in 1939.

I decided that I couldn't accept Mr. Lindsay's generous offer.

A few days later I called Mr. Lindsay at home and told him my decision. He was very gracious.

I stayed in touch with the Lindsay family. When we transferred to New York I finally met my pen pal, Bob, and his family. He set up his medical practice in Worcester, Massachusetts, about 300 miles from New York City.

I'll never forget the Sunday afternoon in 1960 when my family and

I came to visit the Lindsays for the first time. As I drove up the long driveway of Bob's ranch home, his whole family was lined up on the porch, impatiently waiting for us. They all knew my story and the important role the Lindsays had played in my life.

Bob is a big, warm, tall and blond, friendly person with a ready smile and easy personality. Ginny, his wife, immediately made us feel welcome, and our eight children had no problem getting along.

We both cried as we embraced.

"Finally," he said. "It's about time we caught up with each other."

After an authentic American barbecue, Bob asked me to join him in the den. "I want to show you something that I'm sure you'll appreciate."

"Ernest," he looked at me as he slowly opened a small package, "you have no idea what effect you have had on me and my family. When we corresponded before the war, it was through you that I was aware of the events in Europe. When we thought you were lost, it was as if a member of our family had died."

With that, he handed me the open package which contained, in order, all the letters I had sent during the years of our correspondence. I silently looked at my letters, beginning with the first one, dated October 29, 1937.

Dear Robert,

I know you don't know my name. Let me tell you, how I came to your address. Some weeks ago, and I drove with my bycicle to school, there I saw standing at a corner a fine motor car, and many people were standing round this car. I went to it and saw a few men, speaking English. I kould understand some of their words, than I learn English one and half year. I looked to this car and ther a man of this people came to me and asked me, "Do you speak english?" "Yes," I said. "How old are you then?" I answered in English natural, forteen and a half year. (I have birthday on the first of July.) This man was your father. He asked me all in English, weather I will write to you. I was very quickly and he gave me your addresse. I wrote my name in his copybook and some minutes afterwords I went away to school.

Now I am sitting at my writing table, and think about that, what I can write to you.

At first, I must tell you, that I am a Jewish boy. I have still a sister, ten years old. I am still in school, but next Ostern I go out of school. I don't know, what I shall make, if I come out of school, but I shall see all ready.

February 14, 1939
My dear friend Bob,

My best thanks for your last letter. Please will you excuse for my not writing such a long time. But I had to do very much. For the time being I learn English 5 to 6 lessons in day, for i can, if I come to AMERICA very much. In our course, we have 3 lessons of 1 hour; and at home I lern still with a friend 2 to 3 hours. Isn't it very much? Besides that, we can't make anything more, we can't go to the pictures, we can't go to the playground or looking to a football-game, we can't go into another performance or something else. All is forbidden for us. We must stay at home and can't do anything. Isn't it frightful?

It is very honest of your father, that he trouble him so much for me, and I hope, I can ever thank you and your father, what you did for me. It is very fine, that Kennett Square is lying only 12 miles from Wilmington. There we can see and speak us very often, than with the cycle it is only a short hour, isn't it? I'll take my cycle with me to the U.S.A. Shall I do so? Please, will you give me you advice.

On the 10th of November our flat in Mannheim was destroyed. At this time, I lived still in Bruchsal, and there it was too. But I won't write more about this theme. I believe, you know this "nice" things.

Bob was silent as I reread my letters. I thought about the years since I wrote them and was amazed that, despite the hardships I had lived through, there was a tone of optimism in all of them.

"Every member of our family has read your letters," he told me. "We are all proud to know you. You've enriched our lives in ways you will never know."

Bob and I are still close. He and Ginny now live in retirement in California. His father died many years ago. Before he died, I had the chance to meet him in Wilmington and thanked him for being the only person in the world who brought a ray of hope and humanity into the lives of my parents when they were in total despair.

As I conclude this chapter, I can't help but reflect that Lotte's life was saved by the selfless Catholic nuns in France, and that the only family that tried to rescue me was a deeply religious Christian family in the United States.

There is some reason for hope in this world. Perhaps there is a chance, after all, that we can all live together.

22

RETURN TO MANNHEIM

Although I swore I would never set foot in Germany again, on July 1, 1960, my thirty-seventh birthday, I was in Mannheim. I was curious. My wife, Suzanne, and I had arrived the previous day from Israel. I wanted to show Suzanne where I was born and see what had happened to the town of my birth since 1946.

We used money I got from the I. G. Farben settlement of the Wollheim class action suit (*see chapter 24*). I wanted to find my two closest childhood friends, Kurt Hess and Heinz Manz, the two boys who became members of the Hitler Youth and who never spoke to me again after I was thrown out of school. I wanted them to know what had happened to my parents.

I made reservations at the Hotel Mannheimer Hof, the best hotel in the city, and specified that I wanted to stay in the suite where Adolf Hitler had stayed when he visited Mannheim in the 1930s. I still recall that visit and how the whole town lined the streets to welcome the Fuehrer. We had stayed home that whole day, afraid of being seen.

It gave me a perverse feeling of satisfaction to be staying in the same room, to be sleeping in the same bed that the fallen dictator had occupied 25 years before. He was dead. I was alive. The 1,000-year Reich was in ashes. This was a new Germany. I was an American citizen. My publisher from Heidelberg, Theodor Heuss, was now the president of Germany.

First I went to Kurt Hess's house. I told Suzanne that I had a mission I needed to carry out alone. I found the address in the phone book and decided to walk there. The house was damaged but inhabited. I rang the doorbell. An old, gray-haired woman answered the bell. I didn't recognize her.

"Does Kurt Hess live here?" I asked. She looked at me, perplexed. "Who are you?"

"I am Ernst Michel. I lived…"

Her mouth opened in surprise. "You are Ernst Michel?! You are alive?!"

She started to cry, and I had to hold her or she would have fallen.

"I recognize you. The face, a bit older, but it is you!"

She invited me in. By now I knew that this old woman was the attractive, elegant mother of my boyhood friend.

"Mrs. Hess, where is Kurt? Does he live in Mannheim?"

She shook her head, her eyes moist. "Kurt is dead. He was killed in Russia during the war. That is all I know. I don't even know where he is buried."

I sat silently, thinking of my parents and their end in Auschwitz. What irony! Here was the mother of my best childhood friend, and she couldn't even visit his grave.

I told her about my life and my family's fate since my deportation from Mannheim in 1939. Most of the time she listened silently, shaking her head.

So Kurt was dead. Killed in the war. There would be no confrontation. He was dead. I was alive.

Next I sought out Heinz Manz. I found a shop named Manz on the main shopping street. I called the store and asked for Heinz. When the receptionist wanted to know who was calling, I hung up, certain that I had found him. I wanted to see his face when he saw me.

Manz was a beautiful gift shop, probably the finest in town. I walked around a bit, then asked for Mr. Manz. What would he look like now? What would I say?

I recognized him immediately, a second before he recognized me. He hadn't changed much. Of the three of us, he had been the smallest. I didn't say a word.

"Ernst! Is it really you?"

He didn't seem too surprised to see me, because, as it turned out, he had read my articles about the Nuremberg Trials and knew that I was alive. He also knew that I was living in the United States. We had dinner together that evening, Heinz, Suzanne, and me. His wife, he told me, had a serious, debilitating illness and was bedridden. He intimated that she wasn't expected to live very much longer.

Heinz had served in the German army and had been taken prisoner. He knew that Kurt was dead. But whenever I tried to bring up the way he and Kurt cut me out of their lives, he stonewalled me.

"Ernst, that was long ago. We had no choice. We were good, patriotic Germans. We only followed orders."

I had heard that excuse often at Nuremberg. Everyone in the Nazi hierarchy used it. However, I believe human beings always have choices.

"There are more important problems to talk about," Heinz huffed. "Together we have to fight Communism. That is the danger we face today."

He flatly refused to deal with my reason for coming back to Mannheim. He wouldn't allow me to confront him about the way he hurt me and my family.

I really don't know what I expected from the encounter. Was I naïve enough to believe that Heinz would apologize and that he would accept responsibility as a German for the atrocities committed against us? Other Germans were participating in the national denial of guilt and responsibility. Why should he be different?

By evening's end I realized that I had made a serious mistake in seeking him out. I couldn't wait to get back to the hotel. The next morning, before Suzanne and I left for the airport in Frankfurt, we took a long walk to the places I remembered so well. The city was almost new. Although over 90 percent of it had been destroyed during the war, little trace of destruction remained.

Our apartment building on Richard Wagner Street was totally rebuilt. The whole street was new. Every house was rebuilt. My old school was still there, renovated, the playing field which I had loved so much was there. Only the people who were part of my life were all gone. No one was left.

Our final stop was the spot where our synagogue had stood. It was an empty lot. There was nothing left. Very tidy. Nobody would ever know that for almost 100 years a house of worship, a sanctuary, and the center of our lives as Jews in Mannheim had stood in that place. Suzanne left me alone to dwell on my thoughts.

From my earliest childhood, my father had brought me to synagogue every Shabbos morning and every Jewish holiday. I remember when I grew out of "short" pants and was given my first pair of Shabbos knickerbockers. Papi would wear his best suit and tie. Mutti would wear a lovely dress and matching hat. I remember the dark wooden pew we sat in, with its prayer books and *talleysim*, the prayer shawls, neatly folded in their velvet and satin bags.

As a bar mitzvah boy, I accepted my obligation as a Jew in its sanctuary. There, I learned the beauty of being Jewish. Even though we already lived in the shadow of Nazis, I remember how lovely it was that day, when my parents, Lotte, Oma, and I walked to synagogue with Uncle Willie and Aunt Paula. For the first time, I sat on the bima, facing the congregation and waiting to be called to recite my portion of the Torah. I remember seeing Lotte and Mutti smiling in the balcony.

My thoughts were interrupted by a man in his fifties who walked by and gave me a strange look. That spot, there, is where I stood on the morning of November 10, 1938, watching the smoldering ruins. Was he part of the gloating crowd that night?

Before leaving, I walked into the now empty lot, touched the wall of an adjacent building, and silently recited Kaddish, the Hebrew prayer for the dead. Then, with dry eyes, and deep in thought, Suzanne and I walked away.

I was ambivalent when I left Mannheim. I felt empty, cheated. My visit hadn't produced what I had expected, but what should I have expected in the first place? It was too strange. There were only tiny traces of the past. The Germans succeeded in Mannheim. It certainly was *Judenrein*.

I had no business being there. I was sorry I had come back.

23

BUBBA JACKSON, MISSISSIPPI SHERIFF

During the 1950s and early 1960s my responsibility was to organize the UJA campaigns in smaller cities around the country. It was the time of "sit-ins," protests, demonstrations in the South. Tensions were high around the country.

One day, I was in Greenville, Mississippi, to address the town's small Jewish community. The campaign chairman had called me and asked if I would be willing to address the local service club at a lunch. I had accepted.

At that time, Greenville, like most southern towns, was totally segregated. Two-thirds of the town was black. One-third was white. About twenty-five or thirty men attended the luncheon meeting, including the mayor, the sheriff, the local banker, and some other business and professional men. I decided to talk about how it felt to grow up in Mannheim, about the discrimination I faced as a Jew, and about the Nazis' attempt to murder all the Jews. I didn't draw a parallel between the situation in Germany and that of the African-American struggle in the South. However, the audience clearly understood what I was referring to when I stated, "This is what discrimination against Jews led to under the Nazis."

My local chairman squirmed in his seat, and I noticed that the sheriff got up and walked out. When the meeting was over, there was only perfunctory applause. My chairman escorted me back to my hotel and didn't seem very pleased.

"I think you went too far," he commented as we drove to the hotel. "These are sensitive times in this part of the country, and I think you antagonized some people, especially Bubba Jackson, the sheriff."

Before I could reply, I noticed a man standing in the middle of the street whom I immediately recognized to be the sheriff, the one who had walked out of the meeting. He held up his hand, indicating that we should stop.

"Oh no!" My chairman looked at me. "Look what you got yourself into! He can hold you and throw the book at you!"

We both got out of the car. There was nothing else to do. Bubba Jackson took me by the arm and led me across the street into his office in City Hall.

I was scared, almost as scared as I had been when I was picked up after wrecking Henry's car in Chicago. But this time I knew about lawyers and about my right of free speech as an American. Bubba Jackson did not say a word until we were sitting in his office. I tried not to show how afraid I was, but I was sweating.

"Scared ya, didn't I?" he gloated. Then he smiled. "Relax!"

Bubba Jackson was the prototypical Southern sheriff. He was red-faced, heavyset, over six feet tall, and had huge hands. In his sheriff's uniform he was intimidating.

Jackson took a grimy, worn wallet from his desk drawer and put it on the table between us. "I'm gonna tell you a story." By this time I was totally confused. I had expected, at best, a severe reprimand, for what, I had no idea. I envisaged spending the night in jail. Maybe he would order me to get out of town before sundown. Instead Bubba Jackson was telling me a story.

"I was in the Air Force during the war. We were stationed in England. Our squadron flew thirty-six bombing missions over Germany. Of those, most had as their target the town you come from: Mannheim."

I couldn't believe this was happening. Bubba Jackson hesitated and then continued.

"We bombed the shit out of that town and destroyed all the factories, the railroad, the bridges—just about the whole city. I've never been back there, but I know that city well, from a few thousand feet in the air. You're the first person I know who comes from there. I listened carefully about what the Nazis did to you and your family. I heard about that before, but never knew someone like you. I often felt sorry for the people in that town. But no, I don't feel so bad. The bastards!"

He picked up the wallet and held it in his hands.

"When I left Greenville to join the Air Force, my mother gave me a wallet. This is it. I never had a wallet before. My mother put a few coins in it and told me to carry it with me at all times. It would protect me, she said. I kept that wallet. It went with me on all the bombing missions over Mannheim. Lots of guys didn't make it, but I never got a scratch. So this wallet is my good luck piece."

He opened it. It was one of those simple wallets, a coin purse. There were a few coins in it: a quarter, a few dimes, some nickels and pennies. Most of them were green with mold. He lifted a dime from the wallet and carefully placed it on the table.

"Ernie, I want you to keep that dime. I believe it kept me from getting hurt. It came with me on thirty-six missions over Germany. It will bring you luck too."

I sat dumbfounded. There were tears in my eyes. Bubba was moved too. What could I say? Should I take the coin that clearly meant so much to this unusual man? That belonged to a man I had greatly misjudged?

"I can't accept this, Sheriff. It's too much. I know what it means to you."

"I insist. I won't accept no for an answer."

There was nothing to do but assent graciously. I embraced Bubba Jackson and we held each other for a long time. As I left his office, he put his arm around me.

"Ernie, the South is not Germany. There will be changes here. And when you get back north, you can tell 'em about Bubba Jackson, the cracker sheriff who scared you to death and then told you a story."

My chairman was waiting for me in his car, quite concerned about how long it took and wondering what had happened to me.

He could not believe it when I told him about my conversation in the Sheriff's office, and was even more incredulous when I showed him the coin.

"I'll be damned," he repeated over and over. "And here I thought I would have to bail you out."

Bubba Jackson, I don't know if you will ever read this, but you gave a Jewish boy from Mannheim a lot of faith in this country.

I still have your dime.

One of the hundreds of cattle cars that brought 1.5 million Jewish men, women, and children to the Auschwitz extermination camp. This car will be on display at the Illinois Jewish Holocaust Museum and Education Center in Skokie, Illinois, after its opening in 2008.

INAUGURAL EVENT & PREMIERE

I have been made a "Freedom Hero" by the National Underground Freedom Center in Cincinnati, Ohio. Here I am, pictured with five other Freedom Heroes. (*see chapter 31, page 227*)

Freedom
HEROES

From left to right, myself, J. B. Pritzker (chairman of the Skokie, Illinois Holocaust Museum and Education Center), and Sam Harris (president of the Illinois Holocaust Survivors Organization), on a visit to the New York Museum of Jewish Heritage—A Living Memorial to the Holocaust. (*see chapter 32, page 231*)

The sign at the Trinity Church, Manhattan, announcing "Celebrating Our Differences," when I appeared together with the Reverend Jesse Jackson. (*see chapter 28, page 215*)

My sister Lotte (center, dressed in black and purple) at her eightieth birthday celebration, with fifty-eight descendents of her family, including seventeen great-grandchildren. The celebration was held in Jerusalem on Shabbat, November 4–5, 2007. Also pictured is my wife Amy, seated to the left of one of Lotte's son-in-laws (bearded and wearing a white shirt), and my daughter Laurie with her husband (in a blue shirt) on the right. I could not attend due to back problems.

THIS STONE IS DEDICATED TO THE MEMORY
OF OUR PARENTS
OTTO AND FRIEDA MICHEL
FROM MANNHEIM GERMANY
MURDERED: AUSCHWITZ SEPTEMBER 1942
ERNEST W. MICHEL NEW YORK CITY
LOTTE REIN KIBBUTZ EIN HANAZIV
OUR 7 CHILDREN 21 GRANDCHILDREN
16 GREAT GRANDCHILDREN

The stone plaque showing the names of our parents, Frieda and Otto Michel, which Lotte and I placed in a cave at Yad Vashem in Jerusalem in 2007. Inside the cave are hundreds of stones brought by the Holocaust survivors who had come to Israel in June 1981 for the World Gathering, which drew 6,000 survivors and their families from all over the world. (*see chapter 35, page 246*)

Henry Meyer, Auschwitz #104994, and myself, Auschwitz #104995, showing the tattoos on our left arms. (*see chapter 30, page 223*)

Myself and Dr. Peter Kurz, mayor of Mannheim, in front of the Mannheim Holocaust Memorial.

Our parents' names engraved in the Mannheim Holocaust memorial. (*see chapter 36, page 250*)

The Mannheim memorial in the daytime.

My sister Lotte and I telling the stories of our survival at a meeting of the UJA-Federation leadership during a mission to Israel in 2007. (*see chapter 35, page 241*)

The memorial to Mannheim's victims of the Holocaust. Engraved on the inside are the names of the 2,294 murdered Mannheim Jews. It is located on the city's main street.

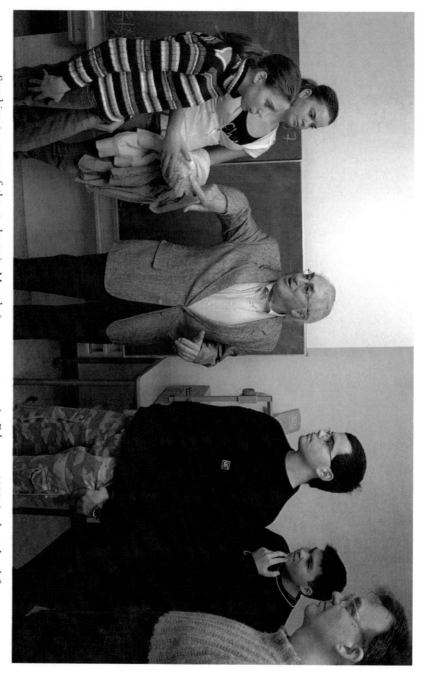

Speaking to some of the students in Mannheim on my return in February 2007, in the school from which I was kicked out at age thirteen in 1936, in sixth grade. (*see chapter 36, page 252*)

24

A MEETING WITH PRESIDENT EISENHOWER AT THE WHITE HOUSE

O n March 20, 1960, the first nationwide dinner of survivors of the Auschwitz-Buna concentration camp was held in New York City. It brought together some 600 survivors and their families and was the first function of its kind ever held in the United States.

Four days later, because I chaired the dinner, I was among five men invited to visit President Dwight D. Eisenhower in the White House. This is how it happened.

A slave laborer from Auschwitz had decided to sue I. G. Farben, the giant chemical combine, for forcing us to work as slaves in the deplorable conditions of Auschwitz. He was the man behind these two related events. I. G. Farben had taken advantage of the unlimited supply of "low-cost" Jewish labor and built the huge factory near Auschwitz to manufacture synthetic rubber called Buna. That's where Walter died and where I worked until I got hit in the head with a rifle butt for looking at an SS guard. Over 130,000 camp inmates, 90 percent of them Jews, died of starvation, disease, beating, or gassing in the process of building the plant, which was never completed and was eventually dismantled at war's end. The slave's name was Norbert Wollheim.

Norbert was born in Berlin and was one of the youngest members of the German-Jewish community leadership. In 1943 he, his wife, and their three-year-old child were deported to Auschwitz. His wife and child went up the chimney with the others. He landed in Buna.

An extremely articulate, courageous, and determined man, Wollheim, who was liberated at Bergen-Belsen, decided to sue I. G. Farben in 1950. He claimed that he was forced to work for two years to build the Buna factory, that he was starved and beaten and never received any payment for his labor. He believed that he had a good case. It took guts to single-handedly sue one of Germany's giant companies. With no funds or support from any Jewish organization, he engaged a sympathetic European-born lawyer, who took the case pro bono.

In 1950 the case of *Wollheim vs. I. G. Farben in Liquidation* was filed in a district court in Frankfurt, Germany. By that time the Allied High Commision had decided to break up I. G. Farben permanently. The company was worth billions of Deutschmarks. Wollheim and his lawyer contended that the conditions under which camp inmates labored in Buna were known to the heads of I. G. Farben and asked for a token DM 10,000 (less than $2,500) in compensation.

The case lingered in the courts for years. I. G. Farben realized that if Wollheim succeeded, thousands of other survivors would file similar claims. It was estimated that some 6,000 to 7,000 survivors throughout the world were still alive.

In 1959, after exhausting one delaying tactic after another, I. G. Farben settled for distributing 30 million Deutschmarks to all the Buna survivors, on condition that no further individual claims be filed. The case received international attention and was taken over by the Conference on Jewish Material Claims against Germany, which handled the often difficult and prolonged negotiations.

Wollheim, who had succeeded in forcing the great German combine to admit its share of the responsibility for war crimes, recruited a few former camp inmates to help him with the paperwork. I was among them. We voluntarily evaluated thousands of applications filed by survivors who claimed to have been inmates of Buna. Similar committees were formed in Israel, South America, Canada, and other countries where survivors had settled.

Each survivor would receive 5,000 German marks or $1,250. In 1960, for many of us that was a lot of money. We were just getting over the effects of the years in the camps and were beginning to earn a living. Many survivors we talked with during the lengthy process of checking claims were in sad shape. Some suffered from recurring nightmares. Others were under constant medical care as a result of the beatings, malnutrition, and similar illnesses. We also encountered a number of survivors who refused to accept any compensation from Germany, although they could have used the funds.

We usually met in the modest offices of URO in downtown New York City, where we evaluated the hundreds of claims. Most were legitimate. Some made the honest mistake of confusing Buna with Auschwitz or Birkenau. We found only a few who tried to cheat. Between us, we were able to determine whether the claimant had actually been in the camp.

I don't remember who had the idea, but we decided to ask all the recipients of the I. G. Farben compensation to agree to make a one-time contribution to establish an Auschwitz-Buna Scholarship Fund. The money would enable a son or daughter of needy survivors to attend college. Our small committee, led by Norbert, all agreed to contribute something from our own Farben checks, and the fund was launched.

Then we decided to organize an Auschwitz-Buna Memorial dinner. Norbert was elected chairman of the scholarship fund and I was elected dinner chairman. Invitations were sent to all Auschwitz-Buna survivors throughout the United States. It explained the goals of the scholarship fund and asked survivors to come together for a dinner in New York, the first of its kind, to celebrate our survival and launch the fund. More than 600 survivors and their spouses made reservations and donations. Even I was surprised at the overwhelming response. The dinner was held at the Concourse Plaza Hotel in the Bronx, in an atmosphere of joy and remembrance.

It was the first time many of us, the alumni of Buna, had seen each other since the death march in January 1945. Scenes of reunion took place at each table and in each corner. Emotions overflowed.

"Aren't you..." and then we'd fall into each other's arms, laughing and crying.

Many who came found fellow inmates they had believed dead. One met a cousin he was sure had perished. These dramatic meetings were worth the exhausting hours we spent organizing the event. The cocktail hour stretched to two. People were too excited to sit down.

The main speakers were Nachum Goldman, President of the World Jewish Congress and a senior leader of world Jewry, and U.S. Senator Jacob Javits. I wrote to Sherman Adams, President Eisenhower's Chief of Staff, to ask the President to designate an individual to accept a specially prepared citation addressed to him, the Congress, and the People of the United States. The citation, signed by all those attending the dinner, eloquently expressed our feelings toward the five-star general who led the Allied Forces to victory and liberated us. In his reply, Mr. Adams informed me that the President had asked Senator Javits to accept the citation on his behalf.

A special scroll of appreciation was also presented to the United Jewish Appeal. It expressed our gratitude for their aid and assistance— for making it possible for us to emigrate to Israel or America and start our new lives.

On the program were Rabbi Herbert Friedman, head of the UJA; Rabbi Herschel Schachter, who as U.S. chaplain helped liberate Buchenwald; Yossele Rosensaft, president of the Bergen-Belsen Survivors Association; and the consul-generals of Poland and France.

The speakers, caught up in the emotion of the evening, ignored the timetable, and the final speaker didn't begin his remarks until well past midnight. Most of the guests stayed to the end. For all of us, it was an unforgettable, emotional evening—and we raised $30,000 for the Auschwitz-Buna Memorial Scholarship Fund. (The funds were eventually turned over to Bar Ilan University in Israel, which is administering the scholarships in perpetuity.)

I sat next to Senator Jacob Javits. Moved by seeing so many survivors gathered for the first time, he passed me a note written on the outside of an envelope. "I'll call the White House tomorrow and suggest you and your committee make the presentation to the President personally. Stay in touch with my office." Two days later we received confirmation from Senator Javits's office that the President would receive us the following Thursday at 12:30 P.M.

A meeting with President Eisenhower at the White House! I immediately called the members of the committee to plan for this extraordinary development. What would we say? How do we make a presentation to the President?

Haskel Tydor, the oldest member of our small group and an Orthodox Jew, proposed that we offer a prayer in the Oval Office in honor of the President.

"But, Haskel, we can't do that," one of us replied. "We can't turn a meeting with the President into a religious ceremony."

"There is a prayer in our religion which is said in the presence of a head of state. It is a brief prayer and totally appropriate," Haskel answered.

We agreed to call Arthur Settel, Senator Javits's key aide, for his opinion. He wasn't much help. He suggested we play it by ear.

We took the morning train to Washington and went to the White House. Our names were listed with the sergeant at the gate and shortly after noon we were sitting in one of the waiting rooms on the ground floor, nervous about the forthcoming meeting. Shortly before 12:30 Senator Javits joined us. He would introduce us to the President. Norbert and I would make the presentation.

We were very quiet as we waited to be taken to the Oval Office. Soon we would be in there, in one of the most famous rooms in the world, in the presence of the most powerful man in the world, the symbol of our hope and liberation. Did we ever imagine, in our wildest dreams in Auschwitz, in Buchenwald, during those years of horror, that we would survive and meet the man who personified everything America represented?

My thoughts were interrupted when a White House aide entered the room: "Gentlemen, the President will see you now." We followed the aide, led by Senator Javits, into the Oval Office.

The President came around his desk to greet each one of us. The first thing I noticed was that he had a small spot on his lapel.

"Mr. President," Senator Javits began the presentation, "last Sunday I attended, on your behalf, a most unusual dinner in New York." He then described to the President the circumstances and asked Norbert and me to present the scroll. We both lifted it onto the President's desk. At that moment I felt a poke in my back. Senator Javits, accustomed to Washington photo opportunities, noticed that I was standing behind the scroll, almost totally obscured, while the White House photographers snapped the pictures which would forever capture this historic moment. I stepped forward. It's good that I did. Otherwise I wouldn't even have a photo as a souvenir.

While all this was going on, Haskel Tydor put on a yarmulke and asked President Eisenhower if he could recite a prayer. I gasped. How could he do this? We wanted to ask the President about his visits to the camps. He had come face to face with survivors and was shocked by what he had seen.

But Haskel was undaunted and, first in Hebrew and then in English, recited the prayer while we all stood silently.

"Thank you very much," the President said, obviously moved.

The President, who had just come from a meeting with British Prime Minister Harold MacMillan, asked about Auschwitz, our liberation, and our new life in the United States. The President was warm and informal and helped us to be very much at ease.

We spent at least half an hour in the Oval Office, and it was only when an aide reminded the President about his next appointment that we took our leave. He again shook hands with each of us and wished us all good luck. We thanked him for receiving us and, as we left the Oval Office, the President said, "This beautiful scroll will eventually be placed in the Presidential Library in Abilene."

I told my kids, who were still a little young, the significance of their father's experience that day. I also sat down and wrote the story of our meeting with the President, and I submitted it to the Reader's Digest, where it won the First Person Story Award for that month.

Here, with permission of the *Reader's Digest*, is the story, as it appeared in the December 1960 issue:

> *From Hitler's Germany to the White House! But even the author could not realize how far he had come until an unexpected incident caused it to be revealed on the face of the man standing behind the President's desk.*
>
> *A Reader's Digest $2500 "First Person" Award*

MY LONG JOURNEY TO EISENHOWER
By Ernest W. Michel

I had been to Washington, DC, and on the flight home I wondered how I would tell my family about this day, the most remarkable in my life. My children were young and perhaps they wouldn't understand its significance, but I so wanted them to.

When I arrived home I kissed my wife, then turned to my three young children standing in their pajamas, faces scrubbed, eyes shining in anticipation of the nightly story. "Tonight I'm going to tell you a true story," I said. "Part of it is very sad, but it ends happily." I paused a long moment. Then I began:

Once upon a time there was a boy—we'll call him Ernest—and he lived in Mannheim, Germany. He loved to play soccer with his best friend, Kurt. But when he was ten years old a wicked man named Hitler seized power in Ernest's country and began to make people hate instead of love. Especially he tried to make people hate Jews. Ernest was a Jew.

On a warm spring day in 1935 Ernest and his friend Kurt ran out onto the soccer field, but the coach stopped Ernest and said, "You can't play soccer any more. You are a Jew." Ernest expected that Kurt would stand up for him. But he didn't. And the following day Kurt arrived at school dressed in a Hitler Youth uniform and he never spoke to Ernest again. It wasn't that Kurt suddenly hated Ernest; he just wanted to be like everyone else. He didn't have the courage to say what he really felt.

As time went on, Ernest found that he couldn't go to the sports arenas, or to the movies, and finally even the public parks carried signs that read: "No Jews or dogs allowed." Then, on the night of November 9, 1938, many synagogues in Germany were dynamited and destroyed. That night Hitler's Storm Troopers broke into Ernest's home, ransacked the place and slapped his mother. Ernest couldn't understand what made normally decent men suddenly act like gangsters.

War began in September, 1939, and six days later Hitler ordered all Jewish youths in Mannheim between the ages of 16 and 20 to report for slave labor. Ernest was just 16. When he left, his father and mother were very brave in front of him, and he was very brave in front of them. Ernest did not know that he would never see his parents again, that they would soon be among the millions of Jews to be killed in Hitler's gas chambers.

For four year Ernest was starved and beaten until he was a skeleton of 85 pounds. Now he was of no more use as a slave; so he was sent to the notorious Auschwitz concentration camp. There the numbers 104995 were tattooed on his arm. These figures indicated the order of his death in the gas chamber. Each day Ernest waited to hear them called.

Then in the spring of 1944 something crept into the concentration camp—it was hope! Eisenhower had invaded Europe! Now Ernest prayed for life for one more month, one more week, one more day…until Eisenhower could arrive to free him.

Early in 1945 Ernest was moved to another horrible camp, called Buchenwald. But as Eisenhower came closer, Ernest and hundreds of other prisoners were marched northeast, away from Eisenhower, away from liberation. And each day the guards methodically murdered two dozen men.

Ernest and two friends decided to try to escape. Late one afternoon as the straggling column breasted a hill, Ernest saw a dense stand of hemlock. He knew that this small forest would be their salvation or their grave. He signaled his two friends and they ran for the forest.

Soon each breath became agony; he crashed into trees but reeled on. At last he fell and could not get up.

But he had escaped. For the first time in six years he wept. Slowly his strength returned and he picked himself up, found his two friends and they all turned west, toward Eisenhower.

A few weeks later the war ended, and the next year Ernest came to the United States. He became a citizen of this great country, and he married a beautiful American girl and he had three wonderful children and a house and a good job. America gave him more than he ever dreamed life held.

But Ernest never let himself forget those terrible days in Germany, nor did he want the world to forget. So he and others who had survived created the Auschwitz-Buna Memorial Scholarship Fund for children of the victims of Nazi brutality. They also decided to thank Eisenhower publicly. They ordered a beautiful big scroll expressing gratitude and loyalty to the United States, and Ernest and five friends went to Washington to present it to Eisenhower, who had become President.

They arrived in Washington and Ernest took a walk. He gazed at the Lincoln Memorial, the Jefferson Memorial and the Washington Monument, and he thought of the wisdom of the founding fathers. And he was a part of it all! He felt very proud.

He returned to the hotel to meet his friends and discuss what they would say to the President the next day. One man, Haskel Tydor, being very religious, proposed to say a Jewish prayer for the President when they met him. The others objected. Ernest was afraid the President might be embarrassed; after all, he was not a Jew. Also, Ernest had just stood proudly before the Lincoln and Washington monuments as an American citizen, and he wanted to act like an American before his President; he wanted to leave the old rituals back in the old country. So he and his friends told Haskel Tydor not to say the Jewish prayer for the President.

At the White House next morning they were ushered into a reception room outside the President's office. Ernest was nervous. He sat, he stood, he paced the floor. He still hadn't been able to decide how he should speak to the President. Suddenly a door opened and a man said, "Gentlemen, the President is ready."

Ernest straightened his coat and his necktie, and his mind raced back through the long journey he had taken to arrive at this door: the years of slavery, the hell of concentration camps, the nightmare of the long march when the very name Eisenhower had made him cling desperately to life. He felt a moment of panic; he didn't want to see the man in person, he preferred to keep him safe in imagination. But it was too late to turn back.

Behind a large desk sat the President. The first emotion Ernest felt was shock of recognition. There was the face he had seen in thousands of pictures; but now it was real and alive and looking straight at him.

The President grasped Ernest's hand firmly and gave him a smile, and Ernest felt himself blushing with emotion. Then in a warm compassionate voice the President asked Ernest and his friends to tell him about the concentration camps.

As Ernest spoke he suddenly realized that all nervousness had left him; he knew that he was in the presence of a man who cared deeply about his fellow men. When Ernest finished, the President recalled grimly his own shock at the horrors of the death camps and denounced those who had looked the other way and had denied responsibility for such inhumanity. He expressed pride that so many victims who escaped had come to America.

The scroll of appreciation from the Auschwitz survivors was presented and the President read it carefully. It was time to go. But, without warning, Haskel Tydor spoke up: "Mr. President, we Jews have an ancient prayer that calls God's blessing on the head of our government. I would like to call that blessing upon you."

Ernest and his friends gasped. Ernest was furious. Haskel Tydor kept his eyes on the President and said, "Do I have your permission?"

"Indeed you have," the President said. He had been lean-

ing against his dek but now he stood erect and bowed his head in reverence.

Haskel Tydor put on a skullcap and opened a prayer book. He recited the ancient prayer in Hebrew, and the President listened to the alien words. Then Tydor repeated the prayer in English, and this time the President could understand. He heard the words, "Blessed be thou, Lord our God, King of the universe, Who has given of Thy glory to mortal man."

Ernest saw tears in Tydor's eyes. Then he looked at the President and saw that he, too, was deeply moved. The President said in a low emotion-filled voice, "Thank you very much."

Now Ernest realized how wrong he had been and how right Haskel Tydor had been. It was wrong to think that they should leave part of themselves in the old world. Here at last they could be whole men, Jews and Americans at the same moment. That was what Washington and Jefferson and Lincoln had said, but Ernest hadn't felt its true meaning until he saw it revealed in the face of the living President, Eisenhower.

And that was the end of the bedtime story. As I put my son to bed he reached up and ran his fingers over my left arm, over the Auschwitz numbers, 104995.

"Daddy, did the President see your tattoo?" he asked.

"He knew it was there," I said.

"When I grow up will I go to see the President of the United States?"

"If you do, my son," I answered, "it will not be because you carry on your arm the death numbers of Auschwitz."

As far as I know, our meeting with President Eisenhower was the first time that a group of Holocaust survivors had been received at the White House. It was one of the most memorable moments in my life.

copyright © 1960 by The Reader's Digest Assn., Inc. Reprinted by permission.

25

THE WORLD GATHERING OF HOLOCAUST SURVIVORS

JERUSALEM, JUNE 1981

I t was 1977, and I was in Israel again. As usual, I visited Kibbutz Nezer Sereni, which is one of hundreds of settlements in Israel. Some were founded more than 100 years ago; Nezer Sereni was founded by Holocaust survivors, and it's located halfway between Tel Aviv and Jerusalem. My friends from Paderborn and Buna were here. They arrived right after the big war and then picked up guns and fought in the War of Independence in 1948.

Many kibbutzim exist on income from agriculture. Others make furniture, machinery, leather coats, or plastics. Some make frozen soy products, others make microchips, some do a few things at once. A few are even in the tourism business.

I make it a point to visit Nezer Sereni every time I'm in Israel. Piese and Onny, who were with me in Buna on Passover in 1943, both live there.

Hilde, Piese's wife, was a member of the infamous Auschwitz orchestra, which played Viennese waltzes as the inmates were marched to the gas chambers. The book *Playing for Time* describes what the orchestra went through. It was made into a TV movie some years ago.

Usually we sit around the coffee table and shmooze, our conversations often interrupted by children and grandchildren. We talk about our families, our friends, and sometimes, not often, about the years in the camps when none of us really believed we would survive. This time our get-together was a little different. When we made the date, Piese told me they had something important to discuss with me.

The weather was hot and humid. We sat in front of Onny's house. Munzie, his wife, had baked a special cake for the occasion. We drank iced tea and soda. After we swapped news about family, Piese turned to me. "Ernst," he said, "we have an idea. It's not new, but we believe it's exciting."

Onny nodded. I had known him since Paderborn. He is a tall, gangly fellow with a ready smile. We worked together in the same *Kommando* unit, cleaning streets and sewers. We were in the same transport, experienced the same dreadful years in Auschwitz. Onny, whose family name is Ohnhaus, is number 105006, which is tattooed on his left arm, just a few digits after mine. Piese got there a few months before we did, so he has a lower number. Both of them, like me, were born in Germany. Like me, they lost most of their family in the Holocaust.

"Ernst," Piese continued, "do you remember an evening in Auschwitz—I believe it was Passover 1943—we were talking about trying to meet with other survivors if we indeed survived?"

I smiled. I remembered that Passover. No matzoh, no nothing, just a dream of liberation, of freedom. "Piese, did anyone really believe that any of us would come out alive from that hell?"

"Well, you did!"

He was right. I did remember. The game that we played was called "What if?" What would we do if we were lucky enough to survive? That Passover someone had suggested bringing all the survivors together. No one believed it could happen. No one believed we would be liberated either.

Munzie cut another piece of cake. They all knew about my sweet tooth. She looked at me. "We have talked about that conversation and went to Jerusalem to see people in the government with the idea of organizing a survivors' reunion."

Onny broke in. "You know what we got? A lot of tea and slaps on the back. Everyone thought it was a good idea, but nobody was willing to really help us."

"Who did you talk to?" I asked.

"Some friends in the prime minister's office."

"Why wouldn't they help?"

Piese got up and started pacing around the room.

"First, they said no one would come. They asked who wants to participate in a reunion of death camp survivors? The only thing you have in common are bad memories. Three: there's no money for something like that. Four: we've got more important problems to deal with. That's it."

There was a moment of silence while I thought about the idea. It intrigued me.

Piese looked at me. "Ernst, you know survivors in the States. You have traveled in Europe and know survivors there. We know Auschwitz survivors here in Israel. Together we can get the names of several hundred people and their children and extended families."

"Who'll pay for this? It would cost money. It doesn't just happen."

"That's why we wanted to talk to you. You have more influence than we do."

"Where would you want to hold the reunion?"

"Here in the kibbutz."

"When?"

"In a year?"

"How many survivors do you think will come?"

"Maybe a few hundred."

"What kind of program were you thinking of?"

He hesitated a moment. "We have some ideas, but nothing specific. We first wanted to hear what you thought about the whole project."

We spent the better part of the afternoon dissecting the idea, batting it back and forth. I tried to be the devil's advocate, raising objections, reacting to some proposals—all the while thinking whether or not this was something I wanted to get involved in. I didn't realize it then, but I really had no choice.

Instinctively and professionally, I knew that the logistics of such a reunion, especially if it involved people from various countries, would be mind-boggling. While there were some active survivor groups (among them the Bergen-Belsen Survivors Association, The Warsaw Ghetto Fighters organization, and various *landsleit* groups) an international reunion of Holocaust survivors had never been attempted.

While Piese, Onny and some of the others were thinking of bringing together those who had been in Auschwitz-Buna, I began to think in much larger terms. Why not all the survivors? Why not include those who had been in hiding, who had lived with false identity papers, who had fought with partisans? Why not make it something really big, pump up the numbers, invite a thousand or more? Why not make this a worldwide event?

The more I thought about it, the more I believed it had possibilities. There were still lots of questions and lots of hurdles, but I felt it was worth a try.

On the long flight back to New York, I made a list of those I needed to talk to. I realized that an undertaking of this kind would take a lot of time and that I couldn't do it without the full support of the leadership of the UJA and my colleague Sanford Solender, my fellow executive vice-president of UJA-Federation.

Sandy was the first one I spoke to upon my return to New York. He quickly sensed the scope of such a reunion and agreed that it had to be done on a large scale, if at all. More, it must include survivors from all over the world. Not just camp survivors, but those who had been in hiding, those who had been partisans, those who left and joined military groups. It had to include any Jew who suffered at the hands of the Nazis.

"Sandy, where can we get the money that's needed?"

"There are foundations, I'm sure, which might respond favorably to this. I would think that UJA-Federation would support this effort as well. Besides, you are the fundraiser!"

I went to see Stephen Shalom, then the president of UJA. He too immediately sensed the unique purpose of such an event and agreed to let me use UJA-Federation facilities and allowed me to give it the necessary time. He went so far as to tell me that he would recommend that the board allocate a one-time contribution toward the budget.

I gave some thought to the cost of organizing the event, and I realized that we would need several hundred thousand dollars. There was no mailing list, no staff, no organization—nothing. At the moment this was just an idea born out of a dream in the hell of Auschwitz.

At a meeting with my colleagues, the professional heads of the major federations from throughout the States, I presented an outline of the plan. All of them were born in America. They all went to college. They were dedicated. They were able, articulate, and tough and they accepted me with warmth and friendship after my appointment to head the New York UJA.

They asked some tough questions, and I didn't have all the answers.

Who will run the show?

Who will handle logistics?

Who will have financial responsibility?

Will you set up an office?

How will you gather the names?

How do you plan to publicize the reunion?

When and where will it take place?

I also contacted the survivors in New York. Norbert Wollheim, who had put together the Auschwitz-Buna dinner, agreed to play a role. His first wife had died in Auschwitz, and his second wife had just died after a long illness. I called Sam Bloch, president of the Bergen-Belsen Survivors Association; also Eli Zborowski, Roman Kent, and others, all survivors and prominent in their various Jewish organizations. From Los Angeles there was Fred Diament and Sig Halbreich, and from San Francisco, Bill Lowenberg. They all agreed to join the effort.

One thing none of us was sure of. Would survivors come to Israel for an obviously highly emotional event? Would survivors be willing to face the past? Would they spend the money, several thousands of dollars, for the trip and incidentals?

During that time I met Benjamin Meed, the president of WAGRO, the Warsaw Ghetto Resistance Organization. Ben, a small man with a round friendly face and penetrating blue eyes, was born in Warsaw, Poland, where his family had lived for many generations. He and his wife, Vladka, are both survivors of the Warsaw Ghetto. Ben, who does not look Jewish at all, survived on the outside, posing as a Christian.

Vladka is a true heroine. She was a courier in Poland and secured arms for the uprising. She wrote a book about her experiences, *On Both Sides of the Wall*.

Ben became a successful businessman but gave it up some time ago to devote himself full-time to perpetuate the memory of the Holocaust. He is a dynamic, imaginative, and driven individual whose total being is devoted to the memory of the Holocaust. The Meeds have two children, both doctors, and four grandchildren. Over the years, we became close friends.

At the suggestion of some of the men I had met, I invited Ben to join the fledgling committee. This turned out to be the best move I made. Ben brought a sense of dedication, an enormous zeal, and a creative imagination to the project. He became my right hand, and he deserves a major share of the credit for the incredible success of what became known as "The World Gathering of Holocaust Survivors."

The second major move I made was hiring a young Israeli conference organizer by the name of Yitzhak Rogov. Born in South Africa, he immigrated to Israel in the 1950s and went into the business of stimulating and running major seminars and conferences. Although we didn't have a nickel in the bank, and only uncertain promises of support, Yitzhak agreed to handle all technical and logistical details. He believed in the importance of the Gathering as much as any of us did. He did it for a minimum fee, and I am sure the Gathering cost him money. He didn't care. He felt the importance of our effort and put his entire organization behind it. Without him the Gathering could not have taken place. It is as simple as that.

The problem of how to finance the reunion was eased when we got financial commitments from the National UJA, the Jewish Agency, and most of the major Jewish Federations around the country. My colleagues from the major cities came through, and I will forever be indebted to them. Major funding also came from individuals I contacted who responded as the plan gained momentum.

We were given office space at the World Jewish Congress and hired a small staff. We called fellow survivors all over the world, and some of us traveled to many countries to personally enlist their cooperation. I went to France, England, Sweden, and Germany. Others went to South America, Mexico, and Italy. Word began to spread after we called a news conference in New York and set June 1981 as the date for the four-day event.

Piese, in the meantime, organized the Israelis.

I was given the name of a young survivor, a woman living in Johannesburg, South Africa, by the name of Miriam Lazarus. I wrote to her explaining what we were trying to do and asked if she would be willing to organize survivors in her part of the world. Miriam, one of the youngest survivors alive, was born in Poland in 1940. Her parents were able to find a Christian couple who agreed to take care of their daughter. After the war, Miriam's father went to find her—her mother had been killed—but the couple would not give her up. After a lengthy court battle her father reclaimed his daughter and they went to settle in South Africa. Eventually Miriam married and had three sons. She had little if any contact with any survivors and knew little about her own background. One day I received a telegram from her:

> *What right do you have to disturb me with the Holocaust? I had thought that I had put it out of my mind. Since receiving your letter, I have not been able to sleep. I am arriving in New York next week and want to meet with your committee.*

She turned out to be an attractive, tall, blonde woman in her late thirties, full of doubt about the Gathering. The news of the planned event had shattered her tranquil life in Johannesburg. She simply could not understand why survivors wanted to get together, but after attending a meeting of the full committee and sensing the purpose of our plans, she became an ardent activist and went back to Johannesburg to organize the survivors living there.

Eventually she brought more than 60 South Africans to the World Gathering. Miriam was given the honor of opening the program. For her, as for many others, the Gathering became a turning point in her life, as survivors were finally able to confront their past and, in doing so, to deal with it in a positive way and come to "closure."

The preparations for the World Gathering took more and more time. Evenings, weekends, holidays—every minute was taken up with the multitude of details involved in organizing such a momentous event.

Support came from many countries. Simone Veil of France, an Auschwitz survivor who became president of the European Assembly, joined us as vice-chairman. So did Elie Wiesel, the future Nobel laureate, and Stefan Grayek, head of the major survivors organization in Israel.

We stayed in constant touch with Piese and arranged for him to come to New York to participate in major decisions about format, agendas, speakers, and so on. Things didn't always run smoothly. There were sharp differences of opinion, based on our varied cultures and lifestyles. While we all had shared the same hardships, we lived in different worlds now and had different concepts of what the Gathering should be.

We did agree on most major points, among them our unanimous feeling that the event should not be a four-day memorial service. We wanted to show the world that we had become active, fruitful citizens in the countries where we lived and that, despite our past, we were able to lead productive lives. The Gathering would be a celebration of our survival and the strength of the Jewish people, while at the same time we would remember, with reverence, our families and friends and all those who perished.

And so it came about that on June 15, 1981, 36 years (in Hebrew double *chai*, meaning twice life) after our liberation, some 6,000 survivors and their children and grandchildren, from 23 countries and four continents, came together in Jerusalem in an outburst of remembrance and emotion.

26

FOUR UNFORGETTABLE DAYS IN JERUSALEM

June 15, 1981 was a warm summer evening. The air was clear, the moon was full. That night 6,000 survivors of the Holocaust gathered in the huge plaza at Yad Vashem, the national Holocaust memorial in Jerusalem, for the opening ceremony of the World Gathering. They brought their families—their children and grandchildren, aware that there we were participating in a moment of grandeur and high drama. Born out of a chance remark by an inmate in Auschwitz in 1943, discussed over a coffee table in Kibbutz Nezer Sereni, and worked on by volunteers and survivors and the Second Generation (their children) for four long years, the magic moment finally arrived. It was the largest event in the history of the State of Israel.

I find it difficult, even as I write this, to put into words what it meant to me. I was torn between my responsibilities as chairman, thinking of all the big and little details that go into such an important event, and my emotions as a survivor whose dream was coming true. I thought of my parents. I thought of my friend Walter. I remembered the day of our arrival in Auschwitz and the agony of our helplessness. I saw the bodies: Leo, Janek, and Chaim on the gallows, and remembered Honzo and me taking them down gently. I saw myself on the death march from Auschwitz and then relived our eventual escape. What had happened to us in our lives? How come I had survived and Walter, Felix and all those others I saw die in front of my eyes did not?

A fanfare interrupted my thoughts. Yitzchak Navon, the president of Israel, was arriving. We all stood up and I went forward to welcome him. He took the seat of honor and the program began.

Among the speakers were Dr. Yitzhak Arad, chairman of Yad Vashem, himself a Holocaust survivor, and Gideon Hausner, Israel's prosecutor at the infamous Eichmann Trial.

Then it was my turn. I stood up in front of that mass of humanity and said many of the things I had said to the people in Port Huron and across the nation during my early years in America. But at Yad Vashem, on that day, my heart was full to bursting, and my words meant more to me.

> Like many of you, I had a dream. Mine was born in the darkness of Auschwitz, nourished by our liberation and finally brought to life four years ago when a few of us met in Kibbutz Nezer Sereni. The dream was that one day—if we live—we, the survivors of one of the greatest tragedies in all of human history, would come and stand together to remind a world that would rather forget, not to let another Holocaust happen—to Jews or non-Jews. Once is enough.

> I remember vividly my arrival in Auschwitz on a gray winter evening in 1943, after endless days in a cattle car, with the SS in their long leather coats, elegant, tall, clean-shaven. I remember jumping out of the car, hungry, frightened and whips lashing down. Then the line moving slowly forward until we came face to face with Dr. Mengele—the Angel of Death—and his thumb went up and down: Up, you live. Down, you die.

> Since they have no graves where we can mourn, we have brought to Israel, in their memory, a piece of rock, a stone. Here is mine. It is a simple stone. On it are written the names of the immediate members of my family who perished. We brought these rocks from all over the world. Eventually they will be built into a monument here at Yad Vashem, so that our children and theirs too can have a place to mourn.

> So here we are, all of us survivors, who came to Israel, sharing memories of a horrifying past, carrying the evidence on our bodies, but proudly standing together to tell a world: We have survived!

We survivors want to tell those who try to rewrite history and deny that the Holocaust ever happened:

Our eyes have seen.

Our ears have heard.

Our nostrils were filled with the acrid fumes from the gas chambers drifting over our camp. Day after day. Week after week. Year after year.

These hands have carried more corpses than I care to remember. Friends, families.

So don't tell us it never happened. We were there. To deny us that part of our lives negates our very existence. We are the living witnesses and we will continue to speak out until the last survivor is no more. After that, only faces on films and our recorded voices will be left to tell future generations.

My fellow survivors, touched by the madness of our nightmare, we have tried to live normal lives. Scarred by the acid of barbarous hatred, we have tried to give love to our children. Forgotten by a silent world, we have tried to avoid cynicism and despair.

Despite all we have known, we affirm life—despite the most ferocious of efforts to steal it from us. While we shall never forget, we will not live with hate. We assert faith and can hug and embrace each other goodbye.

We came to this place in a great burst of love for one another and for the ideals in which we believe—our Jewishness, our Israel, our ancient heritage.

When the final shofar of that closing ceremony sounds, we shall return home and most of us will never meet again. But we will leave with gratitude in our hearts for the miracle of our survival, for that of the Jewish people, and for the rebirth of the Jewish land. Go, my friends—go—knowing that history will tell our story forever.

The gathering attracted radio, TV, newspaper, and magazine reporters from all over the world. We were told that more than 700 media representatives were covering the Gathering. Among them was David Schonbrunn, former chief CBS European correspondent. It was the first time that PBS had agreed to live coverage of an event outside the United States. David, assisted ably by Laurel Vlock, brought the highlights of the four-day event to the United States every night at 10:00 P.M.

The most popular feature of the World Gathering was the survivor village. The Jewish Agency agreed to let us use Binyanei Ha'umah, the Jerusalem Convention Center, as headquarters. One large room was designated as the "Survivor Village." We knew that many survivors coming from different parts of the world had not seen each other since the years in the camps. Some hadn't seen each other since before the war and would be searching for friends and relatives. In order to facilitate this search, we installed a computer system which was tied into the Israeli national system, including the records at Yad Vashem. All day long survivors queued up in front of the computer operators looking, mostly in vain, for long-lost family members.

But there were also heartwarming scenes of recognition as men and women stared at someone.

"Aren't you...?"

"Were you not at Block 9?"

"Don't we know each other from...?"

At the conclusion of one of the meetings, a bald, tanned, well-dressed man stopped me.

"Ernst—Do you remember me from Buna?" I looked at him but couldn't place him.

Julius Paltiel from Trondheim, Norway, looked very different from the fellow in the striped uniform I had known in Auschwitz. He was one of the small group of Norwegian Jews deported to Auschwitz in 1943. Of course, I remembered him. I just didn't expect survivors to come from Norway. I learned that Julius was living with his family in Trondheim, that he was in business there, and that he had built the only Norwegian-style house in Israel. It was where he spent his summers.

Friends gathered from all parts of the world. Some even did find long-lost relatives. We knew the emotional strain was great, and we were urged, by members of the Second Generation, to provide doctors, psychiatrists, and nurses in anticipation of nervous breakdowns and heart attacks. It was a prudent move but none were needed. Not a single survivor needed medical attention. There were tears, yes. There were highly charged emotional moments. But it is a credit to our strength as survivors that not once during the entire Gathering was there even a minor incident to mar the drama of our being together.

On the second day, we broke into smaller groups and visited some of the kibbutzim founded by survivors during the years after the war. In addition to Nezer Sereni, where Piese was host, groups went to Lochamei Hagetaot, the kibbutz of the Warsaw Ghetto survivors.

Among those to address the survivors at Lochamei Hagetaot was the legendary Yitzhak "Antek" Zuckerman, one of the last surviving leaders of the historic uprising of the Warsaw Ghetto. Those who were present will always remember the tall, dignified hero, as he sat quietly in the audience, listening to Elie Wiesel. The next morning the radio announced that Antek had suffered a heart attack during the night and died. It cast a heavy pall on the Gathering as we paid tribute to his memory. He was a man who personified the strength, the willpower—the very best of our people.

Ben Meed and I talked for many weeks about the program for the last evening of the Gathering, the climactic event when we would meet at the Western Wall, the last remaining part of the Holy Temple, which was destroyed 2,000 years ago. Until it was liberated in the Six Day War, it was referred to as the Wailing Wall because, for hundreds of years Jews came here to pray and to mourn the destruction and Diaspora of our people.

We invited Menachem Begin, the popular prime minister of Israel, along with future Nobel Laureate Elie Wiesel, to address the survivors that final evening. The prime Minister had agreed, when Ben and I met with him, to accept the role as Patron of the Gathering, but he didn't commit to addressing the survivors,because he wasn't sure the pressures of his office would allow him to do so. We stayed in touch with his office as we got closer to the date. There was still no final confirmation that he would speak. I asked Yehuda Avner, Begin's advisor, for a meeting with the prime minister. Yehuda, who had been helpful and supportive from the beginning, came through again. The prime minister would see me for a few minutes on the day before the final event.

I was nervous when Yehuda ushered me into Begin's office. I didn't know what he was going to say. Yehuda told me the prime minister had a heavy schedule the next day, including his secretary's wedding in Tel Aviv. It didn't look good.

Begin was most cordial. He had been following the Gathering through the media and remembered very well our last discussion concerning his appearance for the next evening. He told me he had promised to attend his secretary's wedding in Tel Aviv. Before I could feel deep disappointment, he added that he would make a brief appearance at the opening of the session, greet the audience, and then leave for Tel Aviv. There was no way to get him to change his mind. We would have to rearrange the program, but at least the survivors would see and hear the prime minister.

When I got back to the hotel, Ben was making final preparations for what became one of the most memorable moments of that last evening. All the survivors would march en masse through the Old City to the Wall, carrying candles. Six thousand survivors and their families would carry 6,000 candles, each one lit for 1,000 victims.

It sounded good on paper, but the Jerusalem Police nixed it. The March—yes. Candles—no. Ben, undaunted, came up with another idea. The candles would be placed in front of the platform where the program would take place. All 6,000 of them. They would be lit by each survivor as he or she entered the Plaza facing the Western Wall.

And that's how it happened. Ben arranged for the candles. As the sun sank, Jerusalem took on that golden glow she is so famous for. The sky was a deep azure with purple streaks. The mezzuin in the mosque above us sang his evening prayers, as below him, survivors and the Second Generation filed into the plaza, lit their candles, and took their seats.

Then it was night, and the sight of the 6,000 candles flickering in the breeze, with a full moon lighting up the entire plaza left an indelible impression on all of us who were there. In addition to the survivors, the plaza was filled from one end to the other with thousands who stood in the back and wanted to be part of this very special and cleansing moment in Jewish history.

At 7:00 P.M., the Prime Minister arrived in his motorcade. When he saw close to 15,000 people packing the courtyard, he seemed overwhelmed. I could see the astonishment in his eyes as he looked over the huge throng of survivors standing quietly in front of their seats. I saw him motion to one of his assistants. Ben Meed and I came forward to greet him. He turned to us and said, "You go ahead with your program. I will stay until the end." Ben and I looked at each other. We couldn't believe the prime minister had changed his mind so quickly.

Immediately after Mr. Begin took his seat, the program got underway. In addition to speeches, there was one other major part of the program to which we had given a great deal of thought. We wanted the Gathering to be more than a gathering of men and women who had survived the Holocaust. We wanted to leave a legacy which could be passed on from generation to generation, a reminder of the greatest tragedy to befall our people.

Elie Wiesel had agreed to draft "The Legacy of the Holocaust Survivors." It was read that evening by survivors from six different countries in six languages: English, Hebrew, French, Spanish, Russian, and Ladino. Fifteen thousand people maintained total silence. One could sense the emotion running through the crowd. There was an electricity, an unseen bond, as each of the six survivors, born in six different countries read this Legacy:

> *WE TAKE THIS OATH! We take it in the shadow of flames whose tongues scar the soul of our people. We vow in the name of dead parents and children; we vow with our sadness hidden, our faith renewed; we vow, we shall never let the sacred memory of our perished Six Million be scorned or erased.*
>
> *WE SAW THEM hungry, in fear, we saw them rush to battle, we saw them in the loneliness of the night—true to their faith. At the threshold of death, we saw them. We received their silence in silence, merged their tears with ours.*
>
> *Deportations, executions, mass graves, death camps; mute prayers, cries of revolt, desperation, torn scrolls; cities and*

towns, villages and hamlets; the young, the old, the rich, the poor, ghetto fighters and partisans; scholars and messianic dreamers, ravaged faces, fists raised. Like clouds of fire, all have vanished.

WE TAKE THIS OATH! Vision becomes word, to be handed down from father to son from mother to daughter, from generation to generation.

REMEMBER what the German killers and their accomplices did to our people. Remember them with rage and contempt. Remember what an indifferent world did to us and to itself. Remember the victims with pride and with sorrow. Remember the victims with pride and with sorrow. Remember also the deeds of the righteous Gentiles.

WE SHALL ALSO REMEMBER the miracle of the Jewish rebirth in the land of our ancestors, in the independent State of Israel. Here, pioneers and fighters returned to our people the dignity and majesty of nationhood. From the ruins of their lives, orphans and widows built homes and old-new fortresses on our redeemed land. To the end of our days we shall remember all those who realized and raised their dream—our dream—of redemption to the loftiest heights.

WE TAKE THIS OATH here in Jerusalem, our eternal and spiritual sanctuary. Let our legacy endure as a stone of the Temple Wall. For here prayers and memories burn. They burn and burn and will not be consumed.

Then, in response, six members of the Second Generation, our children, rose, one after the other to accept the legacy for themselves and future generations. It was a response drafted by the leadership of the Second Generation on a sticky, hot summer day in New York, and I'm proud to say that my oldest daughter, Lauren, participated in the writing of it all the way from Israel. She stayed on the phone with her New York associates until it was done.

WE ACCEPT the obligation of this legacy.

WE ARE the first generation born after the darkness.

Through our parents' memories, words and silence, we are linked to that annihilated Jewish existence who echoes permeate our consciousness.

WE DEDICATE this pledge, to you, our parents, who suffered and survived;

to our grandparents who perished in the flames;

to our vanished brothers and sisters, more than one million Jewish children, so brutally murdered.

to all Six Million, whose unyielding spiritual and physical resistance, even in the camps and ghettos, exemplifies our people's commitment to life.

WE PLEDGE to remember!

WE SHALL TEACH our children to preserve forever that uprooted Jewish spirit which could not be destroyed.

WE SHALL TELL the world of the depths to which humanity can sink and the heights which were attained, even in hell itself.

WE SHALL FIGHT anti-Semitism and all forms of racial hatred by our dedication to freedom throughout the world.

WE AFFIRM our commitment to the State of Israel and to the furtherance of Jewish life in our homeland.

WE PLEDGE ourselves to the oneness of the Jewish people.

WE ARE YOUR CHILDREN.

WE ARE HERE!

The next moment was one that will forever be etched in my memory, and I must admit I still get the chills when I think of it. I stood on the platform and thought, less than fifty years ago, we were the victims of the Nazi death factory, with little chance of survival. Today we were alive and in the Jewish homeland. Israel was created in 1948, to a large degree because of the guilt of the Western world, which stood by while millions of us were slaughtered. No other prime minister of Israel identified more with the survivors than the man I was about to introduce.

As I approached the microphone, I felt the weight of the moment.

The full moon was directly overhead and cast its glow over Jerusalem. Thousands of us were massed at the Kotel, the Western Wall. It was a sight to behold. I realized then how far we had come, that out of the ashes of the Holocaust we were privileged to see the fulfillment of the ancient dream, the rebirth of the State of Israel. My thoughts went back to my parents. How I wished they could be here to see this moment. But the knowledge that both their son and daughter had survived was denied to them. (Lotte and two of her daughters stayed by my side for most of the four days.) Perhaps here in Jerusalem, where miracles happened and prayers are answered, they joined with us in spirit. Perhaps the spirits of all those who had perished through the ages to sanctify His name, who died because they were Jews, were with us in Jerusalem on that solemn and important night.

I know today that of all the events I have participated in, of all the things that have been part of my life since the escape on the death march from Berga, nothing will ever equal that magic moment when, full of emotion, I introduced Prime Minister Begin to my fellow survivors:

> *And now the moment we have been waiting for. My fellow survivors from around the world: the prime minister of the State of Israel, Menachem Begin.*

I had tears in my eyes as I turned to shake hands with the prime minister. The entire audience rose as one in silence. There would be no applause at any time for any of the speakers—this was a once in a lifetime event that called for a different approach.

Begin began his address, speaking without notes, with the following words:

> *My sisters, my brothers, in pain, in persecution, in fate, in loneliness, in bereavement, in orphancy. From the Baltic Sea to the Black Sea and the Mediterranean, including the island of Rhodes, from the Atlantic Ocean to the Dnieper and the Volga, millions of Jews lived for centuries in many countries.*
>
> *Our fathers and mothers, brothers and sisters, our sages, some of the greatest in our history, philosophers, physicians, artisan, workers, good-hearted people, loving their families,*

devoted to their parents and their children, hospitable, G-d fearing, believers in Divine Providence, loving Zion, believing in the coming of the Messiah and in Redemption, and among them a million and a half of our children.

There was absolute, total silence as the Gathering listened to the prime minister conclude his remarks:

Tonight let us say again, No, there will never be a repetition of the Holocaust. Never! This is our doctrine and our oath. Israel is strong and confident, stronger than the Jewish people has ever been since the days of the Maccabees. Israel is proud and humble, tempered by its experiences, struggles, and commitments.

Israel will never allow an enemy to develop weapons of mass destruction to be used against the Jewish people, never again! The ultimate historic lesson of Masada is to learn how to prevent it. Never again downfall in heroism. Always, when the necessity arises, heroism and victory, so help us G-d!

Slowly, the survivors rose from their chairs and, holding hands, stood for one final moment of togetherness and memories, aware that we had shared a rare moment of Jewish history.

The prime minister too had risen from his chair and, after briefly speaking to one of his assistants, began to walk to the Western Wall, the holiest shrine of our people that has been in our minds and hearts for 2,000 years.

I asked Mr. Begin's permission to accompany him and, receiving an affirmative reply, followed him the few steps to the Wall.

All around people stopped and, recognizing him, made way. Arriving at the Wall, he touched the ancient stones, bowed his head, and prayed silently. I stood a few feet away, caught up in the emotion of that moment.

After a few minutes he turned, looked me straight in the eye, and shook my hand. Not a word was spoken. That single moment, that silent handshake from the prime minister of the State of Israel, was a fitting climax to the greatest experience of my life.

27

MY FIRST RETURN TO AUSCHWITZ

My life as a UJA executive was very hard on my family. Since 1948 I had been very busy, traveling all over the world, dragging my family from coast to coast, continent to continent. There were overseas trips without the family, midnight phone calls, weekends taken up by conferences, meetings, receptions, rallies. There was never enough time to be a devoted husband and father. I was too busy. I needed to put community first. My job took precedence.

Suzanne, who had suffered the slings and arrows of such a marriage for years and years, began to show the strain when we moved to New York in 1970. I must admit that she tried very hard and always provided me with an impeccable home and hearth. But by 1979 she had had enough, and I didn't blame her at all. The children were either in college or out on their own, and we decided to go our separate ways. We stayed close, however; in 1982 she was diagnosed with cancer, and I needed and wanted to support her through the tough times. Our daughters, Lauren and Karen were with her when she died in 1984.

A few months after our divorce in 1979, I was asked to appear on a radio program. I was with Elaine Winik, who is one of the outstanding Jewish leaders in the United States, a past chair of the National UJA Women's Division and past president of UJA New York. My colleague Sandy Solender was with me, too.

The host, a woman named Amy Goldberg, greeted us at the studio. She was utterly self-assured, confident, and knowledgeable. She was also young, vivacious, and attractive. I was intrigued and enchanted. I knew many women, but she really struck a high note. I was the quietest radio show guest in history. I let Elaine and Sandy do the talking while I sat there and studied Amy. I was trying to figure out a way to persuade her to have lunch with me, but I didn't have the nerve to ask.

A few days later I saw her talking to Malcolm Hoenlein, a close friend and colleague who later became executive vice-chairman of the Conference of Presidents of Major American Jewish Organizations. They were in the lobby of the UJA-Federation building, and I stopped to say hi, then left. When I was gone, Amy asked Malcom who I was. She didn't remember me. Wow, what a great impression I must have made!

The next day I decided to call her. I used my involvement in the World Gathering as an excuse and asked her if she would be willing to give me advice on handling the media coverage in Jerusalem. She was an assistant producer at NBC and knew the radio business. It might work. I asked her to meet me at Patsy's, my favorite Italian restaurant in New York.

Well, one lunch led to another, and we began dating. There were ups and downs as the two of us worked on our developing relationship. I, especially, had a tough time adjusting to our age difference, but we finally decided to take the big step. We were married in Elaine Winik's beautiful home in Westchester in the summer of 1988.

Amy knew what she was getting into. I was well known in the upper echelons of the communities as being a total workaholic devoted to my job. There was no doubt that my job would come first. She also knew that I came with the baggage a Holocaust survivor always carries with him—a commitment to the past.

In the spring of 1983 Amy and I were in the process of planning my sixtieth birthday party. Every birthday is meaningful, but as I get older I am increasingly aware of how I beat the odds.

This was going to be a very special celebration. Besides close family and friends, I wanted my fellow survivors to be there to celebrate with me. Honzo and his wife, Martah, were coming.

In the middle of all this excitement, I received a phone call from Bob Loup of Denver, the National UJA Chairman.

"Ernie, this is not an easy call for me to make, and I hesitated for a long time," he began. "I'm planning a national chairmen's mission to Auschwitz and Israel in July. The chairmen of many major and intermediate cities will be there. They are the highest caliber of Jewish leadership on a national scale. Now comes the hard part." He hesitated a moment, and I had an idea of what was coming.

"I'd like you to consider leading the mission."

I had assumed that was what he would ask. I didn't say a word, but I kept listening.

"Ernie, don't give me an answer now. Give it some thought. If you feel uncomfortable about going back to that place, I'll stop right now. You know how much all of us think of you and what you've accomplished. I discussed this with some of the other UJA leaders, and we all feel that your leading the group would have tremendous impact. Noboday can tell the story the way you can."

I didn't say a word.

"Are you with me?"

"Yes. I am listening."

"I want to make it clear to you right away that the decision is totally yours. If you decide not to go, I will fully understand it."

I promised Bob that I would give it some thought. He was coming to New York in a week.

Back to Auschwitz! How could I do it? How would I react to seeing the train tracks where we arrived in March 1943, the barracks, the remains of the gas chambers, the crematoria? Would anyone in their right mind want to do that? Could I do it? I remembered what happened when Suzanne and I had gone to Mannheim. There was no satisfaction in it. And a little piece of me wondered if I should allow myself to be used in this way.

I discussed it with Amy that evening. She thought it was crazy for me to even consider it. "You're a strong person, but that's too much for them to ask."

She was right, of course, and yet I kept thinking about it. Bob had said that my leading the group would have a deep impact, and I believed him. It's one thing to talk about the Holocaust, about Auschwitz, in the abstract. It's another thing for someone to say, "I was here. This is where I stood when...This is where I fell...This is the place where Walter died. Here's where they experimented on Diana. Here's where they hanged Chaim, Janek, and Leo."

I was sure I could handle it, but I wasn't so sure of how I would react.

What made the situation even more bizarre was the fact that the visit to Auschwitz was scheduled for July 1, my birthday.

It was absurd. But the drama of it appealed to me. I would be making a statement to myself and to all those on the mission. I would declare myself. I was physical and psychological living proof that despite what happened here 40 years earlier, I was back, on my sixtieth birthday, to celebrate my survival in the place that had tried to kill me.

So I decided to go. On June 28, 1983, together with 100 top national UJA leaders, chairmen, and executives, I boarded a special El Al plane, the first ever to fly directly to Warsaw.

The first two days were spent in the Polish capital, visiting the site of what used to be the Warsaw Ghetto. We visited Mila 18, the headquarters of the heroes of the Warsaw Ghetto uprising, and not far from it the powerful monument created by the world-famous sculptor Nathan Rapaport in the Umshlagplatz, where they gathered everyone for deportation.

Early on the overcast morning of July 1 we flew to Krakow and took buses to Auschwitz, now a museum and one of the most visited attractions in all of Europe. I sat by myself, looking at the countryside whisking by, thinking of 1943, of the terrifying five-day train ride I took to this place with Ruth and Onny and the others. I thought about how I held onto Ruth one last time. I thought about the selections, the screams, the bodies, the hunger, the beatings. Little details came back to me.

The bus went through the town of Oswiecum (Auschwitz), which I had never seen before. There was the railway station, there were people shopping, children playing. Did they go shopping while we were being killed a few blocks away? Were children playing then too, while Jewish children were being gassed? Were these same people living here 40 years ago? Didn't they smell the fumes from the gas chambers?

How could people lead normal lives while the biggest mass murder in history took place under their noses?

A few hundred yards beyond the center of town was a huge lot where dozens of buses and a large number of private cars were parked. There was a sign: "Auschwitz Museum." The buses had license plates from Germany, France, and all over Eastern Europe. There were hundreds of people milling around, many of them schoolchildren. All kinds of languages were being spoken. Tourists were laughing, eating, and children were running around. There was an ice cream stand, a book store, and another store that sold flowers. The atmosphere was Disneyland. It was so different from what I had expected.

Our mission was divided into groups of 25, each one accompanied by an English-speaking guide. We then set off on foot. Nothing was as I had remembered it. In the museum, a movie theater showed a twenty-minute movie of Auschwitz as it once had been. The administration building had a place to change money, a *vestiere* to check coats, restrooms, a souvenir shop, and a cafeteria. It was not until our group walked through the main gate with the inscription *"Arbeit Macht Frei"* ("Work Makes Free") that I knew I was back in Auschwitz.

Auschwitz was actually three separate camps within close proximity to one another. Auschwitz I was the main camp. This is where the SS commanders directed the systematic killing. It had thirty brick buildings, built for the Polish army in the 1930s. Mostly non-Jews were kept there. It was also where Mengele conducted most of his medical experiments on twins. There was the death wall where prisoners were executed daily after being kept in punishment cells not larger than three feet by three feet. The cells are still visible today and give an idea of the terror methods used by the SS.

Auschwitz I also contains, behind glass partitions in several of the barracks, exhibits of the items brought to the camp by the doomed. There were suitcases, hundreds of them still marked with the names of their former owners. There were combs—thousands of them— shaving brushes, baby clothes, eyeglasses, crutches, prayer books, by the hundreds, by the thousands. Case after case, it was one of the most gruesome exhibits imaginable. Had some of these items belonged to my parents? I wanted to scream, but no sound came out.

The most horrifying case of all contained bales of human hair—blond, brown, black, white—all colors. The hair, bundled into large sacks, was used by the Germans to weave blankets. Inmates from Bergen-Belsen were witnesses to this process. Other items were used for the German war machine and industry. Nothing was wasted. Not even our ashes.

The guide, a young Pole, tried to explain to our group what took place here, never referring to the fact that over 90 percent of the victims were Jewish. He always spoke about Poles, Hungarians, and Czechs. He never used the word "Jews."

I wanted to see Buna, where I spent most of my two years, but the guide explained that the camp had been totally bulldozed and erased. There was only a monument where our barracks had once stood. The roll call place, the Krankenbau, the barracks—nothing was left.

The last place we visited was Auschwitz II, Birkenau, the greatest mass extermination center ever built, the place where four gas chambers and five crematoria worked 24 hours a day. This was where an estimated 1.5 million men, women, and children were put to death, sometimes at the rate of 20,000 per day.

Here was where we had arrived from Paderborn in March 1943. The same train tracks were there, silent. Grass grew through the rails. A few wildflowers were popping through. Could grass grow in Auschwitz?

I closed my eyes to recall that scene 40 years before—the screaming, the dogs, the selection, hugging Ruth once more before she was torn away. I could hear the order of the SS: "Women to the left, men to the right."

The people on the mission left me alone with my thoughts, and I sat down on the tracks, not very far, I was sure, from where I jumped from the car that night 40 years before. It seemed so strange. When I was there, I never realized how huge Birkenau was. Where row upon row of wooden barracks, hundreds of them, had once stood was a huge open meadow of sweet grasses. The only remnants were endless rows of chimneys, which stretched as far as the eye could see. Where once there was a sea of humanity in striped prisoners' clothing, there was now only silence.

The guard towers and the double rows of barbed wire still existed. The sign showing that one of them was electrically charged was still there. I remembered that wire very well. Almost every morning we would find the bodies of prisoners who committed suicide by running into it. Ludwig did that a few weeks after our arrival.

Why did I let Bob talk me into this? If I had been smart, I would have been home celebrating my birthday with Amy, Honzo, my family, and friends.

That evening, after we returned to our hotel, I told the group my story. I didn't have anything prepared. I shared some of my feelings about having come back here on my birthday. As I spoke I realized that coming back had been the right decision. I had survived. I had chosen to help build a Jewish future because I had been an inmate in Auschwitz. I was who I was because of what had happened to me here, in this place.

When I was finished, drained, Bob Loup came over and wordlessly threw his arms around me. Some of the other men also showed, by their responses, how much it had meant to them to listen to an eyewitness account. There was no need to say anything at all. A handshake, an embrace was all that counted.

My talk was a second catharsis, similar to my first speech to the students at the Port Huron Junior College in 1946. The world had changed a lot. I was no longer the same frightened, starving young prisoner. I was part of the leadership of the largest, strongest Jewish community in the world. I was respected not for having survived, which was more a matter of luck than anything else. It was because I had kept my promise and accomplished many things in the memory of those who went up the chimney, by working for the largest Jewish philanthropic agency in the world: the UJA-Federation.

What brought it all home to me, early the next morning, was the sight of the blue and white El Al plane, with its Star of David logo on the tail, as it waited for us on the tarmac at the Warsaw airport. That's when my return to Auschwitz really hit me. The moment I saw the plane, I started to cry. Those were the first tears I shed on the trip, and

I kept thinking that if there had been a Jewish state, a State of Israel in the 1930s, Auschwitz would never have happened. There would have been a place for us to go. No affidavits would have been necessary. No visas. All the suffering would not have happened.

I've never appreciated the reality of the Jewish State and its role in our lives as much as I did that day. On July 2, 1983, when the El Al plane crossed the Israeli coast and landed at Ben Gurion airport, I walked down the gangway proudly, with a big smile on my face. I had survived to see Israel reborn out of the ashes of Auschwitz.

It was a great birthday present.

28

THE REVEREND JESSE JACKSON AND I ADDRESS A SPECIAL SERVICE AT TRINITY CHURCH

I 've always considered myself a liberal. I'll never forget my astonishment when, during my first speaking tour in Texas in 1946, I came across a drinking fountain marked "For Whites Only." I was appalled.

The first American soldier I saw in Germany was a black man. Black men had helped in the liberation of Nazi camps and saved thousands of Jewish lives. Because I suffered discrimination as a Jew, how could I be part of a society that discriminated against African-Americans?

I didn't take an active role in the civil rights struggle, but I supported it. Communally, this support operated on a two-way street. We supported them, and they supported us. Together we were very powerful. But even together, we weren't always able to overcome.

In the spring of 1985, President Reagan and German Chancellor Helmut Kohl went to a military cemetery in Bitburg, Germany, despite the outcry of protest from Americans of all faiths and colors. I was, personally and professionally, furious. What right did the President of the United States have to visit a cemetery where members of the Waffen SS, Hitler's elite storm troopers, were buried?

In order to show my anguish over this unfortunate and misguided diplomatic event, I accepted an invitation to join a group of 40 Americans—Jews, African-Americans, Christians, clergymen, men and women—to fly to Munich when Reagan and Kohl went to Bitburg. The trip was organized by the American Jewish Congress, led by its president, Ted Mann, and its executive director, Henry Siegman. With us were

David Dinkins, the Manhattan borough president, who was elected the first black mayor of New York City in 1989; Wilbur Tatum, editor of the *Amsterdam News*, the largest black newspaper in the country; and Dick Gregory, the comedian and civil rights activist. Betty Friedan, the well-known feminist and author, also joined us.

We chose Munich because it was the city in which a few courageous German students, referred to as the "White Rose," had led a protest against the excesses of the Nazis in 1942. They were all arrested. Some were sentenced to death and hanged. Others were sent to concentration camps. Joined by the handful of German survivors who belonged to the White Rose movement, we went to the cemetery where the dissidents are buried, to lay a wreath and pay our respects. This was where our president should have been. Not in Bitburg.

David Dinkins made a moving speech as we joined the members of the White Rose for dinner. As an African-American, he felt as deeply as I did about the injustice and insensitivity of the President, and he expressed his feelings clearly and unequivocally.

Soon after we got back from Munich, I received a phone call from the minister of Trinity Church in New York. Trinity, which sits at the foot of Wall Street, is one of the oldest churches in the city. He wanted to know if I would be interested in sharing the platform with the Reverend Jesse Jackson during the services in observance of Martin Luther King, Jr.'s birthday. The subject of the joint lecture was "Celebrating Our Differences."

"Are you sure Reverend Jackson will agree to share the podium with me, a Jewish Holocaust survivor?" I asked.

"Yes. He knows of you and is pleased to appear with you. He suggested that you go first and that he follow you. After the two presentations we will have a rebuttal from each of you."

At the time, Jesse Jackson was not the most popular person in the Jewish community. Although I hadn't met him personally, I was familiar with his support of the PLO, his remark referring to New York as "Hymietown," and the fact that many considered him an anti-Semite.

On January 16, 1987, I stood at the pulpit of Trinity Church, next to Jesse Jackson. He was most cordial when we met in the pastor's office, said that he had been looking forward to meeting me and was anxious to hear what I had to say.

The church was filled to capacity. I spoke of the history of the Jewish people, the suffering we had endured over the years, and the similarity of these persecutions with those of the African-Americans. I quoted some of the statements made by Martin Luther King, Jr., referring to his respect and admiration for the Jewish people and Israel, and I voiced the hope that other black leaders would follow his example. I acknowledged, with regret, the strains which were apparent between the African-American and Jewish communities. I concluded with a plea to work together more closely in the common interest and, by doing so, overcoming our prejudices.

The Reverend Jackson, in response, agreed that Jews and African-Americans had much in common and were equally beset by the "insensitivity" of a president who visited Bitburg while cutting social programs and vetoing sanctions against South Africa. These actions, he said, were part of the "spirit of racial disunity" that emanated from the White House.

After the services we spent some time talking about the rift between African-Americans and Jews, and I sensed a willingness on his part to continue the dialogue in a more informal atmosphere. Since I've always believed in the value of open exchange, even where there are strong differences, I suggested that we should bring together a few of my colleagues in the Jewish community who dealt with the process more directly than I did. When I called him a short time later, I found him immediately receptive.

"But," I added, "no TV coverage, no press, no reporters, Jesse. Just a few of us around a table talking to each other to see if we have some common purpose in working together." He readily agreed.

We met a few days later on neutral territory, in the private office of a friend of mine. From the Jewish community, there were three senior executives of leading Jewish communal organizations. Jackson came with three supporters, two of them Jewish. I started off the meeting by talking about our Trinity Church encounter and my strong conviction that an informal, nonpublicized discussion among people with the same common interest could only produce positive results. I asked those around the table to put their prejudices behind them and see if we could find common ground.

The talks, regrettably, went nowhere. Jackson made it clear that he was tired of the constant "Hymietown" accusation and that he had apologized many times for his "unfortunate" remark. He felt it was time to put it behind him. He also made it clear that, while he took no responsibility for anti-Semitic statements by the Nation of Islam leader Louis Farrakhan, neither would he repudiate him.

At that time, these two issues overshadowed any constructive possibilities. My colleagues, who had more experience in interethnic community relations than I did, felt that unless Jesse made a clear, unambiguous statement on these two points, there was no basis for further discussion. We parted on friendly terms and agreed to continue to have dialogues, but I knew that my efforts were not a glowing success. I felt bad about the outcome, but I've never regretted giving it a try.

The Reverend Jesse Jackson has joined hands with Elie Wiesel and prominent rabbis in the New York Jewish community and is bringing the story of the liberators, those heroic African-Americans who saved the lives of many survivors, to the African-American community. The story has touched him deeply. He has made public statements to say that African-Americans are bound to the history of the Holocaust and bonded with the Jewish people in that suffering. He showed the film *The Liberators* to a group of African-American and Jewish leaders at the Apollo Theater in Harlem. He admitted that if he had known this story as a young man, he would have been different. And he feels we need a Jewish-African-American coalition more than ever.

I hope he's right. It could lead to a new beginning.

29

THE 1989 REUNION OF MANNHEIM SURVIVORS

November, 1988: I worked closely with former U.S. Ambassador to Austria, Ronald S. Lauder when he served as chairman of the New York *Kristallnacht* Commemoration Committee. A few days before the fiftieth anniversary of that infamous night of November 9–10, 1938, he asked me to appear with him on "CBS This Morning."

The co-anchors were Harry Smith and Kathleen Sullivan. Ambassador Lauder talked about the commemorations, which were going to take place all over the world, and addressed the importance of remembrance. I talked about my memories of that tragic night in Bruchsal and Mannheim, and the fear that we felt.

I had just retuned to my office when someone at CBS called. A gentleman from Dayton, Ohio claimed to have come from Mannheim and knew me from my school days. Did I want to talk to him? Of course, I said.

An excited voice with a typically German accent came over the wire. "Are you Ernst Michel from Mannheim?"

"Yes. Who are you?"

"I am Robert Kahn. Do you remember me? We sang in the synagogue choir together and we traded stamps. Now do you remember? I saw you on the CBS morning program. So I called the CBS station here in Dayton and they put me through to New York. I didn't know that you were alive!"

Robert Kahn. Yes, I remembered a Robert Kahn, although that was over 50 years ago and so much had happened since then. We chatted for a while, exchanged addresses and phone numbers, and agreed to get together as soon as we could.

The more I thought about the call, the more it came back to me. Sure, I had always been interested in stamps, having inherited that passion from my father, and Bob and I had traded duplicates. We also played soccer together.

The next day the producer from CBS called again. "Ernie, we put the Robert Kahn story, his seeing you on 'CBS This Morning,' on the wire services and there's a great deal of interest. We want to bring him to New York from Dayton and have the two of you meet on the show. Would you be willing to come back?"

Of course I would. A few days later, Robert and his wife Gert, arrived in New York. CBS put them up at the Essex House, where Amy and I met them for lunch the day before we were to appear on the show.

Bob said he still remembered me, although I didn't recognize him. After all, both of us were now in our sixties. He had been able to leave Germany with his parents just before the war. They had settled in Dayton, Ohio, and, after serving in the army, he had become an interpreter. Eventually he had become a civilian employee at the Wright-Patterson Air Force Base near Dayton. He had raised a family and, like me, was now retired. We spent a lovely lunch together and spoke about Mannheim, our youth, and what had happened to us over the years. We also discovered that we are both ardent tennis players and agreed to get together on the courts as soon as we could.

Bob was in touch with many former Mannheimers and brought up the idea of a Mannheim get-together. To me it seemed like déjà vu, another World Gathering of Survivors on a much smaller scale. To my surprise, the issue came up again the next morning during the TV program. Kathleen Sullivan asked if we had ever thought of getting together with some of the people we went to school with. When Bob replied that we had vaguely discussed the possibility, Harry Smith concluded the segment with the promise that, if there was going to be a reunion, CBS would cover it. Well, it didn't happen quite that way, but the reunion did, and it astonished all of us.

Before Bob and Gert flew home to Dayton, he and I talked a bit more about trying to get the names of a few former Mannheimers to see if there was any interest. Since Bob admitted that it was difficult to plan such an event from Dayton, I agreed to bring together a few former Mannheimers in the New York area to discuss it.

The initial letter brought an overwhelmingly positive response. We chose Kutsher's Country Club in the Catskills as the best location, because many were observant Jews and would eat only kosher food. With the enthusiastic support of a small committee, we established a master list of over 500 names from all over the world. Then we began the difficult task of planning a program and handling the details that are always part of an event like this.

In June 1989, 350 Jews from Mannheim, Germany, came together for a four-day reunion that none of us will forget. Many of us hadn't seen each other since we were children in the 1930s. Some came from as far away as Australia, South America, Israel, Germany, and every corner of the United States.

I was strongly reminded of the World Gathering in Jerusalem. This time we asked all the participants to attach photos of themselves as children to their name tags. When people recognized each other, the scenes were unforgettable and moving. All of us met school friends we never would have recognized without the identifying photos.

The most remarkable part of the reunion was the participation of the two rabbis who had served the Jewish community in Mannheim before *Kristallnacht*. Rabbi Dr. Max Grunewald served the community from 1927 until his emigration to the United States in 1937 and was the revered leader of the Jewish community of Mannheim while we were growing up. Rabbi Karl Richter was the rabbi in Mannheim during *Kristallnacht*. I'm sure no other Jewish community in 1989 had two living rabbis whose service went back 70 years. Rabbi Richter was in his early 80s and Rabbi Grunewald was in his 90s. (Rabbi Grunewald passed away at age 93, just before *Promises to Keep* went to press.)

Our beloved rabbis conducted a special Friday night service, aided by the last cantor of the Mannheim synagogue, Cantor Erwin Hirsch. He was in his late 70s. It was poignant to see these three elderly yet vigorous men sing the same ancient melodies, read the same ancient prayers that they had read in our synagogue until that night in November, 51 years earlier.

Rabbi Grunewald delivered the sermon. He spoke in a firm voice without any notes. We sat mesmerized as he evoked memories and obligations, our losses and the miracle of our survival. It was a Shabbat service unlike any other, and we knew there would never be another like it.

Rabbi Grunewald was the last living member of the *"Reichsvertretung der Juden in Deutschland,"* the central governing body of the Jews in Germany. Its last president was Rabbi Leo Baeck, who survived the Theresienstadt concentration camp and came to America after the war. The Leo Baeck Institute was created in his memory, and its purpose is the study and commemoration of Jewish life in Germany. Today I am privileged to sit on its executive committee.

On a very personal note, Mrs. Emma Major, 93 years old, one of the oldest Mannheimers attending our reunion, came to see me on the first evening to tell me a story about my parents.

"Do you know how your parents met?" she asked. I admitted that I didn't.

"Let me tell you the story.

"Your mother came to Mannheim from Norden because she was offered a very fine position at the well-known department store Hirschland. She was a beautiful young woman, and we became friends. She lived, at first, in a boarding house but didn't like it very much. I knew a man, a bachelor, who had a cigar factory and owned a big apartment. This was your father. I arranged for your mother to have a room there, properly chaperoned by servants. That is how your parents met, so I guess I had something to do with your being here. They were married in 1921. I was at the wedding reception."

I was fascinated. It was remarkable to hear the story of how my parents met from a marvelous old lady, Mutti's girlfriend from Mannheim.

30

AUSCHWITZ TATTOO NUMBERS 104994 & 104995

I t all started with a phone call.

The person on the line was Vera Stern, the wife of one of the greatest violinists of our time, the late Isaac Stern. I had gotten to know both of them over the years.

After a friendly hello, she became serious. "Ernie, I want to ask you something. This is something totally unbelievable and it will come as a surprise to you.

"We have a close friend who lives in Cincinnati, Ohio. His name is Henry Meyer. He was a well-known member of one of the great chamber music groups, the La Salle Quartet. We know him well because he and Isaac now teach master classes throughout the world."

I listened carefully. I knew Vera well enough to know that she would not call me just to tell me about Henry Meyer, whose name was totally unfamiliar to me, unless there was a good reason.

"Go ahead, Vera, I'm listening," I said.

"Well, here is what I can tell you. Henry asked me if I knew you. I told him yes, indeed, we know each other. He wants to call you but he doesn't have your phone number and he is also hesitant to call you out of a blue sky. Henry asked me to find out if you would permit me to give him your phone number in New York. This is the reason I called you."

"Vera, since you obviously know him well, you certainly can give him my number. But tell me, what is this about? Why does he want to talk to me?"

"He told me confidentially why but asked me to promise not to tell you about it. It is something he would like to discuss with you personally."

This was strange. I could not for the life of me understand why he wanted to talk to me. But knowing Vera, I was certain there was a good reason for it. So I told her to go ahead and give him my telephone number.

Later that same evening, the phone rang.

"Hello, is this Ernst Michel?"

"Yes, who is this?"

"My name is Henry Meyer. I am a friend of Isaac and Vera Stern. They gave me your telephone number and told me that it was all right for me to call you."

"Yes, I know. Vera told me to anticipate a phone call. But let me ask you. Do I know you? I do not recall any Henry Meyer among the people I have met over the years."

"Yes and no," Meyer replied.

"That's quite an answer," I said. "How do I know you?"

"Let me tell you why I wanted to talk to you without Vera revealing my reason. This may come as a shock to you, just as it was to me when I read your book."

"Go ahead, you've got me curious." I was wondering what would come next.

"I read your book, *Promises to Keep*. You mention in the book that your tattooed number from Auschwitz is 104995."

"Yes, that is correct."

Why would he want to talk to me? What he told me next took my breath away.

"My tattooed number from Auschwitz is 104994!"

I was shocked. My Auschwitz tattoo number is 104995. The tattoo that I have carried on my left forearm since that infamous day in Auschwitz is the number 104995. I would never remove it. I am proud to wear that number. Never as long as I live shall I forget that evening, our arrival in Auschwitz. After five days and five nights cramped in a cattle car with no water, no food, we were beaten out of the cattle cars leaving everything behind. Then came the selection process, with the thumbs up and thumbs down deciding our fates. The women separated from us and the horrible confirmation of what had become of them—"They are already up the chimney."

I will always remember those words being spoken by a camp inmate after we arrived in Auschwitz on March 3, 1943 when I realized at that moment that Auschwitz was not just another labor camp. The reality of what we were facing became clear. This was an extermination camp.

I could not believe it. Henry Meyer had stood next to me that night as we were lined up alphabetically.

"So you really arrived on the same transport as me?"

"Yes, I was arrested in February in Breslau together with other young Jews. We spent over five days and nights in cattle cars. We were over one hundred in that one stinking car and had no idea what was going to happen to us."

"Henry, what was your first name in Germany? Where were you born?"

"Born as Heinz Meyer in Leipzig in 1923."

Nineteen twenty-three, the same year I was born. Later I found out that he was just two days younger than me.

We spent a lot of time reminiscing and talking about what had happened to us since Auschwitz. Henry told me that a camp inmate, a doctor, had asked him what he had done before Leipzig. He had told the man that he was a student of classical music and had learned how to play the violin. He had told him about playing as a child prodigy at a concert in Breslau while such a thing was still possible. By a mind-boggling coincidence, the doctor had come from the same town and had been in the audience when Heinz Meyer had played.

We spoke a long time and then made plans to get together the next time he was in New York. So, a few weeks later, when he was in New York conducting some master classes, we got together.

Henry never married. After many years traveling around the world, he became a professor of classical music at the University of

Cincinnati. Henry and I became close friends. He had the same positive outlook on life as I do and never gave up hope. Here we were, two survivors reminiscing about an event that happened 60 years before, standing next to each other the night we were being tattooed. It was a miracle!

Unfortunately, the story does not have a happy ending. Some years ago, on his way home from a concert in Cincinnati, Henry was seriously injured in a hit-and-run accident and wound up in a wheelchair. No more teaching master classes, no possibility of ever playing again.

Then Henry's beautiful apartment in Cincinnati was co-oped and he could not afford to buy it. He wound up in a home for the permanently handicapped. I visited him regularly in Cincinnati, but I knew that he would never be the same again.

My good friend and fellow survivor, number 104994, died in 2006.

31

I HAVE BECOME A FREEDOM HERO

I f you ever go to Cincinnati, my advice is to visit the National Underground Railroad Freedom Center. A $100 million museum, it is located on the banks of the Ohio River. It is the only museum in the United States devoted to celebrating courage, perseverance, and most important, freedom.

The story of freedom is woven throughout the Center through the heroic legacy of the Underground Railroad and America's determination to abolish human enslavement and secure freedom for all people.

It tells the story of the heroic 300-year African-American struggle for equality in the most effective, high-tech, and up-to-date manner. But it is not just a museum dealing with the history of slavery. Using the Underground Railroad as a lens through which to explore a range of freedom issues, the Freedom Center offers lessons and reflections on the struggle for freedom in the past, present, and future. And it helps visitors discover the power of one voice—shared with many—by speaking out about the meaning of freedom.

How did I, a Holocaust survivor, get involved with the Underground Railroad Freedom Center?

A few years ago I addressed, as I often do, a history class of tenth graders in Cincinnati. A very articulate young student introduced me. Afterwards we spent some time together. She had some very specific questions, which I was happy to answer.

A few months later I received a phone call from a film producer in Cincinnati. He introduced himself as Jim Friedman and told me that he was in the process of doing a film about individuals on the subject of freedom.

"How did you get my name?" I asked.

"A young high school student who knows my work as a producer of documentaries told me about your talk to her class. She was very impressed with what you said and suggested I call you."

That led to a long phone conversation and a subsequent exchange of letters. By then I had learned about the Freedom Center and what the documentary was about. The only thing that bothered me was my being called a "hero." I never felt like a hero.

A few months later the producer and his crew came to New York to interview me for the one-hour production. I learned that I was one of six individuals who would appear on the program, which was eventually shown on PBS nationwide.

The premiere of the documentary *Everyday Freedom Heroes* was on January 14, 2006, at the Grand Hall in the National Underground Railroad Freedom Center, before a crowd of local officials and dignitaries. It was also the first time I had seen the film. I may be a bit partial, but I was very impressed and moved.

I was even more impressed when I met the other five honorees and learned about their accomplishments. All of them were people who rightfully should be considered heroes. I felt privileged to be in their company, especially since I was the only Jew.

This is what the citation says:

> *This Survivor of the Holocaust is not a hero because of what he endured. Ernest is a hero because of the choice he made. He teaches with his pain rather than punishing with it.*
>
> *Ernest's unshakeable belief in the power of hope against all odds is a testament to the power of one voice. His quiet determination to use his horrific experience to underscore the importance of freedom helps ensure that such an act will never happen again.*

32

THE YOUNGEST SURVIVOR

As I am getting older, I dread the winter months in New York. I will never forget the three-day death march from Auschwitz in 40 degree below zero weather. That is why Amy and I decided to spend some time each winter in Scottsdale, Arizona, after my official retirement. Being avid tennis players, we joined the Racquet Club. It has nine beautiful tennis courts.

The first morning after we arrived, I went to the clubhouse, introduced myself, and said I was looking for some doubles partners. I was told there were three guys looking for a fourth. I walked over to the court, quickly said hello, thanked them for including me, and we started to play. I remember we had a great game. It was also the beginning of something much more important.

After the game we sat down and talked. I looked at one of the men in particular. He wore a gold medal around his neck. I kept looking at it.

"You don't know what this is," Sam said.

"How do you know that? It so happens I do," I replied.

"You do?"

"Yes, indeed, I was there too."

"In Israel? In 1981? At the World Gathering?"

"Yes."

"What's your name?"

"Ernest Michel."

"Michel, Michel...That sounds familiar. Aren't you the one who chaired the Gathering?" Sam asked, incredulous.

"Yes, that's me," I replied.

I could not believe it. Here, on a tennis court in Arizona, I had run into a man I had never known but who had attended the 1981 World Gathering of Jewish Holocaust Survivors in Israel, one of the three most important events of my life, the other two being my escape from the death march and my covering the Nuremberg Trials. Sam was born in 1935 and is probably the youngest, certainly one of the youngest, camp survivors I have ever met. In 1942, at age seven, he ended up in the Demblin concentration camp. His parents and older brother had been taken by cattle car to Treblinka and been killed there. Sam, together with his two sisters, stayed in forced labor camps until January 1945. His sisters hid him. This is how Sam miraculously survived. In 1998 an Italian film called *Life is Beautiful* won an Oscar for best foreign language film. It told the story of a father and his five-year-old son being sent to a concentration camp—a story similar to Sam's.

Later he told me the rest of his story. After his liberation in 1945, he spent some time in an orphanage in Poland, then two years in Vienna, where he went to school. In 1947 Sam and his sisters came to the United States. He was adopted through the Jewish United Fund in Chicago by a family in Northbrook, Illinois, a suburb of Chicago. Sam continued his education and graduated from Grinnell College in Iowa. He eventually entered the insurance business. He met and married Dede Keren and they had two children.

We immediately hit it off. Sam, his wife Dede, Amy, and I eventually became close friends. Although he is twelve years younger than I am, he looks toward me as his older brother, whom he lost.

Being as active as I am in the activities of survivors, I asked him if he was involved in Chicago. He told me that he was a member of the Holocaust Memorial Foundation of Illinois. I told him this was not enough. "You are the youngest camp survivor I have ever met, possibly one of the youngest altogether! You must do something. You owe!"

In 1997 I was honored by the New York Museum of Jewish Heritage—a living memorial to the Holocaust—at their annual dinner, and I invited Sam and Dede as my guests. The dinner was held in the dining room on the 103rd floor of the World Trade Center (which was destroyed by terrorists on September 11, 2001), one of the most popular restaurants in New York, with a splendid view over the entire tri-state area. Sam and I looked down and I showed him where our New York Museum was located, facing the Statue of Liberty and Ellis Island. It is one of the greatest locations in New York. It opened in 1997 and I am privileged to serve as a member of its board.

When I saw Sam again, he told me that he had given a lot of thought to our conversation. "Ernie, you are on the board of the Museum in New York. Tell me, how do you get started on something as important as that? How long did it take to do it?"

"Would you believe over fifteen years?" I replied.

The idea of building a New York Holocaust Museum started in the 1970s. A prominent New York real estate developer, himself a survivor, took the idea to then Mayor Ed Koch, who immediately gave it his blessing. It was the mayor who brought the New York District Attorney, Robert Morgenthau, one of the most prominent public officials in New York, into leadership. Morgenthau's father, Henry Morgenthau Jr., had been U.S. Secretary of the Treasury from 1932 to 1946 as a member of Franklin D. Roosevelt's cabinet. Mr. Morgenthau eventually became chairman of the museum and was able to bring in some heavy hitters to help raise the necessary funds. The new wing is appropriately named in his honor.

"Sam," I explained to him, "building a Holocaust museum is a major undertaking. It will take years of planning, building interest, seeing a lot of people, and—most of all—raising money, lots of it!"

Sam is a bright guy, a fast learner. By then I knew that he was committed to the project. He was able to get an appointment with J. B. Pritzker, a member of a prominent Chicago family. He asked him for three minutes of his time. He put his watch on the table. So did Mr. Pritzker. They were identical. Sam spent close to an hour in his office talking about the idea of building an important museum and educational center dedicated to the victims of the Holocaust.

J. B., as he is known, is now the chairman of the Illinois Holocaust Museum and Education Center. Sam is president of the survivors' organization in Illinois. Groundbreaking took place in 2006. The museum is expected to open in the fall of 2008. The state of Illinois contributed $6 million to the project, and Mr. Pritzker himself made a major contribution. So did many others in the community who want to see this building become a reality. Chicago, which boasts the third largest Jewish community in the United States, will join many cities in the country that have memorials dedicated to the six million victims of the Holocaust. Its primary purpose, as is the case in all of the Holocaust museums in the United States, is to educate students about genocide, about the murder of millions of innocent men, women, and children who were killed, not in war, but in peacetime.

The Skokie Museum will house as its centerpiece an original cattle car of the kind that brought Jews from all over Europe to Auschwitz. I was in one of these cars in 1943. So was Sam.

And it all started on the tennis court!

33

GENOCIDE

Over the last several years, a new word has entered our language. The word is genocide.

What is genocide?

Genocide means the killing, starvation, rape, and murder of thousands—millions—of innocent people for religious or political reasons—or no reasons at all—on the orders of elected or self-appointed presidents or dictators.

Since the beginning of the twentieth century, some 100 million innocent men, women, and children in 26 countries in Europe, Asia, and Africa were starved, shot, slaughtered, or tortured by all kinds of means. That is more than half the population of Europe, more than one-third the population of the United States. It is almost twice the number of casualties during World War II, in which some 55 million were killed on the battlefield.

Most of the world did know about it. Our leaders knew. What was the response? Very little. We all know genocide is happening now in Darfur in the Sudan. Some 300,000 have already been killed. Two million lost their homes, everything.

Genocides have been committed at one time or another in 46 countries. Prior to the twentieth century, estimates of the number of victims were very rough, ranging from 90 million to 260 million. It is estimated that sixteen times more victims have been murdered by genocide then in all the wars since ancient times.

The word genocide was coined by a Polish Jewish lawyer named Rafael Lemkin. I consider him one of the outstanding individuals of the twentieth century. It is a tragedy that his name is almost totally forgotten. None of the many films or documentaries dealing with genocide even mention his name.

Lemkin was born in Poland in 1901. When he was in his teens, he read about civilians being killed, among them the two million Armenians killed by Turks during World War I. He read about Nero's massacre of Christians during the first century, and other mass murders.

"I was disturbed by the frequency of evil, and above all, the impunity of the perpetrators," he wrote in his memoirs.

This subject eventually became his obsession. He devoted literally every day of his life to doing something about it. In doing so, he became a nuisance to almost everyone he met. But nobody denied that his ideas and objectives had merit.

After the Nazi invasion of Poland in 1939, he fled his country, was able to obtain a visa to the United States, and eventually wound up in North Carolina, where he took a teaching position at a state university. By then he spoke nine languages, all with an accent. He was both personally and professionally affected by the news of the killings of European Jews, including members of his family, first in the hundreds of thousands and then the millions. That situation only made it more important for him to do something about this plague to mankind. Lemkin was dirt poor and had no permanent job. Eventually, he made his way to New York. Never married, he lived in a one-room walk-up apartment in Manhattan. But that did not bother him. He kept on, undeterred.

Through a member of President Roosevelt's cabinet, he tried to get an appointment with the President. He was asked to reduce his comments to one page. This upset him greatly: "How can you compress the death of millions to one page?"

Eventually he did receive a written reply from the President, which said, "I want to assure you that the United States will issue a warning to the Nazis, and I urge patience."

In 1943 the U.S. ambassador to Sweden sent a cable to Cordell Hull, the U.S. secretary of state: "So fantastic is the news about the extermination of Jews that I hesitate to make it the subject of an official report."

Winston Churchill called it a "crime without a name."

Once Lemkin wrangled a meeting with Supreme Court Justice Felix Frankfurter, who listened to him describing the gruesome methods used by Nazis in killing Jews. He then told Lemkin, "I don't believe you. By this I do not mean you are lying, I simply said I cannot believe you."

He became well known in the corridors of Congress and at the formative meetings of the United Nations. Many people either considered him a nuisance or felt sorry for him.

Always carrying an old briefcase overflowing with papers, he kept on. He wrote personal letters to U.N. delegates, foreign ministers, prime ministers. He cornered religious leaders—bishops, cardinals—and intellectuals such as Pearl S. Buck and Bertrand Russell, as well as members of Congress and other people of influence.

He was jubilant when Trygve Lie, the U.N. secretary general, invited him to prepare the first draft of what eventually became known as the "Convention on Genocide." Finally, on December 9, 1948, after years of delays, the U.N. General Assembly unanimously passed the Genocide Law. It was the first time in all history that an international consensus led to a law making the killing of innocent people a crime subject to punishment.

Among those who congratulated Lemkin was John Foster Dulles, then U.S. secretary of state. Some even suggested that the law be called the "Lemkin Convention." Everyone at the U.N. knew that it was this Polish Jewish lawyer who single-handedly, without any official position, defying all those powerful diplomats who ignored him, had written a new page in human history. Eventually 136 nations, almost all the U.N. members at the time, ratified the Genocide Convention. It is officially called "The Convention on the Prevention and the Punishment of the Crime of Genocide."

Lemkin's entire life was totally devoted to dealing with a curse that has been a part of human history since the beginning of time and that was accelerated to an incredible level in the twentieth century. He was nominated five times for the Nobel Peace Prize but never received it.

Lemkin died of a heart attack in 1959. Seven people came to his funeral, which was paid for by friends. All that happened years ago. As we all know, there have been a number of serious violations since then. The most brutal and most bloodiest genocide since the Holocaust in World War II took place in Rwanda, Africa. One million Tutsis and politically moderate Hutus were murdered, their women raped and violated. All had been Rwandan citizens for generations.

In 1938 I listened on the radio to the strident, shrill voice of Adolf Hitler speaking in the Reichstag: "If international Jewry succeeds in plunging the world into another war, the result will be the end of European Jewry." Nobody paid attention. A year later Germany invaded Poland. During World War II one out of three Jews in the world was killed in the single largest, most devastating genocidal extermination by a single government in all of history.

The number of attempted genocides in the world as well as the total number of victims has greatly declined in the twenty-first century. Right now the only country where this is still going on is Sudan, in Darfur. The very existence of the ICC has made a difference.

Being an eternal optimist, I would like to think that the day will come when genocide will no longer be part of the world we live in but only a sad and tragic part of history.

34

THE TEN MILLION DOLLAR CAMPAIGN FOR NEEDY HOLOCAUST SURVIVORS

Although I officially retired from my position as an executive vice president and CEO of New York UJA-Federation in 1989, I continue my active involvement in the organization as executive vice-president emeritus. I am in my office almost every day. There is always something to do—solicitations, meetings, telephone calls, correspondence. I don't ever want to retire. As long as I feel I can make a contribution, I will continue to do so. Retirement is not for me! There is so much that must be done.

A few years ago I learned that there are some 50,000 Holocaust survivors living in the New York area, over half of them living near or below the poverty line, which statistically is the level at an annual income of $22,000 a year for a family of four and somewhat less for smaller families.

It is estimated that the total number of survivors in the United States is approximately 150,000. In Israel there are some 300,000, Eastern Europe another 200,000 to 300,000, and a few thousand scattered throughout the rest of the world. Most of us are in our 80s and 90s. A few are over 100 years old. This figure sounds like a lot, but it is not surprising. Only young men and women, in their late teens or early twenties, had any chance to survive the brutality of the death camps. We now go to funerals every few days. There is no doubt that within ten or fifteen years there will hardly be any survivors alive.

I was 16 when I was first arrested, 22 when I escaped from the final death march in 1945. I am now 84. I have my good days and my bad days, but considering what happened to me in my youth, I have no reason to complain, and I don't. I am a very lucky guy. I love life; I want to live every day to the fullest. There is so much to be done.

A year or so ago, during a discussion with one of my colleagues at UJA-Federation, I learned that some 25,000 poor, old, and sick Holocaust victims were living in the New York area. I was told that there were plans for a $10 million fundraising campaign to benefit needy Holocaust survivors. They were looking for a chairman who would be willing to take on this responsibility. I had never met survivors like that. It bothered me. Twenty-five thousand survivors living in the New York area under such dire circumstances! Men and women who survived the Holocaust? People like me, who didn't have enough money to take care of themselves?

I was shocked. I asked our staff if I could meet some of them. A few days later I had my first encounter. I could not believe what I found. Mr. X, a man close to my age, was lying in bed suffering from dementia and the after-effects of a stroke. His wife was taking care of him. He was born in Poland, went to Israel after surviving the Holocaust, then came to the United States. Bedridden for several years, he was receiving some Social Security money but only limited funds from the Conference on Jewish Material Claims against Germany, Inc. The couple's children were providing some support.

When I saw them in their small but well-kept apartment in Queens, I asked Mr. X's wife to tell me what she would do if we could provide some extra funds for her.

"I would like an evening once in a while to get out of the apartment, meet some friends, see a movie, just to get out of the house."

After I met two other families under somewhat similar circumstances, I told my colleagues that I would volunteer to serve as chairman of such a campaign if they would have me. I simply could not accept the fact that these were survivors just like me, but who had never been able to adjust to this country, many of them still living with the memories of what happened in their pasts. That is how, as a retired professional, I became chairman of the $10 million special campaign for needy Holocaust victims in the New York area.

I formed a small committee of volunteers who agreed to become part of this campaign. We decided we did not want to have a big dinner or any meetings. It was going to be a one-on-one individual solicitation effort. A member of our staff told me that there was a Jewish family living on Long Island who had come from Germany before the war and built a big business, which they had sold several years ago. They were now contributing some of the money to help worthy causes. They certainly were the kind of people I wanted to talk to. We arranged an appointment in their office.

I had never met them, but they knew my name and my colleagues'. We didn't need much of an introduction. We told them the purpose of our visit. Since they had been lucky enough to leave Germany in the 1930s before the outbreak of World War II, I appealed to their understanding of needy Holocaust survivors who were not as lucky. They asked a number of questions indicating that they were well aware of what I was talking about. At the conclusion of our meeting, I asked them for a one-time contribution, payable over a period of years, in the amount of $2 million. I had been assured by the staff member that they were in a position to donate this amount.

The couple excused themselves and came back a few minutes later. "We want you to know that we understand the purpose of your coming and we are willing to go along with your request for a one-time contribution payable over a number of years."

I couldn't contain myself. I went over to them, embraced them, emotionally affected by their readiness to support our campaign. It was a great beginning to a successful fundraising effort that has surpassed its goal of $5 million, which has already been distributed to those in need.

Incidentally, the woman I spoke to who had the very ill husband now has a sitter every other week so that she can go out to meet a friend or see a movie.

35

LOTTE'S FIRST SPEECH AND OUR FAMILY REUNION

In April 2007 we celebrated the ninetieth anniversary of the UJA-Federation, the organization with which I have been affiliated for sixty years. The plans included a major mission of our organization to Israel, not only to see what had been accomplished over the years, but also visit some of the projects and places where UJA-Federation funds had been put to work. John Ruskay, my successor, asked me to address one of the meetings in Israel and to speak about "the early days"—the 1940s and 1950s—and what role UJA funds had played during those historic years. There are not too many people around who can talk about those early days.

Hundreds of thousands, eventually millions of Jews immigrated to Israel. They came from North Africa, from European countries, from the Far East, from the Middle East, from over 100 countries. In 1948 the Jewish population in what was then Palestine was about 600,000. Today it is over five million. There is no country in the world that has seen this kind of growth.

Israel is the only nation of the 187 member states of the United Nations whose very existence is put into question. It is the only nation that has been threatened by the president of another country, who stated publicly that "Israel should be wiped off the face of the earth!" The same president publicly declared that "There was no Holocaust. It was a myth that six million died."

As I have written in one of my earlier chapteres, my sister, Lotte, lives in a kibbutz in Israel, which was founded in 1946 by a small group of young Holocaust survivors. Its name is Ein Hanaziv and is near Beit Shean in northern Israel, very near the Israeli-Jordanian border.

I had given some thought to what I was going to talk about, namely, the historic years after the end of World War II when hundreds of thousands of survivors were lingering in displaced persons camps, not knowing what their futures would bring. Most of them wanted to go to Palestine. Others wanted to go to other countries.

The longer I thought about it the more it became clear that in talking about the early days, I wanted to talk about the help given to us particularly the United Jewish Appeal, in creating a new life for ourselves. The more I thought about it, the more I thought the best person to talk about it was my sister, whose story I wrote about earlier.

On the spur of the moment, I called Lotte in Israel and told her what I was planning, and that I would want her to join me and talk about how she was saved and her eventual ten day march across the Pyrenees into Spain.

Her response was a firm "No!"

We always speak in German since her knowledge of English is limited.

"Ernst, you are the speaker in the family. This is not for me. I have never done this, never spoken about it, not even with my family," she said. Then she asked, "How many people will be there?"

I sensed an opening, but I had to be honest. "Lotte, there will be about 350 people, all from New York."

"No, I can't do this."

I then called Shlomit, Lotte's daughter with whom I am very close. When I told her what I had in mind and repeated my conversation with Lotte, she said, "Let me try and talk to her about it. I know this is important and it could make a big difference."

Two days later, Lotte called me. "Ernst, I have changed my mind. I will do what you asked me, but I have two conditions." She was very serious. She makes up her mind quickly. "Here are my conditions. First, I want to speak in German and have you translate."

"Accepted. What is your second condition?" I asked.

"That I will write what I am going to say and I don't want you to change it."

"Wow!" I had already thought that I would write it for her, but she gave me no choice. "Okay, accepted. We've got a deal."

That is how on a bright morning at eight o'clock in the ballroom of the David Citadel Hotel in Jerusalem, over 350 mission participants and their families and friends (including my daughter Laurie and her three children, and Lotte's family) had just finished their breakfast.

There was one other speaker and then it was my turn.

I talked about those early days from my experience when I began my career with UJA. That was in 1947, even before the state of SIrael was declared by David Ben Gurion on May 15, 1948. Lotte was sitting next to me, and people were wondering who she was. Nobody had any idea. The only one who knew was the director of our missions department, with whom I had shared what I had planned to talk about.

I began to talk about a young girl, who, all alone, at age eleven, was sent by her family across the German border into France. The family had alerted a cousin who was living in France to be at the train station in Strasbourg and to look for her. This was in May 1939, a few months before the breakout of World War II, when the Nazis invaded Poland. France and England entered the war. Communications between France and Germany came to an end. She was eventually taken in by a Jewish family who had children her age. After the French occupation of Germany, the family tried to get into Switzerland, but they were turned away at the border along with thousands of others who were trying to flee for their lives. This was followed by many months of running, hiding, and temporary quarters—always with the fear of getting caught.

Eventually, she was taken in and saved by Catholic nuns in a convent in southern France. Later, other Jewish children found refuge there. They were never allowed to leave the convent, but were never proselytized by the nuns either. They had to go to church servies every day but the sisters always told them, "You are Jewish, and you should stay that way."

One day in 1943, a sister woke the children up in the middle of the night. She told them to get dressed, and said "Bring sweaters, coats. Only take some personal items and keep your hands free."

"Sweaters? Coats? In July! Why?"

"Don't ask any questions. The less you know the better off you are," she replied. They were taken to a small French border village at the foot of the Pyrenean Mountains.

Lotte, sitting next to me, didn't make a move. She was waiting for me to give her the signal when to start.

I paused and then continued.

"I would now like for you to meet the eleven-year-old girl from Germany who was sent by her parents, all alone, across the border into France in the spring of 1938. She will be eighty in November. She was one of the founders of Kibbutz Ein Hanaziv in 1946, before the State of Israel was born, and has lived there all her life. She has four daughters, fifteen grandchildren, and, so far, seventeen great-grandchildren. She has never talked about her story before. Today is the first time she is doing it.

"It is now with much love, pride, and gratitude that I want you to meet my sister, Lotte Michel Rein, who is sitting next to me."

Spontaneously, the entire room rose and gave her a standing ovation. There was not a dry eye in the room. The moment was filled with emotion. It was truly a unique event, a highlight for my sister and me. The entire dramatic rescue of some 250 Jewish youngsters was financed with UJA funds engineered by a Swiss Jew, Salli Meyer. He bribed German officers with $100 per head in dollar bills for each child who was permitted to leave France over the Pyrenean Mountains to arrive in Spain.

Lotte, speaking in German with me translating, continued her story, describing the harrowing climb across the Pyrenees Mountains in ice and snow for ten days and nights with very little food. Dirty, hungry, with torn clothing, they arrived in Larida, Spain, where they were welcomed by Jewish representatives. They got new clothing and eventually new papers, which permitted them to leave Spain for Palestine in 1944. Eventually Lotte was sent to a kibbutz to study agriculture and, in 1946, founded Kibbutz Ein Hanaziv. She has lived there ever since. Sami died in 1999.

Lotte concluded her story as follows:

We owe our lives to Catholic nuns in a convent in southern France. We have never forgotten them. Without their help, none of us would be here. Several years ago, we invited the senior sister, Sister Jeanne, to visit Israel. We wanted to thank her personally for what she and the other nuns had done. At Yad Vashem, the National Israel Memorial and Museum to the Holocaust, we planted a tree in her honor in the Forest of the Righteous. She received a plaque from Yad Vashem. It was a moment that none of us will ever forget. Sister Jeanne died a few years ago. She always talked about her trip to Israel as the highlight of her entire life.

There was another special family commemoration on the eve of our return to New York. It was an appropriate conclusion to our visit to Israel.

Earlier I wrote about the World Gathering of Jewish Holocaust survivors in 1981 in Israel, where 6,000 survivors from all over the world attended the only worldwide reunion ever held by survivors and their families. In my opening address at Yad Vashem, I had spoken about the hundreds of stones engraved with the names of our families, which we brought to Israel. The stones were eventually placed in a specially built cave at Yad Vashem. They can be seen from the outside. Next to the opening is a plaque, explaining that this cave contains memorial stones brought to Israel in June 1981 by Holocaust survivors from all over the world. There are no graves in Auschwitz, but Auschwitz is the biggest Jewish cemetery in the world.

On my most recent trip to Israel I decided to enter the cave. As much as I looked, I could not find the stone with my parents' names. On the spur of the moment I decided to have a new stone made. A friend, Paul Hunter, a non-Jew, offered to have it done professionally by a stonemason. I called my sister and told her that on my next trip to Israel we should have a ceremony at Yad Vashem and place the new stone with all our family members present—children, grandchildren, and even great-grandchildren. My daughter Lauren and Lotte's daughter Shlomit volunteered to handle the details, invitations to all family members, the agenda, and all other logistics.

So, on a beautiful spring day in Jerusalem, about 40 members of our two families, including two of Lotte's oldest great-grandchildren, assembled in front of the cave to participate in a unique ceremony: the placing of our parents' memorial stone in the cave. It was a simple, extremely moving event that none of us will ever forget. Lotte and I, together, entered the cave and placed the stone with all the others. I am indebted to Yad Vashem, who made an exception for us and organized the ceremony.

That evening, we all met for dinner. Everyone participated. It was an evening none of us will ever forget. The children, shy until then, asked questions of Lotte and me that they had never asked before. One of the great-grandchildren asked to see my number and then just stood there. I gave her a big hug and held back tears. Lotte and I looked at each other with the same thought: If only our parents could have known that between us we now have seventy-two direct descendants. That privilege they were never granted. But although they have no grave, their names are now forever enshrined on holy ground in Jerusalem.

36

MY LAST VISIT
TO MY HOMETOWN

Monday, February 26, 2007, was a remarkable day in my life. As part of a three-day program and as a guest of the city of Mannheim on the celebration of its 400th anniversary, I was invited to address the same school from which, in 1936, I was expelled at the age of thirteen because I was Jewish.

I wrote earlier that there are three events in my life that I consider my most memorable. The first was the day of my escape from the final death march, on April 18, 1945, together with my friends Honzo and Felix. The second was my role, a few months later, as a special correspondent for the German News Agency DANA covering the International Nuremberg War Crimes Trial. The third was my dream come true, the June 1981 World Gathering of Jewish Holocaust Survivors in Jerusalem.

I want to add a fourth event—my last return to Mannheim.

I have been unusually lucky, not only to have survived the Holocaust against all odds, but then to have made a career as a professional in the UJA-Federation Network, a career that has spanned more than sixty years so far. I loved my job from the first day I walked into the Benowitz Men's Store in Ogden, Utah, my first assignment in 1947, and culminating with my eventual role as executive vice-president of the New York UJA, the largest citywide fundraising organization in the world.

That is why I believe it appropriate that the last chapter of *Promises Kept* deal with my four-day visit in February 2007 to the city where it all began, the city where I was born—Mannheim, Germany. I was invited by the mayor of Mannheim to speak at the 400th anniversary of the city about the fate of my family during the Holocaust. The letter from Mr. Widder, whom I had met on a previous visit, came as a complete surprise:

Dear Mr. Michel,

We have already got to know each other during your visit to your hometown and I look back on this event deeply moved. Today, I would like to ask you to visit Mannheim again.

In 2007, Mannheim is celebrating its 400 anniversary. On January 24th, 2007, we celebrate the 400 recurrence of the municipal law's conferment of 1607. Many events will take up the diverse history of Mannheim. We would like to invite you to participate in an event which is especially important for us.

As a former citizen of Mannheim, who had to share with his family an unutterable and inexcusable experience, you have made a unique and incredible moving contribution.

I would really like to ask you to do us and the city of Mannheim, your native town, the great honour to participate in this event and to tell your story at the place where it originated.

I am sure that this is very difficult for you to decide: yet the city of Mannheim would like to make every contribution not to forget the injustice (done) and to bring to mind the importance weight of this horrid part of the last century to all progenies.

To go about this topic with you would be the most important gesture in a year like 2007, in which Mannheim should be presented as it really is.

Dear Mr. Michel, please take your time consider whether you are willing to be our guest and participate in the event on the 25th of February.

Very sincerely,
Gerard Widder

I must admit that I was at first hesitant to accept the invitation, but after talking to my sister in Israel and a friend from my school years who both encouraged me, I decided to accept.

Amy and I were picked up by Rainer Kern at the airport in Frankfurt for the quick trip on the Autobahn to Mannheim. He was the person in charge of the Mannheim 400-year anniversary program and acted together with his colleague, Ulrike Jacker, as hosts during our four-day visit. Both are in their thirties, bright, personable, and deeply concerned about making our stay as memorable as possible. They and their colleague, Susanne Brauer, could not have been more attentive. They instinctively knew how difficult this trip would be for me. I must admit that seldom in my professional career have I met three people who, after knowing them for four days, I today call personal friends. Their general concern, sensing what they knew would be a difficult yet highly emotional visit for me, was clear from our first meeting and only deepened during our stay.

Rainer knew, of course, that in the 1930s we lived, before my arrest in 1939 and subsequent deportation to the camps, on Richard Wagner Street, 26. Like most of the city, the apartment building was destroyed by Allied bombs during World War II. I clearly remember the first time I saw the devastation when I came back in July 1945 (see chapter 21). Our next step was the newly built synagogue, one block from the old one, which, like all synagogues throughout Germany, had been set on fire and dynamited on November 10, 1938, an event that has become known as *Kristallnacht*. The new synagogue was built by the city. The park in front is named in honor of the longtime rabbi and president of the Mannheim Jewish Community, Max Grunewald.

The next step was a surprise. I had known that the city had built an unusual memorial to the over 2,200 victims of the Jewish community who were deported in October 1940 to the French concentration camp in Gurs and from there to Auschwitz in 1942, where all of them were murdered on arrival.

Rainer told me that the mayor had asked to meet with me and wanted to show me the memorial. It is located in the very heart of the city, directly in the center of Main Street, called the Planken, on the busiest corner, like Times Square in New York. Thousands pass it every day. It is an unusual 10-by-10-by-10-foot-square sculpture made of heavy glass. On the inside of the sculpture on all four sides are the names of all 2,265 victims, all the murdered Jews of Mannheim. In front of the memorial, which is lit up from the ground, is a plaque telling the story of the extermination of the Jewish victims. They are not listed alphabetically but at random. It took me quite a while to locate the names of my parents, Otto and Frieda Michel, and my grandmother, Mathilde Wolff. They are there.

I stood there looking at their names, realizing that this sculpture represents the only evidence of their existence in the town where we lived. I found it difficult to tear myself away. It took me awhile to get my composure. Rainer was most understanding. He took us to our hotel. Memories. Memories. Sixty-eight years since my deportation, 65 years since my family was destroyed. Their names are now engraved forever in the center of Mannheim.

There were two other events that were the highlights of our stay.

The first one took place on Sunday morning at a major assembly hall. It was open to the public and there was standing-room only. The entrance fee was twenty euros, or about $28. I had given a great deal of thought to what I was going to say. I decided to speak in German. Although I still understood the language, I had never given a talk in German. Once, several years before, I was interviewed on a German radio network and could not put a coherent sentence together. It was an embarrassing moment and I made a promise to myself never to repeat the experience. This was different. I was the main speaker at a citywide event in Mannheim, with a German audience.

I spoke very openly about what happened to my family and told the audience of my arrest on September 3, 1939, my parents' and grandmother's deportation to a French concentration camp, my subsequent five and a half years in German forced labor and concentration camps, including Auschwitz and Buchenwald, and my final escape in April 1945 on the final death march from Berga concentration camp.

Here are excerpts from my talk.

Never would I have thought that I would speak to an audience of Mannheimers, in the city where I was born and where my family suffered because we were Jews.

I will not discuss the horror, the hunger, the beatings, and the constant fear. Life expectancy in Auschwitz was four to six months. I never gave up hope. How I survived I will never understand.

Why did I accept the invitation from Mayor Widder? Here in this city I lost my youth, my education, my family, my friends—everything. I have reason to hate, but I can't. I won't. Hate destroys you. There is too much hate in this world. Despite my bad memories, despite my mixed feelings, I am glad that I came. You welcomed me with friendship and I return to New York with the conviction that you have proven that good will defeat evil. Remember what happened. Never forget. Only by remembering can we be sure that what happened to me and my generation will never happen again.

Afterwards a well-dressed couple rushed up to talk to me. "You spoke about your school friend, Kurt Hess. Did they live in Karl Ludwig Strasse?"

"Yes, they did. That is where I went when I first came back to Mannheim in July 1945 to look for Kurt."

"Well, he would have been my uncle. Kurt was killed in March 1945 as the Russians moved into Germany."

I already knew that. I'll never forget, on my first return in July, 1945 going to the Hess house, where his mother would not believe that I was alive and told me that Kurt died fighting the Soviet Army a few weeks before the end of the war.

Then he asked me if I could meet him during our stay. "I want to show you something." We made a date for the next afternoon, when he and his wife came to the hotel. He brought with him a photo album of Kurt's family. I recognized Kurt immediately. He also showed me the copy of the last letter Kurt wrote to his parents. He knew that he would not survive. The letter was his final testament.

Kurt's nephew told me that he was chairman of the Mannheim-Haifa Friendship Committee, that he had been to Israel 40 times and had many friends there. Incredible. My close friend Kurt died defending Nazi Germany and his nephew is now a supporter of Israel.

I also tried to find out what happened to my other school friend, Heinz Manz, and was told that he died several years ago. What irony! Here I was, a Jew, destined to be murdered, returning to Mannheim as a guest of the city, and my two closest friends from my childhood were no longer alive. Fate plays strange twists.

My second extraordinary event took place the following day. Rainer, who knew of my having been thrown out of school in 1936 in sixth grade, arranged for me to speak at the Pestalozzi School to a class of teenagers. The building was the same as I remembered. It had not been destroyed by Allied bombs.

So on Monday morning I went to the school where, 71 years before, I was told by my teacher that I would no longer be welcome as a student, simply because I was Jewish. I climbed the same steps and remembered that day so well. It was the first time that I felt as a thirteen-year-old boy that our lives as Jews in Germany would never be the same. Two years later was *Kristallnacht*. The next year began my road to Auschwitz.

That morning, possibly in the same classroom from which I was thrown out 71 years before, I stood addressing students who were close to the age I was at the time. It seemed I had come full circle. In the presence of their teacher and other school officials, including the superintendent of the Mannheim school system, I told the class what happened to me that day in 1936. I still remember every moment.

My teacher's name was Mr. Christ. I will never forget him. When the last class of the day was dismissed, the teacher asked me to remain in my seat and then asked me to come forward. "Ernst," he addressed me, "I have to tell you that this is your last day at school. Effective immediately, you are no longer permitted to come to classes in this school." I looked at him, totally bewildered. I couldn't understand it. What had I done? I had tears in my eyes as Mr. Christ put a hand on my shoulder.

"You are Jewish. Jews will no longer attend public schools in Mannheim. All Jewish students are being informed today. Your parents will be informed about this."

My talk at the school was covered by a reporter from the local newspaper. Also in attendance were other city officials. They were curious to listen to how a young boy born in Germany who had been kicked out of school in the sixth grade would tell his story to today's generation. I must admit it was an incredible experience for me. This was not just a talk. I was talking about the "Final Solution." I tried to put it in a way that young students could understand.

I asked if there were any questions. There were none. I sensed that the students were so shocked by my story that they just could not ask questions. However, after the class was dismissed, they came over and asked me all kinds of questions. They couldn't understand how this had taken place in their own town, in their own school.

The next day Amy and I left Mannheim. Rainer drove us back to the airport. It was not just the end of a chapter in my life, it was the last time I would ever go back. At age eighty-four, having seen the worst a human being could endure, I was on my way back home to the United States, the country that had given me the opportunity to start life all over again and make up for the past. I am a very lucky individual. I love life. I not only survived one of the greatest mass murders in all of history, but I have been privileged to try to make up for what happened to me and the Jewish people so that it will never happen again, to anyone, anytime.

WHERE ARE THEY NOW?

My oldest daughter Lauren, her husband Chaim, and their three children live in Jerusalem, Israel. He is an architect; Laurie is a professional tour guide and is in great demand.

My second daughter Karen, her husband Rabbi Brian Daniels, and their three children live in Albany, New York. Karen is a clinical social worker, and Brian is Associate Commissioner for the Office of Family and Children's Services in New York State.

My son Joel and his wife Terry live in Independence, Missouri. He drives a limousine. Terry teaches art.

Honzo Marek, with whom I worked in the infirmary in Auschwitz-Buna and with whom I escaped on April 18, 1945, remained one of my closest friends. Each April 18th, together with Amy and his wife, Martha, also a Holocaust survivor, we celebrated as our birthday. They retired and moved to Virginia. Honzo died ten years ago from a heart attack. I visited him only a few weeks before his death when the Blacksburg, Virginia, high school put on a play about his life and survival.

Felix Schwartz was the third of our trio. We worked together in the Buna infirmary and escaped together. He never married and lives in a small village in Pennsylvania. Felix has no recollection of the past and totally erased it from his memory. I met him once and I must admit it was a great disappointment.

My mentor, Lieutenant Albert Hutler, his wife Leonore, and their daughters Susie and Frankee became my family after my arrival in the United States. Al and Lee died in the 1980s. I will be forever grateful to them for the role they have played in my life.

Dr. Samuel Samuelides was born in Greece and arrived in Auschwitz Buna with a transport of Greek Jews in 1944. He was a doctor in the Auschwitz Buna infirmary where Honzo, Felix and I worked. He is one of the many to whom I owe my life.

Gerd Hartog was my close friend in Paderborn before we were deported to Auschwitz. He became a Capo in the camp. The last time I saw him was on the death march in January 1945. All efforts to try to find what happened to him were unsuccessful. I must assume he died before the end of the war.

Of the approximately one hundred inmates of the forced labor camp in Paderborn, (see Chapter 4) who arrived in Auschwitz in March 1943, all women were immediately sent to the gas chambers. Of the men, five are still alive, among them my close friends Piese and Onny, who live in a kibbutz in Israel.

Stefan Heyman is the man most responsible for my being alive (see Chapter 7). He survived the death march, was liberated, returned to Berlin, and became Minister of the Interior of the East German government. He is no longer alive. I will be forever grateful to him for being responsible for saving my life.

Ben Meed, my friend and co-chairman at the World Gathering of Jewish Holocaust Survivors in Jerusalem in 1981 (see Chapter 26), became the founding Chairman of the American Gathering of Jewish Holocaust Survivors. He held this position until his death in 2007 and was responsible for creating the largest database of survivors. He is sorely missed.

Bob Lindsay and his wife Ginny (see Chapter 21) live in retirement in California. We have stayed in touch throughout the years and make it a point to see each other. Bob's family has played a major role in my life. I will never forget that it was his father who arranged for an affidavit for me to come to the United States.

Joseph Mengele, the death doctor in Auschwitz who conducted the horrible medical experiments on Auschwitz inmates, including Diana (see Chapter 15), escaped to Argentina and lived there for many years under an assumed name. He drowned. His remains have been positively identified.

Rudolf Hoess, the commandant of Auschwitz, appeared as a witness at the Nuremberg War Crimes Trial. I was there the day he testified as a witness for the prosecution (see Chapter 6). He was sentenced to death by a Polish court and executed on a gallow overlooking the camp where he killed so many. Of 617 SS defendants tried in Polish courts, thirty-four were sentenced to death.

EPILOGUE

I am writing these lines in the fall of 2007. It is a beautiful evening, crisp and clear, as I write the last chapter of *Promises Kept*. I look out the window of our weekend home in upstate New York, at the lake, the trees. It is quiet. The sun is going down.

I am now 84 years old. I was 70 when I wrote my earlier book. I have lived a full and productive life, but tell myself "It ain't over yet." Considering what I have lived through I can't believe I have made it this far. I am a very lucky man.

The days of playing tennis are gone. My legs and my head don't get along too well. They don't do what I tell them to do. I walk slower than I used to and have trouble with my balance. But otherwise, I am fine.

I was sixteen when I was arrested and sent to my first forced labor camp, not yet twenty when I arrived in Auschwitz, and twenty-two when I escaped from the final death march.

The number of survivors is shrinking. In ten, maybe fifteen years hardly any survivors will be around. Then, only books, documentaries, films, museums and Holocaust education centers will be left to tell the story of the most devastating genocide in history.

I have been given a gift, the greatest gift of all—the gift of life against all odds. Never would I have believed I would live to see the year 2007. I love life! I cherish every moment. I wake up in the morning and greet every day as a present. I hope you can, too.

I love America and will never forget the sacrifices made by so many to make it possible that those of us who survived would enjoy the freedom and liberty we all have in this country.

I never gave up hope, even when it seemed hopelessness was the only choice. I have tried to make up for what happened. That is why I have written *Promises Kept*. One of my greatest satisfactions is the ability to communicate with students in schools, colleges, universities, not only about what happened to me and my generation but about our obligation to do everything we can so that what happened in the past shall never happen again—to anyone, anywhere, anytime.

Every person has ups and downs. That is life. When things get tough, there is always hope, always a new day. Never forget this.